THE INDIAN FRONTIER WAR

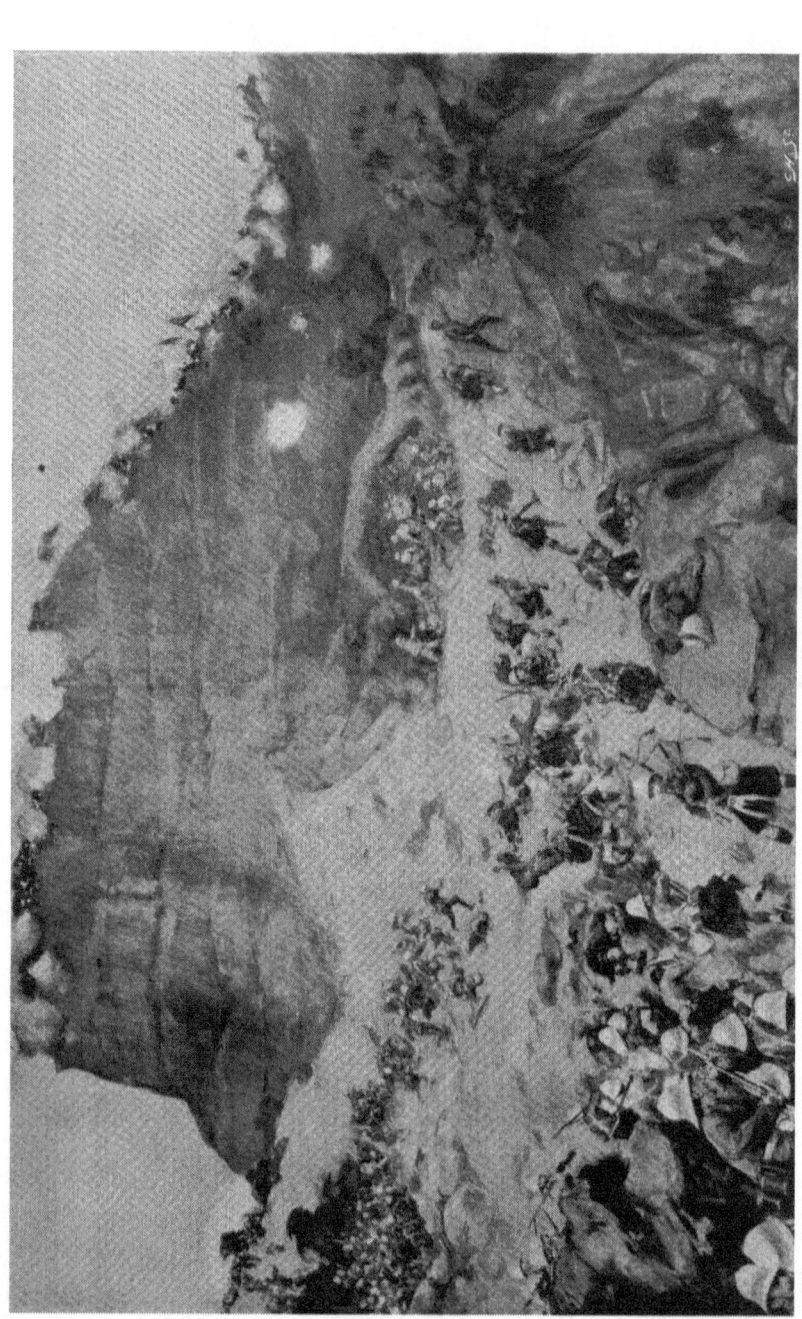

THE ASSAULT ON THE DARGAI HILL

October 20

See page 129

THE INDIAN FRONTIER WAR

BEING AN ACCOUNT OF THE MOHMUND
AND TIRAH EXPEDITIONS

1897

LIONEL JAMES
REUTER'S SPECIAL CORRESPONDENT

WITH THIRTY-ONE FROM SKETCHES BY
THE AUTHOR AND PHOTOGRAPHS,
AND TEN MAPS AND PLANS

The Naval & Military Press Ltd

Reproduced by kind permission of the Central Library,
Royal Military Academy, Sandhurst

Published by
The Naval & Military Press Ltd
Unit 10, Ridgewood Industrial Park,
Uckfield, East Sussex,
TN22 5QE England
Tel: +44 (0) 1825 749494
Fax: +44 (0) 1825 765701
www.naval-military-press.com
© The Naval & Military Press Ltd 2005

In reprinting in facsimile from the original, any imperfections are inevitably reproduced and the quality may fall short of modern type and cartographic standards.

THE AUTHOR

DEDICATES

THIS VOLUME TO

MR. J. O'B. SAUNDERS

PROPRIETOR OF "THE ENGLISHMAN" CALCUTTA

AS A SMALL RETURN FOR THE GREAT

KINDNESS HE HAS SHOWN HIM

PREFACE

From the way the public Press has called for explanation upon certain points connected with the campaign, it has appeared to me that the public barely appreciate what was asked of their army when it was sent to invade Afridi and Orakzai Tirah. Having been present at the Campaign, I would that my readers should start from as fair a standpoint as possible, for I feel sure that, after really grasping the circumstances of the campaign, they will appreciate the reasons why I have abstained from criticism. Be it understood that casualties must occur, and in a mountainous country like the Afridi the casualties must be in proportion to the efficiency of the transport. The Government of India chose to *equip the force with an inefficient transport*, and the General Officers could only do their best with what was served out to them.

Those who have no knowledge of frontier warfare can form but the faintest conception of the adverse conditions under which the campaign took place, and it would be well for the public in general to refrain from forming any judgment on the matter till the whole question has been properly threshed out. Let us consider for a moment the task that lay before General Lockhart when he took over the command of the Tirah Expeditionary Force. He was given a conjectural map of the theatre of war, and was led to understand that no small part of his duty was a fairly accurate survey of the unknown country. He had, it is true, at his disposal perhaps as fine a body of fighting men as could be found in any part of the world, but with this army he had to carry a larger army of non-combatants and followers, and a multitude of transport animals—an array which would strike a Continental soldier dumb with amazement. On the day the first shot was fired on the Changru Kotal there were no fewer than 43,810 transport animals attached to the Tirah Expeditionary Force. This was, be it noted, in addition to the transport of the Peshawar and Kurram columns. Even given that this enormous baggage train was in efficient order, which it was not, and had to operate over level and metalled roads, it would still have remained a source of weakness to those responsible for its protection.

How much more, therefore, must this unwieldy train have been a thorn in the side of our fighting men when it had to be protected, and pushed and driven through perhaps the most difficult country in the world! General Lockhart was called upon to take this undisciplined multitude across mountains where there was not even a vestige of a goat-track; along river-beds strewn with boulders, where the only path was knee-deep in icy water; through gorges where two animals abreast closed the passage; up gradients which in their initial stages defeated (and this is a hard saying) even mountain battery mules; down descents which were almost precipices; through barren places where food there was none; and into extremes of climate which destroyed the weaklings and consequently increased the loads of the more robust. Even had there been no opposition, the passage through such a country of an army so handicapped would have been a great feat. But there was bitter opposition. Each pathway was disputed and every covering ridge held bands of well-armed enemies. And such enemies! The fighting on the slopes of the Safed Koh is not the fighting of which one reads in books. Those who have not seen half a dozen men armed with weapons of precision and posted on the top of a cliff stopping and even throwing into confusion the baggage train of a whole division can never realise what an undertaking is the coercion of these wild tribesmen in their mountain fastnesses. Things are not now as they were fifty or even twenty years ago. In those days we had only to dislodge a few ill-armed cragsmen, whose one advantage lay in the natural positions which their country gave them. Now the conditions are vastly different. The Pathan, while still possessing the natural advantages of country and physical hardihood, is further armed with weapons as precise and deadly as our own. He has been skilfully trained in their use, and from a dozen sources comes his supply of ammunition. He is as active as a gural or mountain goat; he can carry a week's rations on his back; and experts maintain that he is as deadly a shot at eight hundred yards as the Boer is at four hundred. Moreover, he is clever and crafty, and is fighting in his own country, where every hill path and position for ambuscade is known to him. Long training in fighting, whether as a soldier in our service, or in the endless war of Pathan sept against sept, has made him learned in the task of taking life while carefully preserving his own. Indeed, it would be difficult to imagine or discover a better method of defending a mountainous country than the Afridi has shown.

The critics at once conjure up the deadly effects of screw-guns and Maxims. But what tribesman was there who did not know before the Sampagha was crossed that the nine-pounder could not demolish a decently constructed sungar, and that the hail of the Maxim was of no avail against a rapidly moving line of irregular skirmishers? Indeed, on many occasions our batteries and machine guns only furnished larger targets for hidden riflemen. Knowing exactly our weaknesses and where their own strength lay, the Afridis in crafty council at Bagh determined, when their choice was war, to avoid all massed opposition, and reserve their fighting strength for the system of guerilla warfare which they understand so well, and in which all the disadvantages lie with the invader. Thus they lay in wait upon the flanks of straggling baggage; marked down the range of kotal, ridge, and defile; stood close hidden while advance-guards and fighting bodies moved past them in the early day, only to close upon and harry

PREFACE

tired and day-worn rear-guards in the hope of delaying them until they were benighted, trusting to destroy them at leisure while entangled in an impossible country. Those who have never been under a continuous fire do not realise how constant rear-guard actions tell upon the soldier ; how weary and dispirited he gets, and what resource and skill and courage must be displayed by officers to stave off disaster. Yet because men are lost, because tired followers are panic-stricken in the face of an enemy dropping, as it were, from the clouds, critics call for explanations and the wrecking of military careers. If only such critics could have stood on December 13 in the fighting line, and seen the magnificent display of skill shown by the officers of General Westmacott's Brigade while men dropped fast, they might perhaps understand the difficulties under which a rear-guard retirement is carried out. And it has been a campaign of rear-guards. I would have my readers realise how easy it is for a cragsman armed with a breechloading piece to cause casualties, while he himself is secure on a hilltop, and how rear-guard accidents may occur at the close of a short winter day, when baggage has to be driven and carried for miles down the bed of a mountain torrent.

LIONEL JAMES.

WAINI, T.S. RAILWAY, INDIA.

The Publisher is indebted to the Proprietors of "The Graphic" for their kind permission to reproduce the drawings from the war-sketches made for them by the Author.

CONTENTS

THE MOHMUND EXPEDITION

I. Fanaticism the chief cause of the Pathan revolt—Influence of European affairs on Asiatic minds—The Amir's pamphlet —And quotation from it—" The Mad Fakir " Pp. 4—15

II. Concentration of troops—Formation and despatch of the Mohmund Field Force—List of officers . Pp. 16—23

III. The Gundah Plateau—March from Shabkadr—Reconnaissance of the Jarobi Road and the Nahakhi Pass—Punishment and fines inflicted on the Upper Mohmunds
Pp. 24—35

IV. Attack on the Camp—Death of Captain Tomkins—Ill luck of the 38th Dogras—Gallant conduct of Lieutenant Watson, R.E. . . . . Pp. 36—44

V. Helio connection with General Blood's force—Position of the enemy—Night attack on General Blood's camp by the Ghazis . . . . Pp. 45—55

VI. General Westmacott's camp at Kuzchinari—Advance on the Badmanai Valley—Attack by enemy and "prettily fought engagement" . . . . . Pp. 56—61

VII. Suffering of the wounded—Progress of the brigade up the Jarobi Valley—Effect of burning and tower blasting on the tribesmen—A short and satisfactory campaign Pp. 62—72

CONTENTS

VIII. Difficulties to contend with—First action of Patiala Infantry under Captain Cox and Lieutenant Davidson—The splendid work of the 20th Punjab Infantry   Pp. 73—79

IX. Lower Mohmunds fined and punished—End of campaign within view—An account of the Mohmunds and their characteristics . . . . . . Pp. 80—87

THE TIRAH EXPEDITION

X. The Amir's influence—Routes to the Tirah Valley—Conflicting rumours . . . . . . Pp. 91—98

XI. Start of General Hamilton's Peshawar column—Order of advance of troops to the front—Stupendous task entailed in moving the army—Accident to General Ian Hamilton—Advance up the Dargai Ridge—Its position and surroundings . . . . Pp. 99—113

XII. Storming of the Dargai Heights—Gallant charge of the Gordons—List of killed and wounded . Pp. 114—123

XIII. Determination of the tribesmen to fight—The story of the buried standard and its effect on the Afridis—Arrival of General Hart, V.C.—Persistent firing into camp throughout the night . . . . . . Pp. 124—134

XIV. Advance up the Khanki Nullah—Description of the pass—Defence of the pass . . . . . Pp. 135—143

XV. Events *en route* to the "Promised Land"—View of Tirah from the Arhanga Pass—Choice of the camping ground—Description of the mosque at Bagh—Daring attack on the baggage . . . . . . Pp. 144—152

XVI. Description of an Afridi homestead—Attack on a foraging post—Difficult position of Captain Rowcroft and two companies of the 15th Sikhs—General Westmacott punishes the Zakka Khel villages—The kotal of Saran Sur—Arrival of Sir William Lockhart and withdrawal from the summit commenced . . . Pp. 153—169

CONTENTS

XVII. Rapid movements hampered by wounded—Political outlook—Terms of surrender—Zakka Khels, the "Thieves of the Thieves" . . . . . . Pp. 170—176

XVIII. General Hart's brigade at Mastura engaged in more hostilities—Good news from General Kempster's detached brigade—Story of the Bagh mosque—Military opinion with regard to the future—The "dwelling of the saintly mouthpiece of the Prophet"—Heavy day near Camp Maidan . . . . . . Pp. 177—191

XIX. Treacherous attack on Major O'Sullivan and officers prospecting for camping ground—Bodies of missing Dorsets found—Tribal representatives of the Khumber Khels, Aka Khels, Malikdin Khels and Kamrai Khels received by Sir William Lockhart and Sir Richard Udney
Pp. 192—199

XX. Advance into the river-bed below Bagh—Yeoman service of the little Gurkha scouts—Sharp fighting with the enemy—Arrival of the force at Datoi—Anxiety on account of the baggage not arriving—Sir William Lockhart's determination to return to Bagh—Retirement from Datoi continued . . . . . . Pp. 200—211

XXI. Advancement of Colonel Collins and half of the Queen's into the Massuzai Valley—Magnificent sight of a burning valley—Bravery of Sir Pertab Singh—Advancement upon Esor . . . . Pp. 212—222

XXII. The Chamkannis resist—Retirement of Colonel Hill and the left column—Bravery of the scouts and the difficulties they overcame—Good work done by the Gurkha scouts The return to Bagh camp . . . . Pp. 223—231

XXIII. Evacuation of Maidan commenced—Attack by the enemy on Colonel Pulley's regiment—Borderers dislodge the enemy from the hillside—Discomfort of the troops in camp—Strange scenes in camp—Order of advance from Datoi—General engagement of all troops . Pp. 232—247

CONTENTS

XXIV. The troops meet with no opposition on the march through the Zakka Khel country—The baggage take the wrong road, which causes a grave delay—Serious position of Major Downman and his soldiers—Captain Uniacke's bold conduct in attacking a village—Anxiety in the Sher Khel camp—Search party sent out—Block of General Westmacott's column in the river-bed—Afridis' *coup* in attacking the column—The march of Lockhart's 2nd Division a great military achievement—General Lockhart's order to G.O.C. . . . . Pp. 248—268

XXV. Khyber Pass reported deserted—Ali Musjid occupied without a shot being fired—Colour-sergeant Walker captured and retained as a hostage . . . . . Pp. 269—273

XXVI. Christmas Day and letters in camp—Account of Chena village—Enemy engage the Yorks in a smart flanking skirmish—Sir William Lockhart's plan of campaign changed—End of winter campaign and its result.
Pp. 274—284

XXVII. The Tirah Field Force . . . . Pp. 285—300

ILLUSTRATIONS

	To face page
The Assault on the Dargai Hill . . .	Frontispiece
Pathan Mountaineers	6
General Elles's Advance on the Mohmund Plateau . . .	20
General Jeffreys's Force Repelling Night Attack . . .	34
The Capture of Hadda Mullah's Village	66
General Westmacott Conducting the Retirement from Jarobi .	70
The 1st Devonshire Regiment Entering the Kohat Pass . .	100
Ruins of Saraghari Post	106
Fort Gulistan	108
Camp at Shinwari	110
Fort Lockhart	112
Dargai Cliff	116
Front View of the Bluff of the Dargai Ridge	120
After the Battle of Dargai	122
The Khanki Valley and River	126
Camp at Karappa—Khanki Valley	130
A Native Mountain Battery in Action near Karappa . .	132
The Taking of the Sampagha Pass	138
The Final Assault on the Summit of the Sampagha Pass .	140
Akbar Mullah's Mosque	148
Camp at Maidan in Afridi Tirah	150
The Arhanga Pass	150
Camp at Maidan Tirah	152

ILLUSTRATIONS

	To face page
The Northamptons Returning down the Nullah	166
The Attack on General Kempster's Rear-Guard	186
The Defenders of Gulistan	210
The Attack on the Chamkanni Tribe	226
General Westmacott's Brigade Drawing out the Enemy	244
The Enemy Opening Fire on the Advanced Guard	246
Saving the Baggage in the Rear-Guard Action	256
General Sir William Lockhart's Personal Staff	290

MAPS AND PLANS

	Page
Map of the Khyber and Bazar Valleys, showing Routes Taken by the 1st and 2nd Brigades . . . . (to face)	3
Map of Theatre of Operations of the Mohmund Field Force, showing Principal Engagements	6
Plan of General Blood's Camp at Nawagai, Attacked on the Night of September 20	53
Map of Theatre of Operations of the Tirah Field Force, showing Routes and Chief Engagements	93
Plan Showing Disposition of the Troops at the Storming of the Dargai Ridge and Position of the Enemy . . .	118
Map of the Mastura Valley, showing the Route taken by Lockhart's Advance and Actions at the Sampagha and Arhanga Passes	140
Plan showing Disposition of Troops at the Rear-Guard Action at Saran Sur	165
Map of the Upper Waran Valley	184
Map of Theatre of Operations of the Force in the Bara Valley, showing Camps and Detached Entrenchments . . .	249
Plan of House defended by Kempster's Rear-Guard on December 11	253

THE MOHMUND EXPEDITION

A

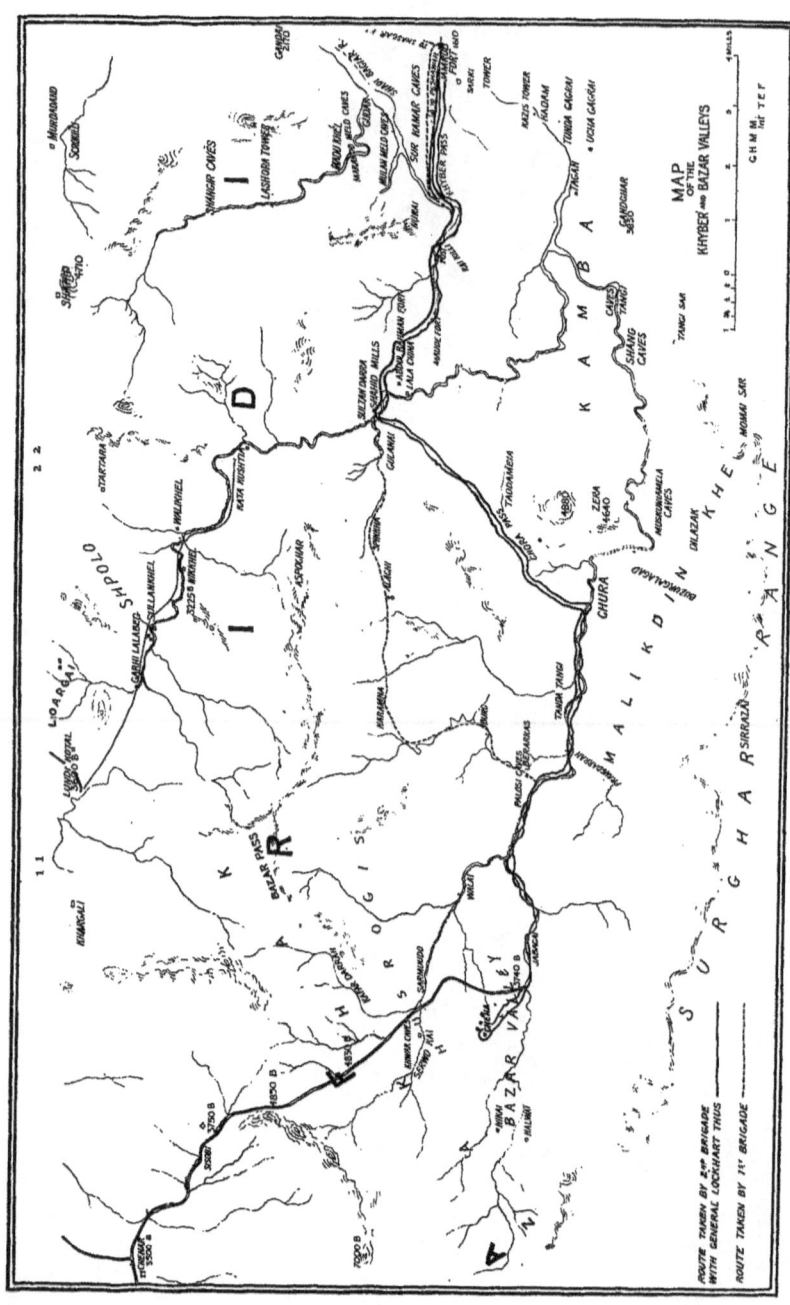

I

Fanaticism the chief cause of the Pathan revolt — Influence of European affairs on Asiatic minds — The Amir's Pamphlet — And quotation from it — "The Mad Fakir."

To pretend that the following is a complete history of the Pathan Revolt on the North-west Frontier of India would be absurd : for it will probably be years before a complete narrative, embracing the full details of the wave of fire and sword which has swept from Tochi to Bonair, is placed before the public. All that the present volume pretends to furnish is a simple narrative of the heaviest undertaking upon which the Government of India ventured, to crush out a rebellion which at any time might have exercised the worst possible influence upon the whole of the Indian Empire. Neither does the narrative profess to be more than a rough diary of a campaign, told in the simple language of a war-correspondent, unembellished with profound reasonings on the political situation which led up to the result. It is a brief description of those scenes of the frontier drama at which the author was present, and in chief is a diary of the operations of General Sir William Lockhart's force against the Orakzai and Tirah Afridis.

To speculate upon the causes which led to the Maizar attack, the rising of the Swat-Bonair tribes, the Mohmund raid, and the upheaval of the Afridis from the Khyber to the Kurram, would open a chapter of argument which would leave but little space for the history of events. But after having studied the attitude of the tribes from the first burst of their energy, through the varied phases of their resistance, and the final collapse of the majority of sections, one is inclined to sum the causes of the outbreak up under three heads: the first of which is fanaticism; the second, fanaticism; and the third, *fanaticism*. There is no doubt that there have been many influences of late years tending to a definite conclusion of the frontier question. Though no statesman could tell when the actual outbreak would occur, yet those who best understood the uncertain temperament of these wild borderers knew that the late policy, though it acted well for a time, must sooner or later end in open friction, for there is no limit to the extent to which the self-conceit and independent up-bringing of the tribesmen could carry them. Especially as their traditions fostered their belief in their own prowess. The Afridis, Mohmunds and Bonerwals, though they had often been arrayed against the Indian army's forces, could boast that they had never been attacked with success, and in two cases that their land had never in all time seen the white invader. Moreover, as they yearly became better armed and imbued with training in arms, they grew more confident in the security of their independence. And, to the feeble reasoning of the illiterate Oriental mind, it took but little argument to impress upon the younger generation that the subsidy which the Indian Government paid the Khyber tribes was a simple tribute given rather through fear than in accordance with a stated policy. With a youth tired of inter-tribal feuds, and yet trained to the use of arms of precision, the tribal temperament easily lent itself to the first wave of fanaticism which swept across the frontier hills and valleys. It is not necessary to give the meaning of the word fanaticism. Wherever Islam is the creed there will be found disciples prepared to preach its cause and to fire the undercurrent of feeling which forms part of this weird belief. All that such preachers ask is that a crisis may arrive which shall stir the popular feeling out of the narrow channels of trade, commerce, and homeside agriculture. And in 1897—by strange chance a year which marked a great era in the growth of the British Indian Empire—pathetically enough, this crisis came.

At the time much was written and said about the present upheaval, much that had bearing upon the subject and much that was irrelevant. But taken in a nutshell the real cause of the whole business may be claimed to be the successful attempt of the Mullahs to 'seize a moment of unrest and work upon the fanaticism of the tribesmen. The riots at Calcutta and the Greek fiasco could have but little effect alone to originate such an outburst of feeling; though doubtless, as the documents subsequently found in Said Akbar's dwelling in the Waran Valley showed, they were contorted so that they became incentive factors in keeping the flame alive. Practically what happened is this. The Mad Mullah played upon the veneration which the whole frontier has for the late Akhund of Swat, and having represented

himself as that worthy's successor by divine selection, he preached from the text most hateful of all to the Pathan borderer, "Annexation by the Infidel," and his trump card was this: "There is holy Swat practically annexed, a garrison at Malakhand, a permanent post at Chakdara; yet in the original proclamation a short occupation was all that was

PATHAN MOUNTAINEERS

THE MOHMUND EXPEDITION 7

promised!" The Mullah made the most of this, and prophesied an extension of it. This was enough to unsettle the Pathan mind, and the conflagrated border was the outcome.

Nor has the Amir's pamphlet been an unimportant factor. The work itself is a cunning production by a cunning man, and even in the English translation you can perceive the double meaning between the lines. The summoning of the Mullahs to Kabul alone was a sufficient foundation for the latter to work upon. Such quotations as the following—and the Amir's book bristles with them—could not but be weapons in the hands of fanatics : "The need of those persons who defend the frontier of Mohamedan territories for one prayer is equivalent to five hundred prayers of those who stay at home and do not proceed to the frontier for keeping watch." Again : "O true believers, when ye meet a party of infidels, stand firm and remember God frequently, that ye may prosper. . . . When ye meet the unbelievers marching in great numbers against you, turn not your backs from them, for whoso shall turn his back unto them on that day, unless he turneth aside to fight or retreateth to another party of the Faithful, shall draw on himself the indignation of God, and his abode shall be Hell: an ill journey shall it be thither!"

How far the Maizar outrage was an outcome of the general wave of fanaticism which swept across the frontier it is difficult to say, but there is no doubt that ever since the publication of the Amir's book the Mullahs had taken the cue, and a religious crusade was being preached throughout Islam in the

East. And it may be that the back-wash of this preaching influenced the Calcutta rioters, since many weird suggestions found publicity in the Moslem Press at that period, which at the time were treated with levity and derision, as that portion of the Mohamedan outburst faded as rapidly as it ignited. If, however, Maizar was a herald of the coming storm, it failed to attract attention to the whole line of the frontier, though it was known politically that the fanatical Mullahs of the frontier were restless, especially the Mullahs Powindah, Najmat-ud-din of Jarobi, Said Akbar the Akakhel Afridi, Indrej of Bazar. Then suddenly an unheard-of prophet arose in the land in the person of a Bonerwal-Swat madman known as the "Mad Fakir."

According to native report he was a native of Swat who travelled to Central Asia and eventually settled in Mazar-i-Sharif, the Amir's chief cantonment in Afghan Turkestan. He is said to have lived there for ten years and then to have gone to Kabul. This summer, according to the same report, he visited Bajour, the Utman Khel country, and Buner, preaching the necessity of waging war against all enemies of the Faith. He is supposed to have been in league with Najmat-ud-din, the notorious Mullah of Hadda, whose fanatical hostility to the British Government is well known. Whatever truth there may be in this story, one point is clear: the "Mad Fakir" appeared in Upper Swat in July, and the fame of his preaching spread far and wide. He gradually worked his way down

THE MOHMUND EXPEDITION

the valley, with a rabble of men and boys at his heels, and on July 26 he was at Landakai, within hail of Chakdara. On that day he took the final step which brought about the rising. He claimed to be inspired to work miracles; the Heavenly Hosts were, he said, on his side; and he announced that with or without help from his listeners he would sweep our troops from Chakdara and the Malakand in eight days. His excited appeals to the fanaticism which exists in every Pathan were responded to in a manner little short of marvellous: his progress from Landakai to Thana and thence to Aladaud, both villages in view of Chakdara post, must have been a triumphal one; the villagers flew to arms; our levies hastily retired, except such as joined his standard; all the headmen, with one solitary exception, were carried away by the popular enthusiasm; and by nightfall a resolute body of tribesmen was on the move to attack the Malakand, while another party turned their attention to Chakdara. The Mullah had roused the whole valley, and his standard afterwards became the rallying-point for thousands of fighting men from Upper Swat, Buner, the Utman Khel country, and even more distant parts.

On July 29 the whole of India rang with the news that the tribes had risen and that the Malakan had been attacked; that Chakdara, the fortified post on the Swat River, was invested; and that the tribes this side of the Panjkora were up. The tension throughout India was great, especially when the fate of the little garrison of Chakdara seemed to hang in the balance. Then came the news that the post had been relieved, and it seemed that the first wave of fanaticism had been checked; and with the wounding of the Mad Fakir himself and the heavy losses inflicted upon the tribesmen, it looked as if the frontier trouble was over, and the meting out of punishment to the tribes implicated would end the affair. But the public anxiety was barely assuaged when from Peshawar camp the startling news that the Mohmunds were up, and that Shankarghar, a village within our frontier, had been raided and gutted. The battle of Shabkadr, which took place on August 9, showed that the raid was not the work of a small party of marauders, and with the vague rumours which reached Simla from the Samana, India became convinced that the country was on the eve of a crisis as serious as it was unexpected—a general upheaval of the Pathan transfrontier tribes. Nor was this a mistaken view, for within the next few days the Samana was invested and the Khyber in the hands of the tribesmen. On the very day that General Sir Bindon Blood's punitive division left Amandhara to carry out the operations which were planned to stifle the spark of revolt in Swat-Bonair, and to make an example capable of being felt all along the frontier, Gulistan and the Samana were invested and an Afridi Lashkar had closed upon the Khyber.

A few days previous to August 8, 1897, the Hindu Baniahs of Shankarghar deserted their bazar, saying that they had been warned that it was to be sacked by the Mohmunds. The Baniahs being so scared,

THE MOHMUND EXPEDITION

the Peshawar movable column, consisting of four guns of the 61st F.B. under Captain Blacker, two squadrons of the 13th B.L. under Major Atkinson, the 20th P.I., and two companies of the Somerset L.I. under Major Lumbe, was sent out to Shabkadr. There was no difficulty in crossing the Kabul River, which was bridged, until the third branch of the stream was reached; so the force made for the Kadir ferry, the 13th B.L. swimming across it. Major Atkinson and the 1st squadron reconnoitred towards Shabkadr, flames at the same time being visible. Lieutenant Turner reached the fort at 8 A.M. and found Shabkadr bazar burned, and that the enemy had taken up a position facing the fort on a plateau about a mile and a half distant. Lieutenant Turner then acted with his squadron in compact formation until Major Atkinson brought up the other squadron of the 13th B.L., the infantry arriving somewhat later. The cavalry, skirting the cultivated ground between the fort and the plateau upon which the enemy was in position, pushed them backwards and forced the Mohmunds into the low hills which skirt the border, with considerable loss to horses and men. The next morning the enemy were seen still to be in possession of the lower ranges of the hills, but did not appear in great force, so Colonel Woon moved out to attack them. Taking his course viâ Shabkadr village, he gained the plateau which the enemy had held on the preceding day.

Here the infantry halted, as the artillery, to which the 13th B.L. were acting as an escort, were not up, having taken the direct route and found difficulty in the cultivated ground. The infantry being in such small numbers, only about seven hundred, the enemy conceived the bold idea of completely enveloping them and cutting off their retreat to the fort. They were found to be in reality in great force, at least seven thousand. The numbers enabled them to show a strong front, at the same time to detach a force to operate on Colonel Woon's left flank, and also a further strong detachment to work as cutting-off party. The flanking party came down under cover of the Gundab Nullah, while the third party, completely concealed by the low hills, so far achieved that object that the small force of Somersets and 20th P.I. were forced to fall back. The enemy were greatly assisted by ravines and the broken nature of the country.

This same plateau has always been the battle ground of the Mohmunds, and all past histories point to their employing a similar method of attack. Colonel Woon's infantry retired in two sections, the one supporting the other. But the tribesmen, as usual, interpreted an orderly retirement to be a defeat, and pressed on with great determination, at times being within a hundred yards of the Shabkadr force. While the infantry were thus returning by alternate bodies on the fort, the artillery were able to come into action, and this freed the cavalry, which were directed by General Elles, who had arrived from Peshawar during the engagement, to manœuvre outwards so as to join the enemy's flank. Making their way up one of the ravines, the 13th were able to execute this manœuvre unperceived by the enemy,

THE MOHMUND EXPEDITION 13

and forming in a nullah, they made one of the most timely charges which cavalry has made in India.

Led by their British officers, they took the inner fringe of the advancing enemy and charged them from end to end. Taking the entire length of the plateau, a matter of about a mile and a half, they over-rode the whole of the attacking front, and the enemy, broken and demoralised, fled to the hills in disorder. During the earlier part of the morning the cavalry had been supporting the guns, but on the arrival of the 3rd Field Troop from Peshawar, Major Atkinson's squadron was free to act as it did, and to deal a salutary lesson to the over-confident tribesmen. The incidents of this charge were that Major Atkinson had his horse shot under him at the end of the charge, four hundred yards in front of the position originally occupied by the infantry, and Lieutenant Cheynes was hit a few yards beyond. To attest the severity of the morning's fighting, sixty per cent. of the force engaged were returned as casualties. All previous experience with the Mohmunds had been endorsed, in that a small force is able to keep in check even overpowering bodies of the enemy; and at no moment during the engagement was there any doubt but that the party could have held their own back to the fort, though severely pressed. The action is significant of the benefit of infantry playing into the hands of cavalry and the efficacy of their mutual co-operation.

From the 9th until it was determined to send a force into the Mohmund country, the force has been a corps of observation, and the duty has been exceptionally severe, as with an enemy audacious enough to attack the very fort of Shabkadr—to attempt to axe-open the door and to burn the environs—there was no saying what they might not attempt. The cavalry was out patrolling day and night, and one squadron of the 13th B.L., under Major Balfour, reconnoitred all three main routes into the Mohmund country, which are due north-south of the Alikandi route, through Pindiali's villages (North Mohmund) the Gundab Nullah, the direct route, the southern boundary of which was the scene of Colonel Woon's fight and which leads to the centre of the country, and lately the Shinoli route, which leads into the southern portion of the valley by Afghanistan via Lalpura. It has not been possible in any case to reconnoitre beyond a five-mile radius from camp, because the enemy's pickets have invariably fired on any attempt being made. All the main kotals have been held in strength, at times to as many as a hundred to two hundred rifles.

As soon as the authorities realised the really serious extent to which the wave of fanaticism had spread, it was determined to despatch without delay a division into the Mohmund country. The original programme which the Malakand division would have followed was altered, and it was so ordered that the Malakand and Mohmund field forces were to carry out the work of punishment through the stretch of land lying between Lalpura and the Swat River up to Bajour in concert. It was estimated that a month would be sufficient time to allow for the complete punishment of the Mohmunds and Mahmunds; and

THE MOHMUND EXPEDITION 15

while these active operations were being carried out, the organisation of the Tirah Field Force, the big and crushing undertaking of the campaign, was being pushed on, so that the force might start as soon as the Mohmunds had been sufficiently dealt with. General Elles was given the command of the division which was to operate direct into the Mohmund country, the same being drawn chiefly from the Peshawar garrison, and the reserve brigade, which had been watching the mouth of the Khyber. By September 11 most of the force had concentrated at or about Shabkadr Fort, and the commissariat had arranged for a general advance by the 15th of the month.

II

Concentration of troops—Formation and despatch of the Mohmund Field Force—List of officers.

Shabkadr Fort,*
September 12th.

THE daily cavalry patrol reported heavy firing at 7 A.M. at the mouth of the Karapa defile in Gundah Nullah. Major Balfour moved out and supported the patrol, and found that a party of tribesmen, about three hundred strong, presumably Halamzais, had come down into the Tarakzai hills, and had planted three standards on the side of the left boundary of the defile, which is clearly visible from Shabkadr. They saluted the act with a fusillade of not less than fifty rounds. This may be taken as an act of defiance, and the supposed friendly Tarakzais must have allowed them into their country to make the

---

* Shabkadr Fort itself was built by the Sikhs. It stands on a mound and has walls fifty feet high, so is practically impregnable to any force without artillery. Shankarghar was an old Sikh Cantonment bazaar, and it is inhabited chiefly by rich Hindu moneylenders, who have had very profitable dealings with the tribesmen on both sides of the border, distant only three miles away. Shabkadr, when attacked, was held by forty or fifty Border Police, who were attacked from about 4 P.M. to 5 A.M. They accounted for some forty of the tribesmen without loss to themselves. The appearance of the troops on Saturday morning caused the Mohmunds to withdraw to a respectful distance, but they were full of fight when

exhibition. A trader on his way from Periarwa to Kuner reported that his caravan of donkeys had been looted in the pass. On arrival of the cavalry the tribesmen uprooted their standards and disappeared into the defile, and the cavalry had orders not to follow them farther.

SHABKADR CAMP,
September 14th.

The whole of General Elles' force concentrated within two miles of the site of Colonel Woon's action of the 9th of last month, and stood ready to move at a moment's notice, it being believed that the start would be made on the 15th. General Elles inspected all arms on the two days before the actual advance took place, General Macgregor's Brigade (2nd) being turned out on the 13th, General Westmacott's the following morning. The first-named comprises the Oxfordshire Light Infantry; the 9th Gurkhas, Colonel Woodhouse; the 37th Dogras, Colonel Mills; the 1st Patiala Infantry and No. 2 Mountain Battery. The Oxfords turned out in condition, and it was impossible not to notice their workmanlike appearance,

Colonel Woon made his attack. The ground on which the action was fought must be much the same as that on which Sir Colin Campbell in 1852 with six hundred men met and defeated six thousand Mohmunds, and again in January 1864 Colonel A. Macdonnel, of the Rifle Brigade, with one thousand seven hundred and fifty men, defeated a body of five thousand, who held the low hills facing Shabkadr. His success, like that of General Elles, was due to the cavalry, the Mohmunds being tempted into the plain and then charged. A squadron of the 7th Hussars on that occasion made three successive charges, which enabled the infantry to act with decisive effect against the enemy's broken line.

and that eagerness which betokens confidence in the ranks both in themselves and their officers. The 9th Gurkhas looked well, but being Khas Gurkhas are a different stamp of men to what one has been used to. That they are of the right sort was amply shown when the whole regiment volunteered on the first orders of mobilisation to carry down the baggage of the regiment, which lay with them at Lansdowne. The 37th's record is too recent to require further eulogising.

The Patiala Sikhs called forth admiration on every side. They are as fine a body of the great fighting race as one could wish to see, and entirely officered by native officers. It was pleasing to notice that under the inspection they were as self-controlled and confident as if it was not their first appearance on active service. They are safe to fulfil the high opinion already formed of their military efficiency. The P.A. Somerset Light Infantry unfortunately wore the stamp of the malaria-driven station which they have garrisoned, and a month in a Shabkadr swamp had told its tale. The 20th P.I. are the pick of native infantry which we have seen lately. The 1st Gurkhas also turned out admirably; and when one considers that General Elles' cavalry is the 13th B.L., after yesterday's and to-day's inspection one feels confident that as fine a force is concentrated on the Mohmund border as could be chosen on the frontier.

The recent record of 13th B.L. calls for no further remarks, but the horses of the regiment show up wonderfully fit after a month of hard patrolling

THE MOHMUND EXPEDITION 19

on the frontier. There are three Maxims with the force, two attached to the Somersets, and the 16th Lancers' Maxim detachment under Lieutenant Campbell attached to the 13th B.L. The latter equipment is one officer, eight men, eleven horses. The gun and tripod carriage are carried on one horse the ammunition-boxes on another. This equipment seems the most practicable for hill fighting and uneven ground, as the gun can be brought into action at a gallop, and the unbuckling of a couple of straps finds it in action.

The orders for the advance were out early on the 14th. The 1st Brigade under General Westmacott to advance at 5.30 A.M. on the 15th up the Gundab Valley making for Azim Killa, a fortified village twelve miles up the pass. Two battalions of the 2nd Brigade to act as support and the rest as baggage-guard, two squadrons of the 13th convoying the baggage later. The march should bring the force into contact with the Tarakzai, Bharankhel, and Halimzai Mohmunds. The Lower Tarakzai on the left of the Gundab Gulley are reported friendly, and it was in order that their patrols, showing a specified headdress, were not to be fired on. But the other two tribes have distinctly shown that they are hostile, and it is from them that the first opposition is anticipated. If the march is not unduly delayed the 16th or the 17th should see the Peshawar force into the Kumali Valley, which may be taken as the key of the Mohmund country. Towards it converge the three routes from the Peshawar Valley and the Lalpura Nullah. It is also practically equidistant from

Nawagai with Shabkadr Fort. It is the country of the Kwaizai section, and is reported to be highly cultivated. It was arranged that the two invading forces should concentrate here, as thus the whole of the Mohmund country would be in their hands, for the concentration meant twelve thousand troops against a reported possible nineteen thousand tribesmen, if the latter stretch their organisation to the full. Thus their only course would be to make a last stand at Inzarai Jaroba in the Baizai section, or to set their standards up upon the Kabal Sapar range, from which point it is impossible to conjecture the future, as they would have by the latest demarcation the Amir's territory as their retiring ground. The line of advance after Had Kili or the Kamali Plain is practically unknown, though it is evident that the main commissariat positions of the country are the above-mentioned points. Approximately the fighting strength of the Tarakzai Halimzai and Isshakhels is one thousand respectively, and the Bazai, who were the most interested in the Peshawar advance, two thousand.

The Governor-General in Council sanctioned the despatch of a force as detailed below, to be styled the Mohmund Field Force, to move into the Mohmund country from Shabkadr, and co-operate with a force under the command of Major-General Sir Bindon Blood, K.C.B. The force was composed as follows :

First Brigade.

1st Battalion (Prince Albert's) Somersetshire Light Infantry.
20th (Punjab) Regiment of Bengal Infantry.

GENERAL ELLES'S ADVANCE INTO THE MOHMUND PLATEAU

THE MOHMUND EXPEDITION

2nd Battalion 1st Gurkha (Rifle) Regiment.
Sections A and B, No. 5, British Field Hospital.
No. 31 Native Field Hospital.

Second Brigade.

2nd Battalion Oxfordshire Light Infantry.
9th Gurkha (Rifle) Regiment of Bengal Infantry.
37th (Dogra) Regiment of Bengal Infantry (six companies).
Sections C and D, No. 5, British Field Hospital.
No. 44 Native Field Hospital.

Divisional Troops.

13th (Duke of Connaught's) Regiment of Bengal Lancers.
No. 3 Mountain Battery, Royal Artillery.
No. 5 (Bombay) Mountain Battery.
28th Regiment of Bombay Infantry.
No. 5 Company Bengal Sappers and Miners.
1st Patiala Infantry (Imperial Service Troops).
Detachment 16th Lancers, with a Maxim gun.
Detachment 1st Battalion Devonshire Regiment, with two Maxim guns.
Sections C and D, No. 63, and Section A, No. 45, Native Field Hospitals.

Commands and Staff.

General Officer Commanding the Force (with the local rank of Major-General).	Brigadier-General E. R. Elles, C.B.
Aide de-Camp	Lieutenant M. R. Elles, R.E.
Orderly Officer	Captain K. MacLaren, 13th Hussars.
Extra Orderly Officer . .	Captain R. E. Grimston, 6th Bengal Cavalry.
Assistant Adjutant-General . .	Major C. L. Woollcombe, 2nd Battalion King's Own Scottish Borderers.
Assistant Quartermaster-General .	Major G. H. W. O'Sullivan, R.E.
Deputy-Assistant Quartermaster-General (Intelligence)	Captain F. A. Hoghton, 1st Bombay Grenadiers.
Field Intelligence Officer . .	Lieutenant C. E. Macquoid, 1st Lancers, Hyderabad Contingent.
Commanding Royal Artillery .	Lieutenant-Colonel A. E. Duthy, R.A.
Adjutant Royal Artillery . .	Captain W. MacLeod, R.A.
Field Engineer	Captain F. H. Kelly, R.E.

THE INDIAN FRONTIER WAR

Assistant Field Engineer	Lieutenant W. A. Stokes, R.E.
Assistant Field Engineer	Lieutenant C. B. L. Greenstreet, R.E.
Principal Medical Officer	Surgeon-Colonel E. Townsend, A.M.S.
Superintendent Army Signalling	Captain G. C. Rigby, 1st Battalion Wiltshire Regiment.
Provost Marshal	Major P. Massy, 19th Bengal Lancers.
Field Treasure-Chest Officer	Lieutenant W. M. Grimley, 20th Punjab Infantry.
Senior Veterinary Officer and Veterinary Inspector	Veterinary Captain F. W. Forsdyke, A.V.D.
Chief Commissariat Officer	Captain G. Westropp, Assistant Commissary-General, 2nd Class.
Assistant to Chief Commissariat Officer	Captain G. R. C. Stuart, 1st Battalion East Lancashire Regiment.
Divisional Transport Officer	Captain F. A. Rideout, Assistant Commissary-General.
Assistant to Divisional Transport Officer	Lieutenant W. M. C. Vandeleur, 2nd Battalion Essex Regiment.
Ordnance Officer	Major T. E. Rowan, R.A.
Survey Officer	Brevet-Major W. J. Bythell, R.E.
Section Commandant	Captain W. C. Knight, 4th Bengal Cavalry.

First Brigade.

Commanding	Brigadier-General R. Westmacott, C.B., D.S.O.
Orderly Officer	Lieutenant R. C. Wellesley, R.H.A.
Deputy-Assistant Adjutant-General	Captain W. P. Blood, Royal Irish Fusiliers.
Deputy-Assistant Quartermaster-General	Captain F. J. M. Edwards, 3rd Bombay Cavalry.
Brigade Commissariat Officer	Captain E. Y. Watson, D.A.C.G.
Brigade Transport Officer	Captain D. H. Armstrong, 1st Battalion East Yorkshire Regiment.
Regiment Commissariat and Transport Officer	Lieutenant N. G. Fraser, 4th Bombay Cavalry.
Assistant Superintendent Army Signalling	Lieutenant H. W. Field, Devonshire Regiment.
Veterinary Officer	Veterinary Lieutenant F. U. Carr, A.V.D.

Second Brigade.

Commanding	Colonel (with temporary rank of Brigadier-General) C. R. Macgregor, D.S.O.
Orderly Officer	Second Lieutenant E. W. C. Ridgeway, 29th Punjab Infantry.
Deputy-Assistant Adjutant-General	Captain G. M. Gloster, Devonshire Regiment.
Deputy-Assistant Quartermaster-General	Captain H. Hudson, 19th Bengal Lancers.
Brigade Commissariat Officer .	Lieutenant D. H. Drake Brockman, D.A.C.G.
Brigade Transport Officer . .	Lieutenant R. G. N. Tytler, Gordon Highlanders.
Regimental Commissariat and Transport Officer	Lieutenant F. W. Birch, 29th Punjab Infantry.
Veterinary Officer . . .	Veterinary Lieutenant W. J. Tatam, A.V.D.

III

The Gundab Plateau—March from Shabkadr—Reconnoissance of the Jarobi Road and the Nahakhi Pass—Punishment and fines inflicted on the Upper Mohmunds

GUNDAB FORT,
Thursday, September 16th.

THERE are many records of heavy marches on the North-west Frontier, yet there can be few to equal the advance which was made yesterday into the heart of the Mohmund country. Now that we are here on the much-talked-of Gundab Plateau, it seems difficult to realise what a labour it was to get here. The 1st Brigade fell in at 5 A.M., at Shabkadr, and at 5.30, as the day was breaking, a party of the 28th Pioneers and the 20th Pathans marched off first towards the low hills and ravines which mark the entrance to the Gundab Nullah. The 20th were advance-guard, a place they had earned on account of the hard time which they had with these very tribesmen a month ago. The Somersets came next, and then followed No. 3 British Battery, under Lieutenant-Colonel Cunningham. Then the 1–2nd Gurkhas, rear-guard. This was the order of advance of the 1st Brigade. From the very commencement the path was but a water-way covered with shingle and boulders. For the first few miles the country showed signs of habitation, but as soon as the path which skirts the nullah and leads towards the Karapa defile was reached, the country began to present a most desolate and arid appearance. Low lines of hillocks, intersected with ravines and solitary spurs, rose gradually above each other, and but for a limited scrub jungle there was no trace of vegetation, not even occasional trees, while after the fourth mile no water or sign of water was visible for ten miles.

The heat of the sun as the day advanced was terrific, radiated and intensified by the face of this arid wilderness. The political information was that our object, the Azim Kila, was about twelve miles inwards, with a good road quite suited to camel transport. Again has it been proved how absolutely unreliable is this transfrontier information; for, after the force had advanced as far as Dund and begun to cross the Karapa, it was evident that no camel road existed, and it afterwards proved that the destination was nearly twenty miles away, over a country which was all but impassable to mule transport. About Dund the enemy were reported, and a few shots were fired into the 20th advance-guard; but they proved to be only a few scouts, and the flanking parties sent out reported all clear. After which nothing further of opposition was met. But from this point began one of the most trying marches that troops ever made in India.

The heat, as was said before, was awful, and a couple of hours of it saw the water-bottles empty.

Men, mules, and ponies struggled on until a halt was called at one o'clock, immediately after the steep ascent of the Karapa had been made. The heat told terribly on the British soldiers, and all the weaker were forced to fall out and wait for the water mules. But after the halt the gradual rise to the pass which leads into the Mohmund Plateau commenced. The road undulated more as the force advanced, until when the rapid ascent of 1000 feet to the plateau level commenced it was nothing but a stairway of boulders, up which the transport literally had to be hauled—great stepping-stones more like the ascent of the Egyptian pyramids than anything else. The path, or waterway to give it its correct name, ran up this almost sheer ascent, and it was not until the sun was sinking that the advance-guard of the 20th debouched on to the plateau plain on the far side of the pass. Here were met the first signs of cultivation. The plateau for two miles is a pleasant plain, ended by the fortified village of Gundab. Beyond this is the Gundab River and a further plain of about ten square miles, with a fortress to right and left, while beyond the hills which intervene between the Kabul range rise perpendicularly to about 2000 feet above our present level.

The whole of the range, which flanks the road to Gundab, was found to be sungared and recently prepared for defence, but the valley from end to end was deserted, though every evidence showed that the desertion had taken place almost as soon as the 20th topped the pass. In fact, the fires in the houses were alight and some live stock still about,

THE MOHMUND EXPEDITION 27

while the hills across the ravine were covered with refugees. It is expected that the tribesmen never anticipated that our force could arrive at their plateau the same day that they left Shabkadr, and that the aid which they were promised from the Hadda Mullah never arrived. The fact remains all the same that they missed a great opportunity, for if the pass had been held, Gundab could never have been made that night. It was altogether a march beyond the capabilities of British troops, and the sufferings of the men in the heat during that weary climb without water were beyond all conception. Men of the Somersets were seen offering mule-drivers all the money they had on their persons for a suck at the dregs in a water-bottle. It was this march which was responsible for the breaking up of the Somersetshire Regiment. Saturated with malaria, the men gave out, and so trying was the day that men who would probably have mended as the campaign proceeded went sick, so that the regiment fell to pieces during the severe work which followed, and was unable in the end to take the place allotted to it in the original constitution of the Tirah Expeditionary Force. It was a terrible blow to the whole regiment, especially to the officers, better men than whom could not have been found. As was to be expected, but little of the transport arrived on the first night into Gundab, for the road was worse even than the tracks on the Chitral Expedition. The village made an excellent camp for such of the force as arrived, and the baggage was packed, as well as was possible, as it stood on the pass.

GUNDAB,
September 17th.

By this date the 1st Brigade was now fairly installed on the Mohmund Plateau, but the arrival of the commissariat of necessity was slow, as the Karapa proved a harder business than was anticipated. Two squadrons of the 13th Bengal Lancers arriving on the 16th made the strength of the force encamped at Gundab up to three thousand fighting men. The place itself is built after the fashion of all frontier forts—that is, it is a confused collection of square flat-roofed huts with occasional towers, and is completely surrounded by a wall. It stands on the extreme edge of the tableland overlooking the Gundab ravine. The place has every evidence of the extreme poverty of the inhabitants, and the house of the Khan is but a bare hut.

General Elles and General Westmacott made a reconnaissance up the Jarobi road on the 16th, taking as an escort a field troop of Jodhpur Lancers and 13th Bengal Lancers. They found the road viâ the Gundab bed excellent for four or five miles, and that the valley increased in fertility, and was more generally inhabited as they advanced, the fortified posts being numerous; in fact, every spur was commanded, but there was no sign of an enemy in force, and but for a few stragglers, twelve of whom were captured, the valley was completely deserted. The Nahakhi Pass was explored and found to be passable, and not so severe as the Karapa, though all information points to the road to Jarobi being

THE MOHMUND EXPEDITION 29

almost devoid of water, which will make the advance of even one brigade a difficult matter.

News arrived in camp on this day of General Jeffreys' rear-guard action in Bajour. Details are scarce, but the fact of a Lashkar being in force on the far border probably accounts for the clear advance which this force has made. It points to the possibility that these Mohmunds never anticipated that a force could make its way up to Gundab as rapidly as we have done, and concentrated to oppose General Blood's advance, which is a direct advance into the best part of their country, if such a country can have a best part. Whether they will return to give us a taste of their night attacks or not it is impossible as yet to say. Probably they will have their spirit broken on the Bajour side, and will return here with folded hands, asking to be spared, as they have never opposed us; this being their general custom. A small Jirgah has already come in to see the Political Officer, and this seemed to be the purport of their visit.

CAMP ISUFKHEL,
September 18th.

General Westmacott's Brigade, consisting of two squadrons of the 13th B.L., under Major Atkinson; No. 3 (British) Mountain Battery, under Colonel Cunningham; 20th P.I., Colonel Woon; and one company of the 1st Gurkhas, marched out of Gundab into the valley which runs north behind it, and proceeding five miles encamped for the night at the village from which this is dated. The General made a reconnaissance with the cavalry up to the summit of the Nahakhi Pass, which is the northern outlet of the valley. The whole of the Isufkhel Valley is fertile as Mohmund fertility goes, and every half-mile brings you upon fortified villages. Apparently these people evidently live in a constant state of hostility, for each village is surrounded by a wall which is flanked with towers, and the majority of them have keeps in the centre. The structure is stone and the construction in all cases crude, mortar or mud being rarely used except for the roofs— shale-stones fitted in seem to be the extent of their masonry material. What impresses one most in this valley is the fact that, though fertile, the villages are too numerous for the area capable of cultivation; therefore one presumes that the Mohmunds are more thieves than husbandmen.

The General's reconnaissance of yesterday was of great importance. In the first place he found that the pass out of this valley was far more practicable than was anticipated, and that three days would make it passable for all transport. Also news was locally obtained that General Blood's cavalry has been seen in the valley,* and while the General was on the kotal we distinctly heard six reports far up the further valley, which could only have been artillery in action. Thus we suppose that General Blood's force was engaged yesterday, and this presumably accounts for the extraordinary action of the Lower Mohmunds in leaving the advance of General Elles' Division unopposed. The country had been

* This proved to be Wodehouse's reconnaissance from Nawagai towards Mittai.

THE MOHMUND EXPEDITION 31

drained of its fighting men so that the Bajour advance could be opposed.

There can be no other interpretation of the position, since almost impregnable posts have been left unguarded, and there has not been a sign of opposition since the Shabkadr watchmen fired on the advance-guard the first day of our advance. It is hoped that we shall open communication with General Blood to-day, and it is possible that a junction may be made between the outposts of the two forces. The prospect, as the plain beyond the Nahakhi Pass shows, is bad. As you stand on the pass a great arid plain stretches away in front of you, with an area of perhaps sixty square miles before the next range is reached.

Of this plain possibly a hundred acres on the near side of the pass are cultivated, the rest is a desolate sandy wilderness, broken only by gaping ravines and sandy hillocks. Water apparently there is none; and it is evident that the next two marches in this country will be as severe as any General would care to make with cavalry, mountain artillery, and mule transport. To-day promises to be an interesting one in the annals of this unsatisfactory campaign.

GUNDAB,
September 19th.

Yesterday was a day of many important events in camp. In the first place the reconnaissance which General Westmacott pushed out to the Nahakhi Pass found helio connection with General Blood's Division about 10.30 A.M. We had just climbed to the ascent of the kotal when a runner came in with a letter from the converging force. And it transpired that we had not been mistaken in the supposition that they had had an engagement. The Khan of Gairat, with a following of about four thousand men, had fallen foul of the cavalry patrols, and had killed a couple of horses with their fire. The guns had been brought up and the Khan's position shelled, but no more forward action was made that night. The helio brought the news that General Blood's force was rather pressed for food, and he asked for ten days' supplies, or in default he could work his end with five days' supply. This, of course, even if the plan of operation had not been changed, would have been impossible, as we have barely yet got up three days' supply for ourselves, though now that the camel road has been so much improved, stores should arrive rapidly.

As soon as connection was found by helio with General Blood's force, General Westmacott made a cavalry reconnaissance up the valley towards the hill on which the signal station stood—it must have been twelve miles away, and the cavalry could make no junction. They found the country which they crossed arid and, as they proceeded up towards the boundary hills, sterile. Water there was practically none. It is evident that water will be the chief trouble of the advance. The two plains on the far side of the Nahakhi Pass are found to be the Kamali, which was believed to be a most fertile valley, but which proves to be an arid stretch, occupied and

THE MOHMUND EXPEDITION 33

inhabited, it is true, but the inhabitants are dependent upon rainfall to stock their reservoirs, which are tanks. There has been recent rain, but the opinion formed by the reconnaissance is that it will be severe work for the force advancing the two marches from Nahakhi to Jarobi.

Two squadrons of the 13th B.L. under Colonel Deane, made a further reconnaissance to the left of General Westmacott's position, searching for the Khappak Tangi Pass, which they are not sure if they found, but they also found a land almost devoid of water supply, tanks alone acting as reservoirs, and these being of such slight depth that the transport would exhaust them in twenty-four hours. But by far the most important news in camp is that owing to General Jeffreys having come into contact with the Mahmunds in Bajour, General Blood's Division has been ordered back to pacify the Bajour Valley. It is believed in camp that General Jeffreys had a tough fight and is in a tight place, but direct news is as yet impossible here. Consequently we push on with all expedition to bring about conclusions with Hadda Mullah, who, with Gairat Khan, has a following some ten or twelve thousand strong between Mittai and Jarobi. His men are locally reported to have been reinforced by a number of swashbucklers from across the Khandhari frontier. This is not to be confused with Khandahar; it is a local name of a valley in the Amir's territory. The supposition is that, unless we move with rapidity and take the initiative, the Mullah's adherents will take General Blood's covering movement as a sign

c

of weakness, and thus taking heart, make a severer task of General Elles' advance.

Such is the attitude at present of Hadda Mullah and the Upper Mohmunds. Commissioner Merk has dealt with the Lower Mohmunds, and they have completely surrendered as far as Jirgah promises go. The punishment for their share in the Shabkadr dacoity is a fine of 5000 rupees, of 2400 maunds of grain, free forage for our troops as long as we occupy the country, surrender of all breech-loading rifles and Enfields, three hundred firelocks, and three hundred swords. The Jirgah has been given seven days to fulfil its promises.

The terms of this treaty call for some reflection. One would have preferred when treating with Pathans to have blood for blood—village for village. It is the method which they understand, and which they are most likely to feel and remember. But looking to the poverty of the Lower Mohmunds, and believing their excuse that the Mullah with a show of force coerced them, the punishment is considered adequate. Still, the first good season will erase the memory of the fine from their minds, when ruined villages and fire-blackened towers would have been a lasting memorial of our visit.

The telegraph office is up to Gundab, the field wire having been laid over an execrable road at the rate of seven and a half miles a day, when the guarantee is three to four. This promptitude reflects great credit on the officer in charge of this department. The Gundab office was opened at midday on the 18th, and we marched on the 15th.

GENERAL JEFFREYS'S FORCE REPELLING THE NIGHT ATTACK

September 19

THE MOHMUND EXPEDITION 35

It will be seen that while General Elles was pushing up towards Kamali, that General Blood had crossed the Panjkora, and having left Brigadier Jeffries to punish the Mohmunds, had himself with Brigadier Wodehouse pushed on to Nawagai. It was while General Blood was approaching Nawagai that the severe engagement referred to took place.

IV

Attack on the Camp—Death of Captain Tomkins—Ill luck of the 38th Dogras—Gallant conduct of Lieutenant Watson, R.E.

INAYAT,
September 24*th.*

WE have had plenty of work to do since the 14th, and there has been no time for writing letters, but we have an off-day to-day, and I will attempt to give you an account of what has been going on here in these parts for the last few days. The 3rd Brigade advanced from Ghosana to Watelai on the 12th, and the 2nd moved up beyond Khar on the 13th, and the 11th Bengal Lancers reconnoitred the passes south leading towards the Mohmund country. On the 13th the Political Officer with two squadrons of the 11th Bengal Lancers moved up the Mahmund Valley, and with the assistance of the Khan of Jhar an attempt was made to get the Jirgah to come in; but this proving unsuccessful, an advance was made up the valley, and some sheds were burnt in a village known to be implicated in the attack on Chakdara, and in which there was a horse that had been stolen from the cavalry. On the 14th a squadron of the 11th Bengal Lancers reconnoitred the Salarzai

THE MOHMUND EXPEDITION 37

Valley and one of the passes north. An armed picket was posted on the hill, and in some places armed men were seen about, but generally the people seemed quiet. They expressed a fear that at any time some tribes might come down and attack our camp, and so implicate them. That day the 2nd Brigade camp had been moved some miles nearer the Rambat Pass; the Buffs and Sappers had been moved up to hold the pass, and preparations had been made to cross in the morning. There was no suspicion of any contemplated attack on the camp. About 8 P.M., however, some shots were fired into camp, and every one was on the alert at once. The Guides occupied the east face of camp, the Sikhs the south, and the Dogras with the cavalry and guns the north face. The first attack was made against the Guides and continued about two and a half hours, the leaders every now and then making every effort to bring their men on to the charge. About one hundred yards from the east face there was a deep nullah, and the ground on the far side commanded the camp. The enemy, I believe, had carefully reconnoitred the camp by daylight, and located the headquarter camp, as all night a steady fire was kept on this from the points of vantage east of the nullah, and had the officers whose tents were in that locality not been employed elsewhere they would have fared badly. Several shots were fired into some grain bags which were put up to shelter the General.

After about two and a half hours' firing from the east face the enemy moved off, evidently to hold a council of war. They then came on against the Dogras, their leaders again trying to bring them on to the charge and imploring them to shoot lower. A bugler also tried to sound, but only succeeded in making weird noises. There was a large percentage of rifles used against us, and the shooting was very close, as will be seen from the number of animals killed and wounded, about thirty-five being killed and sixty wounded. The 38th Dogras had exceedingly bad luck, losing three officers. Permission had been granted to Captain Tomkins to make a sortie, and orders had been passed down the line to cease firing, when suddenly the order for the sortie was countermanded, and Captain Tomkins was going down the line passing the order to commence firing again, when he was shot in the mouth and fell. He must have offered a clear mark in the moonlight. Lieutenant Bailey had just brought up an order to his commanding officer from the General Officer Commanding, and was shot in the side close to Colonel Vivian, and died in a few minutes. Lieutenant Harrington was lying in the trench with his men with his head against the parapet, when a shot came from over the other side of the camp and hit him on the back of the head. Great sympathy is felt for the 38th Dogras for their extreme ill luck on this occasion. About 2 A.M. the enemy suddenly stopped firing and began to clear off. At 6 A.M. Captain Cole was ordered to move off with a half-squadron of the 11th Bengal Lancers, and see if he could find any traces of the people who had attacked the camp.

THE MOHMUND EXPEDITION 39

Outside the camp a crowd of people was seen, who said that they were the followers of the Khan of Khar and had come to help the Sirkar. One of these gentlemen who had said that he had come to help the Sirkar was then asked who had attacked the camp, and where they had come from. Of this he declared absolute ignorance, until a little persuasion was brought to bear on him by a few sowars, when this ignorant gentleman crawled on to his pony and led the party straight off after the enemy. After going some six miles the right flank patrol reported men going away to the right front; the direction was at once changed, and after a gallop of two miles the tail end of a party of tribesmen was overtaken and a number speared. They were followed into a gorge, where the cavalry dismounted and opened fire. The enemy now having reached ground where they knew themselves to be safe, turned and opened fire, and those on the hills also began firing. The position being a most disadvantageous one for cavalry to act in, it was considered advisable to return at once. Directly the enemy saw the movement they came swarming down the hill, but the retirement was carried out with the loss of one horse killed and one wounded only, and the enemy followed to within four miles of camp, keeping at a respectful distance and with one eye on a nullah. Three miles from camp the cavalry were supported by the Guides, infantry, and four guns, but it was then too late to take the offensive.

On the 16th three columns moved out to the north to punish the enemy who had attacked us.

The right column under Colonel Vivian, with the 38th Dogras, a section of Sappers, and two guns; the centre one, under Colonel Goldney, one squadron 11th Bengal Lancers, four guns, 35th Sikhs, and Buffs; the left column to operate near camp, under Major Campbell, with the Guides. The cavalry with the centre column soon came up with the enemy, who had collected on a knoll at the foot of the hills some three hundred strong. On the appearance of the 35th Sikhs they moved off north, keeping close to the foot of the hills, and the 11th Bengal Lancers followed them, dismounting, and firing volleys as opportunity occurred. The 35th then came up again, keeping close to the foot of the hills for about an hour and a half, but the enemy had disappeared among the rocks and hills. The 35th then moved half right against the village of Shahi Tangi. The tribesmen were sniping at them, but here was no resistance. The village of Shahi Tangi was reached and burnt, and then it was deemed advisable to retire. Directly the retirement was commenced, the enemy appeared from all sides, rocks and nullahs, and came on very boldly—people from the west of the valley coming over to join in the fight. The Sikhs were pressed very heavily down the hill, the enemy coming up to within forty yards. When they reached the foot of the hill and got on to open ground the charge was sounded, and fixing bayonets, the Sikhs charged and cleared their immediate front again, and a company of Buffs coming up covered their subsequent retirement.

The 11th Bengal Lancers had all this time been

THE MOHMUND EXPEDITION 41

watching the left flank, and had kept the enemy in check for a certain time until they saw the success of their movement against the 35th, when they at once advanced against the cavalry. They were held by dismounted fire for half an hour, when, having turned the left flank of the cavalry obliging them to retire, they immediately closed in on the left flank of the Sikhs, taking advantage of cover afforded by the nullahs. The cavalry, hearing heavy firing in front, moved forward again, and suddenly saw a company of Sikhs surrounded on three sides having a hot fight. The advance scouts of the 11th Bengal Lancers were seen to be very excited and signalling wildly; the squadron came up at a gallop, and charged the right rear of a party of tribesmen closing on the Sikhs. Unfortunately a nullah intervened, into which the enemy threw themselves, and the cavalry were unable to charge home. However, they came up with such a yell that the moral effect of cavalry was seen, the enemy not only clearing across the nullah, but out of the village on the far side from which they had driven the cavalry three-quarters of an hour before. The Guides infantry came up a short time after, and swept the enemy away back on the left flank. The General Officer Commanding now came up. The guns were ordered up to a position covering Shahi Tangi, and the 35th and Buffs were commanded to go for the enemy holding that village. One company, 35th, who had been acting as escort to the guns, was ordered up the hills on the right (Captain ▨▨▨'s company). The Buffs and Sikhs soon cleared Shahi Tangi, and after a halt retired again without much opposition to the position held by the guns.

A halt was now made, and the towers and fortifications were destroyed by Sappers. At about 3.45 a general retirement was ordered, and about this time a message was received from Captain Ryan that he was being pressed, and he was ordered to retire at once; but apparently this message never reached him. A half-company of Guides was also sent to support him. Captain Ryan after some time saw the retirement of the Brigade, and attempted to conform, but was very heavily pressed, and could only do so very slowly. As the brigade retired the enemy came on from the west of the valley again and pressed; but as the brigade cleared the place where the enemy had been first found by the 11th Bengal Lancers in the morning, the tribesmen seemed to have got news of the company of the 35th on the hill, as they moved rapidly across to the east of the valley to cut off this company. The Guides were now sent to assist the 35th, and the brigade was halted on a small plain. The Guides moved up to the foot of the hills, and took up a position to cover the retirement of the Sikhs. The retirement of the Sikhs was made down a long spur ending in a level ridge followed by two small knolls. A half-company of Guides reached the Sikhs just at this level spot, and as the enemy's swordsmen were running in among them. The men were dead beat; they had had no water and a very heavy climb, and a very hard-pressed retirement.

The Guides gallantly carried the wounded Sikhs

THE MOHMUND EXPEDITION 43

down the hill, and soon the little party came under the steady covering fire of the Guides at the foot. Still the enemy pressed on. Lieutenant Gunning was cut over the back twice in the nullah at the foot of the hills by a man who got in rear of him as he was using his revolver at three men facing him. He had already been shot in the face at the commencement of the retirement, so he was now in a bad way, but was carried safely into camp. When the Guides had been ordered to the relief of the Sikhs the brigade halted for some time, but as the Sikhs were reported near the bottom of the hill, orders were given to march on. Darkness came on, and by some ill chance the guns, a section of Sappers, with a small escort of Buffs and the General Officer Commanding, became separated from the column, and found themselves left behind.

The General Officer Commanding, finding himself in this position, made for a small village; but unfortunately the enemy got there at the same time, and the escort was not strong enough to turn them out. Lieutenant Watson, R.E., with five men of the Buffs, made two gallant attempts to go back for reinforcements, but he was shot down, wounded in three places. Several other unsuccessful attempts were made. A position was taken up under the eastern wall of the village and a trench thrown up to afford some protection, but the enemy were firing at ranges from five to twenty-five yards. The darkness of the night and the dead bodies of the battery mules certainly saved a number of lives, together with the fact that the enemy were afraid to face the guns. As the moon rose Major Worlledge, 35th Sikhs, who with four companies had been also lost in the darkness, and who was on the plain about eight hundred yards off, sent a sowar of the 11th Bengal Lancers to see if any assistance was required. This man quickly informed him of the critical situation; the four companies were brought up, and at once the enemy bolted. The party was left undisturbed for the rest of the night. The remainder of the brigade had reached camp about 9 P.M.

At daybreak the 11th Bengal Lancers and 38th Dogras went out and brought in everybody.

Since then we have had a fight nearly every day, but nothing of great importance has occurred. Now the Maliks are seeking for terms, and have been informed of the terms on which they will be received.

V

Helio connection with General Blood's force—Position of the enemy—Night attack on General Blood's camp by the Ghazis.

CAMP NAHAKHI,
September 20th.

THE whole of the 1st Brigade, with headquarters and divisional cavalry and artillery, are now across the Nahakhi Pass. One cannot say enough in praise of the Sappers and Miners and the Bombay Pioneers for the way in which they have made the pass over the separating range from upper and lower Mohmund land passable for all arms and camel transport. When the cavalry first reconnoitred into the Upper Mohmund Plateau, two days ago, it was as much as men and horses could do to scramble down, the horses stepping from boulder to boulder, with the sowars hanging to their tails to keep them from overbalancing when the landing purchase was small. It took the cavalry two hours to climb over the two miles of pass on the 18th, and on the 20th laden camels made the passage in three-quarters of an hour. The news from General Blood, with whom helio connection has never been lost since first established on the 18th, is that the enemy is still in force within reach of him, but has retired a little farther up into the hills. They made a half-hearted attempt upon his camp last night, which was easily countered. Our own news is that the Suffi Mullah has been detached by Hadda Mullah to attempt to prevent us from conjunction with General Blood's force. The spies reported this force to be in the hills, about three thousand strong, six or seven miles north of Nahakhi, and the 13th B.L. have gone out to look for them.

No news as yet has been received from the reconnoitring column. When connection was fairly opened yesterday with General Blood's force, orders came through from India that General Blood was to retire and arrange punitive measures in the Mohmund country as a set-off against their attack upon his rear brigade. Yesterday General Blood helioed through that it would be disastrous if he retired in the face of the enemy, that General Jeffreys was strong enough to do all that was required at present, and that a conjunction with General Elles was imperative. For that reason the whole of General Elles' 1st Brigade pushes forward to-morrow to Lakarai, which is within four miles of General Blood, so that a concentration must take place to-morrow. And from this will date the precise measures of the operations against Jarobi and the Haddah gathering. The days are hot, but the weather is not severe, the health of the force being extraordinarily good. Of the force which marched from Galanai (Gundab) this morning not a single man fell out, and the hospitals are barely occupied.

THE MOHMUND EXPEDITION

Nahakhi Pass,
September 20th, 9 p.m.

General Elles and General Blood are timed to meet to-morrow somewhere near Lakarai, and, as I said in my last letter, the future of the expedition dates from their meeting. Important news has come into camp to-day from General Blood's column, but being by helio, of necessity it is in places broken, and deficient in detail. It appears that General Jeffreys was out with a punitive column, and that he met a certain amount of opposition, and that the tribesmen retired before him, and his column pursued until late in the day. On retirement of the column towards their camp, the enemy, augmented in numbers, returned to the attack, and pressed their advance so hard that General Jeffreys was forced to occupy a large village on the hillside, his column not being long enough to prevent it; the enemy occupied the far end of the village, and it was from this position that the fire was so disastrous, and it was only upon support coming from the camp that the enemy were sufficiently driven out for our casualties to be carried away. Telegraphic messages have been sent with the casualties, which show the severity of the fighting. General Blood was ordered, from Simla, I believe, to retire from his position about Nawagai, and to concentrate his division about Inayatkila to punish the Mohmunds and Salazais who had attacked his rear column. But General Blood has found it impossible under existing circumstances to make this retrograde movement. In the first place, the Hadda Mullah, with a considerable following, is in position at Badmanai, and upon General Blood's falling back he could, without doubt, swoop down upon Nawagai and wreak a severe vengeance on the Khan for his loyalty to the Kaffir. Secondly, a retrograde movement on the part of General Blood's force is rendered difficult, if not impracticable, owing to the nature of the ground, which here is scored by deep nullahs which would afford suitable cover to an enemy interpreting a judicious retirement into a retreat. Therefore General Blood, reporting his rear column in sufficient strength to hold its own, stands fast until General Elles' Division can cover his retirement.

The position of the enemy, as far as the latest intelligence goes, is as follows: The Hadda Mullah, with what following he has got, is watching General Blood's force from Badmanai; but hearing of General Elles' advance, he has detached the Suffi Mullah, an inhabitant of the Amir's territory, it is believed, to Kung, ten miles up the Kamali Valley. The Suffi Mullah is said to have two to three thousand men with him, and the spies give it that his orders are to prevent our marching up the Kamali, but if we attempt to concentrate with General Blood, he is to return and rejoin the Hadda Mullah. Some complexion of truth is given to this story by the fact that the 13th B.L. reconnaissance to Kung to-day found the enemy in some force and were fired at by them from long ranges. Lieutenant Macquoid, Intelligence Officer with General Westmacott's Brigade, while sketching the country towards Kung,

THE MOHMUND EXPEDITION 49

was also fired upon. That the enemy mean fighting is evident from the show of force which General Blood helios they made in the valley six miles from his camp two nights ago. The tribesmen were indulging in a Chuttack dance. Moreover, they made a small attack on his camp last night, but finding the force on the alert quickly retired. This is the situation up to the latest news received in camp, and the situation has become at last interesting. It is believed that upon our force advancing far enough to cover a retrograde movement by General Blood that he will retire, and, concentrating his division, proceed with the punishment of the tribes concerned in the attack on General Jeffreys, while General Elles' Division alone takes the initiative against the Hadda Mullah. But this is conjecture as yet. In the meantime, General Jeffreys is proceeding with the punishment of the tribes about Inayatkila with every success, though the fact that he has had two killed and six wounded shows that he has met with further opposition.

CAMP LAKARAI,
September 21st.

General Elles marched out from Nahakhi this morning with General Westmacott's Brigade for Lakarai, five miles this side of Nawagai, where General Blood was encamped with General Wodehouse's Brigade. The 13th B.L. formed the advance-guard, being followed by the mountain batteries, the 1st Gurkhas, the 20th Punjab Infantry, and the Somerset Light Infantry. The higher

D

Komali Plain was found to be very fertile and dotted with numerous towns and villages. This plain was quite the most populated valley that the force has yet passed. Tank-water only was available, but up to date there has been plenty. As the advanced-guard crossed the spur of Lakarai into the Nawagai, it was met by an escort of the 11th B.L., which was with General Blood. Exactly at a quarter-past ten Generals Blood and Elles met in a tope of trees, and there was a general handshaking as the two staffs met. There was plenty of news from the Nawagai Column, for they confirmed the news that the enemy was in force at Badmanai. Their camp had been most vigorously attacked the preceding evening.

The camp had just settled down to rest for the night, when, about nine o'clock, a heavy volley was poured into the camp and a rush of swordsmen followed.

Tents were struck as rapidly as possible, and the fire of the Queen's and Sikhs stopped the swordsmen, so that the enemy, for a time, confined themselves to sweeping the camp with rifle fire. They had evidently in the daytime marked down the seat of the General Officer's tent, for the centre of their fire seemed to be here, and it was here that General Wodehouse was wounded below the knee, the bullet passing through the flesh. But the Ghazis were determined to have their sword play, for they again organised a charge, and three sides of the entrenchment were attacked simultaneously: and so fiercely was the attack pressed that many almost reached

THE MOHMUND EXPEDITION 51

the ditches. In fact, in the morning bodies were found within a few feet of the muzzles of the mountain battery. At this point the gunners fired a few star shells, which enabled the men manning the trenches to clear the plain up to the hills. But this did not stop the firing into camp, which was hotly maintained until two o'clock in the morning, when the moon rose.

To show how severe the engagement was, there were no fewer than over thirty casualties to combatants, while among the three squadrons of the 11th B.L. nineteen horses were wounded. deaths. It was impossible to estimate the enemy's losses, as under cover of the darkness they carried away most of their dead and wounded, only leaving those who were close up to the lines. These were sufficient to show that the Lee-Metford, now that it has the Dum-Dum cartridge, is a weapon in which the soldier may have every confidence. What it hits it stops; so much so that the question of its capabilities of stopping a rush of Ghazis need never more be discussed.

These are the details of the fighting of Monday as far as we are aware. General Blood returned to his camp at Nawagai and General Westmacott's Brigade encamped five miles from Nawagai in the same plain, and with General Blood's camp full in view. The camp was heavily entrenched and all sorts of precautions taken against a repetition of the tactics of last night. All reports agree that the assault showed method and tactical organisation, for the men armed with breechloaders covered the advance of the swordsmen. It must also have taken some military knowledge of the camp and of camp attack to organise a simultaneous attack on three sides at once. The persistent way in which the General's position was fired upon showed that the enemy were aware of the internal arrangements of the camp. They must have got their information from spies, and, indeed, one spy who was recognised as a deserter from a Punjab infantry regiment was captured.

Camp Kuzchinari,
September 22*nd.*

The following is a rough sketch plan of the camp at Nawagai which was so severely attacked on the night of September 20. The valley ranges due north, and in this outline one is looking across the gorge, the left-hand side of the sketch being to the north. The chief rushes were made from the north and ~~east~~ *west* sides, a nullah within three hundred yards giving them great cover. Further information says that though the attacks were the severest, and though the fire of those of the enemy on the spurs about six hundred yards away swept the camp from end to end, yet at no time was there any disorder, and the firing of the Queen's was in volleys from the beginning to the end of the action. The brunt of the attack fell upon the Queen's and the 22nd, a series of stone walls up to within fifty yards of the Queen's front and a sungar within a hundred, affording ample shelter for the Ghazis to form before making their assaults. To

THE MOHMUND EXPEDITION 53

show how severe was the breechloader fire, there is not an officer of the force whom I have yet met who has not had some portion of his camp furniture broken by a bullet. It is impossible to speak too

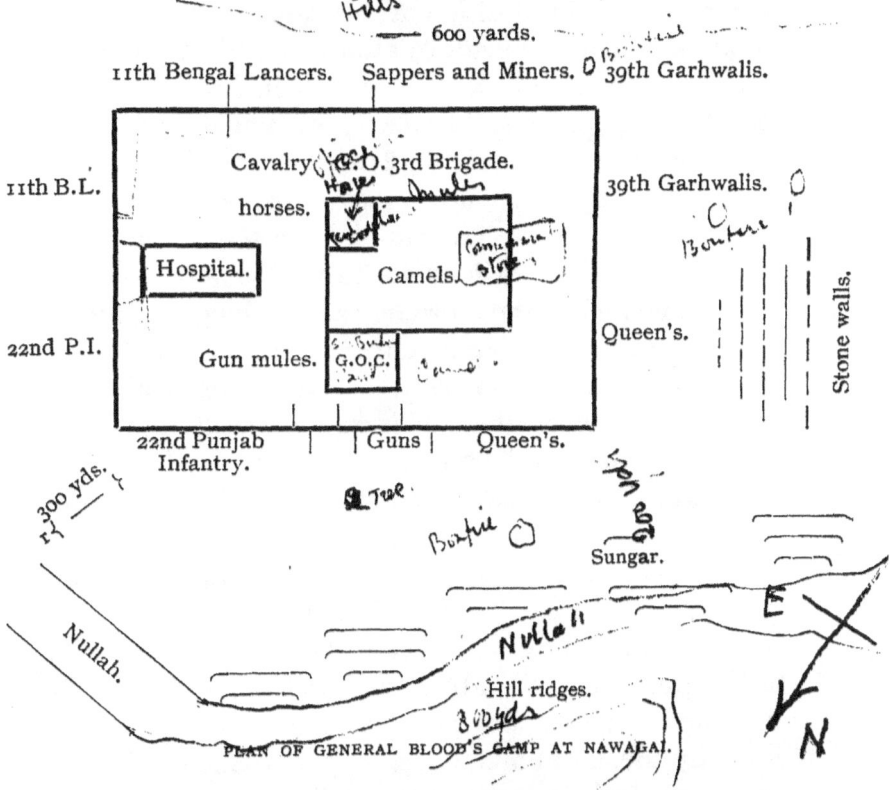

PLAN OF GENERAL BLOOD'S CAMP AT NAWAGAI.

highly of the discipline maintained by all concerned, and the confidence which they had in General Blood, for the most trying situation was reached when the defenders were hit in the back by a fire aimed at the opposite point of defence.

ADVANCE TO CAMP KUZCHINARI,
September 22nd.

Nothing happened in General Westmacott's camp last night, though a feeble attempt was made upon General Blood's position at Nawagai. It is hardly thought that they meant to attack there, and possibly a few had come back to look for their dead, for they had the previous night buried a few under stones on the ridges above the camp, where they had been discovered by the Garhwalis. The only hostile demonstration with General Westmacott's Brigade was that the friendly feudatories of Nawagai, whom we had passed in the morning calmly ploughing their fields, attacked a belated convoy of goats, killed two of the drivers, and so badly cut up two others that there is little chance of their recovery. It appears that General Blood had warning from the Khan of Nawagai that he was to be attacked on the 19th, and that the camp was in readiness to receive it, but that night only a few men came down and sniped. The next day the enemy debouched into the plain and had their usual afternoon demonstration, ending with a Chuttack dance. More to impress the Khan of Nawagai than to do damage, a few rounds were fired by the mountain guns. This seemed to have the effect of collecting the tribesmen, for they swarmed into the plain and attacked, as has been already narrated.

General Westmacott's Brigade advanced this morning up the Badmanai Valley from Lakarai, Colonel Graves, who has assumed command of Colonel Wodehouse's Brigade, advancing similarly from

THE MOHMUND EXPEDITION

Nawagai, General Blood having returned to Inyatkila to General Jeffreys's column. Advanced-guards of the 13th and 11th Bengal Lancers, under Colonel Deane and Major Delamaine, found the enemy in force upon all the spurs which cover the advance to the Badmanai Pass. They opened fire from the lower villages before retreating upwards, and a horse of the 13th Bengal Lancers was killed. The day was too far advanced to carry the pass, so camp was formed for both brigades at Kuzchinari, which is situated about two miles from the pass.

As I sit writing, I can see the white flutter of the standards which the enemy have set up along the range of hills in front of us. The men seem very determined, and it is the general opinion that we are upon the eve of the one engagement which is to terminate the Mohmund operations. Probably we shall be severely fired into in camp to-night.

Many of the villagers who are implicated in yesterday's raid have been brought in. They have been handed over to the Khan of Nawagai for punishment, as they claim to be his feudatories. It is possible that the news of General Jeffreys's engagement has put heart into the Upper Mohmunds, for they showed great front to the advance party of the 13th and dismounted fire did not dislodge them. They only moved over the crest of the spur and returned to the attack as soon as the cavalry had retired.

VI

General Westmacott's camp at Kuzchinari—Advance on the Badmanai Valley—Attack by enemy and "prettily fought engagement."

TORAKHWA,
September 24th.

WITH the news of General Blood's night attack still fresh on our minds the force settled down into camp at Kuzchinari quite prepared for a repetition, as the cavalry reconnaissance had shown that the enemy were in earnest. The two brigades had just settled down, when bonfires were seen on all the neighbouring hills, and firing opened just as two guns sounded "lights out." It was a harmless fire; but General Graves's Brigade fired some volleys in return. The enemy evidently satisfied themselves that the camp was prepared, and the shots dwindled out before midnight. At seven in the morning the two brigades fell in to assault the pass. General Graves's Brigade, consisting of the 22nd P.I., the Queen's, and 39th Gharwalis on the right, the three batteries, No. 3 British, No. 1 Native, and No. 5 Native, massed under Colonel Duthy, in the centre, and General Westmacott, with the Somersets, 20th P.I., 1st Gurkhas, and the Bombay Pioneers,

THE MOHMUND EXPEDITION 57

on the left. The left was the main attack, the enemy defending from this flank. Roughly the position was as follows: a kotal bushed with holm oak covered the access to the pass, and at its foot stood a fortified village; to the far left a conical hill, crowned with a sungar and fort, covered the advance to the foot of the kotal. Beyond the kotal to the left front the hills rose up in ridges to 2000 feet above the Kuz camp level, while a series of spurs and ridges sank away in succession down into the Badmanai Valley, which is the most fertile part of the Mohmund country that we have yet been in, and which is thickly populated. On the far side of the valley similar spurs led up to the great hills, within which lies Jarobi, the object position of the advance.

At 7.30 General Westmacott threw out the 20th P.I. as his advanced-guard. The regiment being supported in the fighting line by the 1st Gurkhas, the Gurkhas being followed by the Bombay Pioneers; the Somersets, with the exception of two companies, which were detached to hold the conical hill and sungar on the left, being ordered to furnish the escort to the artillery. The two brigades marched simultaneously, but the brunt of the day fell on General Westmacott's Brigade. As the foot of the kotal was reached, it was evident that the enemy were in force, as they could be distinctly seen dodging in and out of the bushes and taking up posts of vantage. At 7.45 they fired the first shot, and then a general fire broke out from their position. Without an answering fire from the 20th, skirmishers slanted up the hillside, taking cover and advancing as deliberately as if it were a field day. The ascent was very rough and steep, and it was not until the advanced line of skirmishers was within forty yards of the summit that the enemy fell back. The glitter of cold steel was too much for them, and they streamed up towards the left. But Lieutenant Logan, with the Maxim detachment of the Devons, had covered the left, and they could only retire to the succeeding ridge. The Maxim came into action at 8.13, at which time the top of the kotal was won. The fighting line was then halted, as it was found that the enemy held a very commanding position on the ridge in the direct rear. Up to this point the advance had been made simply with the support of the machine guns, and the first defended position was won without the aid of artillery fire. But before a further advance was made Colonel Cunningham was ordered up with No. 3 (British). On his arrival General Westmacott, who personally conducted operations in the front of the fighting line, ordered the 20th to carry the second ridge while the mountain battery shelled a crest at 1750 yards upon which a standard had been set. As soon as the 20th left cover they were met by a brisk rifle fire from the parallel ridge, and it was evident that picked marksmen had been posted, for General Westmacott and his Staff at once became the centre of a galling fire. The 20th, covered by the Gurkhas, having got their wind again after the first steep climb, simply skirmished magnificently. They lost no chance of cover, and when the distance between them and the enemy was narrowed down, with a cheer that was heard above the reverberation

THE MOHMUND EXPEDITION 59

of the battery fire, they tried to close in with the bayonet. But the tribesmen, though they disputed every inch with severe rifle fire, would not wait. Knowing the country and retiring in parties, they were always ready on the succeeding ridge after each spur was carried.

It was after the second crest had been rushed that the action developed, and as the hills expanded so had the fighting line to be extended, the Gurkhas here coming into action. Detachment after detachment of skirmishers pressed forward, while the guns dispersed any prominent gathering. General Westmacott, in spite of his being marked down by the sharpshooters, coolly directed the action. At one time the General and Captain Wellesly, his orderly officer, had a rock near them ploughed and splintered by a volley. The Afridi Company of the 20th, with the Maxims, took the lower spurs and had a separate engagement to themselves. A party of forty of the enemy ensconced themselves in a *ziarat* and declared defiance by beat of drum and well-sustained fire. A detachment of the Afridis of the 20th worked up to them in spite of the Martini fire by which they were received, and collecting under a pathway rushed the position with the greatest pluck. The tribesmen, drum, standard and all, had not the *morale* to stand, and fled precipitately down into the villages below and streamed across the plain, where Lieutenant Logan dispersed them with his Maxim, which he had forced up an almost impracticable roadway. By this it was twelve o'clock, and the position had been won, the tribesmen having made their way either across the plain or into the impossible heights above. The left advance had easier work to perform; they found the enemy in places, but Colonel Duthy's artillery broke up all collections of tribesmen at long ranges, and when at 12.30 a party collected to oppose the advance-guard of the 22nd P.I., Lieutenant Logan ranged them with his Maxim at 1800 yards and the gathering broke, climbed over the rear walls of the village, and fled up to the passes above. It is difficult to assess the enemy's losses—probably they are not heavy, as they were all wonderfully skilled cragsmen and rarely showed above cover, and they never were massed in force, but were broken up in small defending parties. Our casualties were one Gurkha killed, one wounded, two 20th Punjab Infantry wounded, one follower and one hospital assistant wounded, and several casualties in the mules of the mountain battery.

It was a prettily fought engagement, and might have been a field day, so methodically was the advance carried out. At the close of the fighting General Elles, who had watched the engagement from the pass, helioed up to General Westmacott: "Beautifully done by 1st Brigade; work of 20th Punjab Infantry and Maxim detachment could not have been done better." It would be unfair to draw comparisons, but the work of the Afridi Company of the 20th is almost unparalleled. They were a detached picket the night previous to the assault, and they joined their regiment without food or water and fought through the battle, being fourteen hours under arms without water, as they were too eager

THE MOHMUND EXPEDITION 61

for the front to wait for the water mules. And there was never a murmur. By three o'clock the baggage was streaming up the pass, which is a very easy one, and General Westmacott's Brigade took up its position for the night under the walls of Badmanai Fort, the headquarters having moved up also.

VII

Suffering of the wounded—Progress of the brigade up the Jarobi Valley—Effect of burning and tower blasting on the tribesmen—A short and satisfactory campaign.

Camp Bohar Dag,
September 26th.

From Badmanai the force moved down to Torakhwa, and on the following morning marched out of the fort there to the punishment of the Jarobi Valley, the key of most of the trouble which has taken place in this quarter of the frontier. General Westmacott marched his column out with the Somerset Light Infantry as the advanced-guard, the Gurkhas following, then the two mountain batteries with the Bombay Pioneers as escort, while the 20th P.I. furnished the rear-guard, General Elles and Staff, including the Maharaja of Patiala—Sir Pertab Singh, by the way, is still in hospital—accompanying the advanced-guard. A short pass had to be crossed before the opening to the Jarobi Plain was reached, but it brought no difficulties, and there followed a march of five miles over as desolate and arid a country as one could ever imagine: tier upon tier of dusty waste-stretches, the force winding its weary way along the shingled and bouldered nullahs and

THE MOHMUND EXPEDITION 63

waterways which serve this casual people for roadways. It seemed that Jarobi, the valley of the Mohmunds which overflows with milk and honey, was but a myth, for it appeared that the barren waste between it and Torakhwa ended in a solid range of hills. But the Patiala Cavalry, which were furnishing the advanced scouts, came back and reported a gorge, and this was the promised land. A reconnaissance up this gorge made by Captain Houghten and Lieutenant Maclaren was fired on by the enemy, on the heights on either side, to the number of two or three hundred, and on return parties could be seen by the advanced-guard. Two guns of No. 3 Battery were called up to disperse them, and a couple of ringed shell with a volley from the company of the Somersets was sufficient to do this. But it was at once apparent that the valley was a most difficult one to approach from a military point of view.

It was narrow and winding and surmounted with precipitous hills, which were so high that it would have been heavy work turning them if they had been occupied. But though the tribesmen could be seen collecting on the summits, they made no attempt to arrest the advance of the troops up the valley. Captain Kelly at once set to work, and flames showed on either side that Shabkadr was being avenged. At the first gorge General Westmacott left the Somersets with No. 5 Mountain Battery, and a half-battalion of the Gurkhas was sent up a spur which commanded the left approach up the valley, while a company of the 20th was detached to take a similar position on the right. The force then advanced, and a square tower standing prominently in the centre of the waterway showed where the valley opened out to the right into the Jarobi Valley proper. The main advance toiled up the bouldered way, and then, when the tower was reached at last, the beautiful valley which no Kaffir had gazed upon before broke upon the view. After the country we have been in for the last ten days it certainly was a picturesque spot. The valley opened out and the far side was lost in a lofty range. On the right the hills were lower and gracefully wooded with walnut and pine, while as stepping-stones to the centre of the valley the green fields of Indian corn rose in succeeding tiers, and there on a knoll with a deep grove at its foot stood Jarobi proper, nestling against the wooded spurs which rose away from behind it, melting away into the bleak barrenness of the separating range.

As the first white men shaded their eyes to the scene, the elements joined, and, as if in disapprobation of the sacrilegious advance, dense stormclouds rolled over the peaks and vivid lightning played above the sacred spot, while the artillery of heaven reverberated across the peaceful valley : an ominous forecast of the rude awakening which was about to come. And even as the force halted in the entrance the flames of destruction began to lick upwards in the posts which held the gorge, and the commanding tower stood a moment and then melted away in a cloud of dust and smoke as the destroying cartridge took effect. After a temporary halt two companies of the 20th and the Sappers were sent forward to burn

THE MOHMUND EXPEDITION

Jarobi. As they came abreast of the village the heavy clouds brought up rain and hail, and a bitter wind chilled all to the bone as they plodded up the pass. Colonel Woon was in command of his two companies, and beyond the knoll he found the road which was said to lead to the Mullah's retreat contracted into a narrow defile with almost sheer cliffs on either side. The Sappers had applied the fatal torch to Jarobi, and Colonel Woon was still pressing up the defile, and yet there was no hostile demonstration. Then suddenly, when the roadway became still narrower, a blaze of fire was poured in from either side, and it was evident that the defile was held by the enemy in force.

Under a hail of bullets a party of the 20th Punjab Infantry pushed on through the defile to the mosque of the Hadda Mullah, led by a Bajauri Subadar. A dozen swordsmen stood ready to defend the spot, but a Martini volley dropped half that number and the rest made for the boulders. Colonel Woon then began to withdraw, and worked back up the defile under cover of the fire of the half-battalion of Gurkhas which had by this invested the flaming remnants of the Jarobi village. The guns also were shelling the left. Thus was the object of the expedition attained. The Hadda Mullah has fled to Asmar or some part of the Shinwari district across the Afghan border. He has been a stout celibate and is advanced in years. These two facts are probably responsible for much of the influence which he undoubtedly has held over the Mohmund frontier.

While the advanced-guard action was taking place, the main body were having an unhappy time with the elements, in the broader valley. A chill wind brought up hail and sleet, and the men, wet through to the skin, lighted huge bonfires to keep themselves warm. Standing inactive in this weather was miserable work, and many broke off corn cobs from the fields and cooked them in the fires. But if it was wretched for the sound, it was far worse for the wounded who began to come back from the front. One could not but admire the fortitude of several: one man shot through the thigh, and another with the bones of his foot splintered by a Snider bullet, walked down a mile and a half on that awful road before doolies and medical treatment could be arranged. But the engagement did not end here, for as soon as the enemy perceived that the force was retiring from the valley they at once pressed forward to the attack, lining both hillsides, and with their knowledge of the country keeping perfect cover. The guns were withdrawn, and the Gurkhas passed through the Bombay Pioneers, which regiment covered the retirement of the whole force with half-battalion volleying. General Westmacott and Staff stayed with the Pioneers, and as they held the last gorge the situation became critical, for the enemy grew bolder, and in the last quarter of an hour four more of the Pioneers were wounded. The force was then withdrawn and returned to camp at the mouth of the first gorge. The night was a lively one, as before "lights out" was sounded the enemy commenced firing into camp and engaged the

THE CAPTURE OF HADDA MULLAH'S VILLAGE

The last rush on the Mosque at Jarobi

THE MOHMUND EXPEDITION 67

picket of the Gurkhas in a severe fire. But the camp was never alarmed, though four men were wounded as they lay asleep, and a camel-driver killed, this making the total casualties eighteen for the twenty-four hours.

It will be seen that by returning from Jarobi by way of the Bohar Dag, General Elles would have thrown, when he reached Kung, almost a complete circle round the most fertile portions of the Mohmund country, and returning along the Kamali from Kung he practically had visited the whole of Western Mohmund. A detachment from the 2nd Brigade had already been ordered out from Nahakhi to Kung, to be prepared to co-operate against the tribesmen in the Bohar Dag if necessary.

During the progress of the brigade up the Jarobi Valley a party of tribesmen demonstrated on the left of the baggage as it was forming up into camp. Major Massy, 19th Bengal Lancers, who was in command of the rear-guard, sent out as many of his men as he could spare to clear the heights within reasonable distance of the camp. The report on this action is as follows: "At 12.20 the enemy, numbering some eighty men, appeared on the ridge running east to west and above the spot where the head of the baggage-guard had arrived and was awaiting orders. This unexpected move created some consternation, but Major H. S. Massy, Provost Marshal, at once collected all available details and regimental escorts on the threatened flank, and sent out a company of the 20th Punjab Infantry against the enemy, who slowly retired before them. Meanwhile about two hundred of the enemy appeared on the peaks to the west and opened fire on the baggage, but at too long a range to do any damage. Two more of the five escort companies of the 20th were now called up, and under Captain Handcock, 26th Punjab Infantry, ascended the rocky cliffs and peaks to the west, and gradually drove back the enemy, being engaged with them throughout the afternoon. The baggage was then packed, and Major Massy, assisted by Captain Houghton, D.A.Q.M.G., Intelligence Branch, finally drove off the enemy."

On the following day General Elles took two battalions and a battery and punished the Atma Khels, burning Maizar Chini. General Westmacott with the rest of the brigade proceeded to Bohar Dag, burning and destroying all the towns by the way. We were again in the desolate-looking country which borders on Kamali. Jirgahs began to come in and to talk reasonably to Mr. Merk, the Chief Political Officer, for the sound of tower blasting was beginning to have its effect upon the tribesmen. But the Kuda Khels, reported to be the best armed and richest section, sent in a formal challenge, and on the 29th General Westmacott moved out against their valley. Their towers and fortified villages lie on a sloping rise which, standing on a deep ravine, leads up into the higher ranges which spur out from the Kabul Supar. The force, with Colonel Sage's Gurkhas thrown out as an advance-guard, worked up the valley, and there seemed no sign of the enemy. We began to believe that theirs had been but an idle threat, and that the position was deserted.

THE MOHMUND EXPEDITION 69

But it was not so, for suddenly at about six hundred yards a heavy rifle fire was opened from the villages, while the whole front of hills, extending over quite a mile, was found to be occupied. The first volleys from the village and towers were so heavy that four of the escort to the guns were hit and the horse of Captain Knapp, commanding No. 5, wounded. The terraced cornfields gave cover for the advance-guard, and the General Staff, which was with it, came under a really hot fire, it being marvellous that no one was hit, each member having narrow escapes. The Staff taking cover in a nullah, the guns were ordered to shell the villages, and a few rounds, making excellent practice on the towers, saw the enemy, about four hundred strong, streaming into the deep ravine and making for the hills. The commanding crests were then covered with smoke puffs and the action became general. The tribesmen were ensconced behind sungars, and in spite of ringed shell stuck to their defences with a tenacity which they have not shown in the previous engagements of the campaign. The Oxford Light Infantry having arrived from Kung just as the guns came into action, General Westmacott directed them to take up a position on the left, and with Lieutenant Logan's Maxim detachment to cover the advance of a company of the Bombay Pioneers sent to dislodge the enemy from the left spurs, the Gurkhas covered by the guns being sent on a similar errand on a high conical hill on the left, from where the enemy still kept up a harassing fire.

As soon as the heights were cleared the enemy

fell back to corresponding spurs, about 1000 yards
distant, where they had already erected sungars.
From here they kept the two parties in action as
long as they remained on the frontal position. In
the meantime the hand of the destroyer had been
at work, and frequent explosions showed that the
Sappers were destroying towers on every side. By
twelve the whole valley was in flames, and General
Westmacott proceeded to withdraw his force. Two
companies of the Oxfords were moved up to cover
the retirement of the Bombay Pioneers, and the guns
took position and covered the retirement of the right.
The enemy at once occupied the crests as soon as
they were evacuated, and fire upon the main body
recommenced. But the excellent practice of No. 5
Battery and the irritating rattle of the Maxim kept
them from following down. And though the retirement was, of necessity, slow, covering as the front
did a mile of country, yet it was beautifully carried
out, and General Westmacott cleared his force out
of the valley without further casualty. The guns
and Oxfords covered the complete retirement. The
force encamped under the hills at Kung and has
halted all to-day. Jirgahs are coming in, and the
whole of the Khwazais have come to terms. Practically the expedition is on the homeward turn.

NAHAKHI,
September 29th.

General Elles' force halted at Kung all yesterday,
this being the first halt since the force left Nahakhi
on the 20th. The whole of the day was given up

GENERAL WESTMACOTT CONDUCTING THE RETIREMENT FROM JAROBI

THE MOHMUND EXPEDITION 71

to Jirgah receptions from the neighbouring tribes. The Political Commissioner, Mr. Merk, has succeeded in making terms with the majority of the Kamali tribes. The following tribes having agreed to the terms attached to them in brackets :—Kamali proper (100 guns, 100 swords, 1500 cash), Bharan Khel (100 guns, 100 swords, 1000 cash), Issa Khel the same, Atmanzai the same, Dawazai (150 guns, 150 swords, 1500 cash). All to be paid in by October 3. The Jirgah of Kung could not make up their minds, but the young bloods made them up for them, and the Kung camp was fired into for several hours on the night of the 28th, therefore before leaving General Elles caused all fortified portions therein to be razed. This was done by 8.30 A.M. As the rearguard, the 13th Bengal Lancers, left the place a few shots were fired at them from small collections on the hills. Lieutenant Macquoid, of the Intelligence, when reconnoitring to the Sangagaki Pass with a squadron of the 13th, was fired upon, but though Lieutenant Turner had a narrow escape no harm was done, and the tribesmen hastened on the arrival of their Jirgah to explain that they had been misled by the smoke from the Kung towers into believing that the survey party was a hostile demonstration.

Colonel Graves's Brigade passed over the Nahakhi Pass to-day *en route* to Peshawar, and under existing arrangements General Westmacott will stand fast with his brigade at Nahakhi, while General Macgregor with the 2nd Brigade marches to Yakdung and the Atmanzai country to levy fines. The 20th Punjab Infantry also march down to Peshawar to-morrow, presumedly *en route* to join General Meiklejohn's force at Malakhand, which, it is reported, will operate against the Bunerwals, but this is only a camp rumour, and I have been unable to trace its origin. One may now say that the chief object of the campaign has been accomplished.

All the tribal gatherings have been broken up, the Mullah's refuge has been destroyed, the Upper Mohmunds have been severely punished, and the Lower Mohmunds have complied and are complying with the Political's terms. A short and satisfactory campaign.

Orders had come for the 20th Punjab Infantry to return to India to join the Malakhand Brigade. As only the short expedition to Yakdare and Danish Kol remained, General Elles sent down the 20th from Nahakhi on September 30. Before they marched out of camp General Elles took the opportunity of thanking them for the splendid service which they had rendered during the brief fifteen days' campaign, complimented them on their success, and shook hands with every officer and sirdar in the regiment. In consideration of the Afridi element in the regiment it had been considered politic to remove the regiment from close proximity with the expedition about to advance into Tirah. But to do a fine regiment justice, I must say that during the Mohmund Campaign, though they knew too well what was happening in and about their homes, the Afridi companies never once showed anything but the finest spirit when called upon to meet fellow Pathans in open fight as enemies of the uniform they wore.

VIII

Difficulties to contend with—First action of Patiala Infantry under Captain Cox and Lieutenant Davidson—The splendid work of the 20th Punjab Infantry.

PESHAWAR,
October 4th

As was pointed out in a previous letter, the fortune of war induced the Hadda Mullah to make his stoutest attack against General Blood's Column at Nawagai, but in spite of that when the Upper Mohmunds were reached General Elles' Division had three smart engagements, and the force returns to Peshawar with a casualty list of between thirty and forty. But a successful campaign is not to be simply judged by the butcher's bill, and much of the success of General Elles' force must be credited to the fine work of the Bombay Pioneers and Captain Kelly's Sappers and Miners. The description of the Kharappa and Nahakhi Passes you have already had, but it speaks volumes for the road-makers when a pass, over which horses and laden mules had literally to be levered, is made passable for laden camels in three days. The passes were the chief obstacles which had to be overcome.

Next in military order comes the dearth of water,

which at one time promised to delay the whole of the operations. Once the Candab stream was left behind, water became scarce until Badmanai was reached. And if it had not been for the dust storm which so disturbed the camp at Ganalai on the night of the 16th, matters must have become most serious. But the storm brought heavy rain in Kamali, and on arrival at Nahakhi the tanks were found to be full. But the tank supply in Mohmund land did not go far when the transport for a division had to be watered, and the water supply continued a source of anxiety to the Officer Commanding throughout, and stringent arrangements were made and guards habitually placed over all supplies to prevent misuse and fouling. This dearth of water consequently brought double work upon the cavalry, as the whole country had to be reconnoitred to find sufficient to supply the wants of so large a body. It was not until Badmanai had been passed that the enemy came to the conclusion that the draining of the tanks was the best means by which they could delay the advance upon Jarobi. As the advance-guard crossed the kotal which leads out of the Badmanai Valley parties of the enemy were seen attempting to cut a tank in the valley beyond. No. 3 Battery opened on them at 4000 yards, and with such accuracy that a ring shell was planted fairly in the tank in question. Farther up it was found that most of the tanks had been cut, but so hurriedly in many cases that sufficient water remained for the use of the force.

And last of the three chief obstacles, which could easily have been the first, comes the opposition by

THE MOHMUND EXPEDITION 75

the enemy. One cannot conceive why, as they meant fighting, the tribesmen did not oppose the advance over the Kharappa Pass and the Nahakhi Kotal. Both passes lent themselves admirably for defence, especially the former, as it could only be reached by a rough march of ten miles at least, with only such water as could be carried. There can be only a choice of two reasons: either the tribesmen were deceived into the belief that a force advancing from Shabkadr would be forced to make two marches before the Gundab Plateau was reached, or they were not in force enough to oppose both General Elles' advance and General Sir Bindon Blood's at the same time; yet events showed that when the attack was made upon the Nawagai Camp the Suffi Mullah had been detached to operate against the Peshawar Column if the latter advanced on Jarobi viâ Kung— that is, by the same route as that by which it eventually returned. The first shot fired upon General Elles' force, if we except the straggling fire opened on the advanced guard in the Gundab Nullah on the 15th, was after Colonel Graves's Brigade had been made over to him, and on that day the 13th Bengal Lancers' reconnoitring parties were fired upon, a horse being shot, and both Lieutenants Steele and Macquoid narrowly escaped being hit. That night the camp was fired into from several points without a casualty, and in the morning General Westmacott's Brigade fought the first action, forcing the heights on the left flank of the pass. The enemy were not in great force, but they were well posted, had a succession of positions to fall back upon and a clear line of retreat. Thus when they found that they could not prevent the advance of the 20th Punjab Infantry and Gurkhas, they split up into numerous groups and retired fighting. These groups perhaps only numbered ten to fifteen men and half a dozen rifles each, but they stuck to each position which they took up until the final rush was made. It is probable that the Mullah and his advisers anticipated that the force would be marched to his stronghold viâ Mittai, for the Malakhand Brigade on the following day found Mittai strongly invested, probably by Musa Khels, who were the Mullah's strongest adherents. It was during this reconnaissance that the 13th Bengal Lancers found to their cost that it is impossible for the present cavalry carbine to hold its own against long-range weapons such as have now found their way into the tribesmen's hands.

Here the Patiala Infantry first came into action. The cavalry retiring reported three villages to be held by two hundred men with fifty rifles, and it was necessary to dislodge them by infantry before they could be destroyed. The Patiala Infantry were detached under Captain Cox and Lieutenant Davidson. The men advanced very steadily and drove the tribesmen out. Havildar-Major Mehtab Singh has been promoted for gallantry in this brush, and on leaving Nahakhi H.H. the Maharaja presented the men of the regiment with Rs. 1000. After Badmanai a few shots were fired into camp at Lashkar Kili, but there was no real opposition until the Jarobi Defile was reached. Here the tribesmen, presumably the dwellers in the valley, followed the

THE MOHMUND EXPEDITION 77

same tactics as are usual with them. They made little show of opposition until the force was well up into the defile and the sun was setting. Then, when the troops had to be withdrawn, as Jarobi Valley was not the place a General would care to encamp in for the night, the enemy took heart, and galled the retirement with a harassing fire. That night also the camp was severely fired into, and the outlying pickets at times became hotly engaged. It was evident that the Upper Mohmunds were then on the warpath, for numerous armed gangs were about in the neighbouring hills, and while Jarobi was being invested, the Koda Khel contingent made a demonstration against the rear and baggage-guard of the force.

On the morning after the demolition of Jarobi, the work of tower destruction continued without further contact with the enemy, and it was not until the Koda Khel Valley was reached that fighting recommenced. This engagement has been fully detailed, and with the burning of Kung on the following day it may be said that hostilities closed. A few shots were fired on the cavalry rear-guard as they left Kung; but since then there has not been another shot fired. As has been pointed out, the Mohmunds are a poor people, so the punishment must have been severe; seventy-two stone towers have been destroyed by gunpowder and forty fortified positions burned. The force has lived for three weeks upon the country at an estimated cost of Rs. 4000 a day. Eight hundred swords and eleven hundred guns, including some rifles, have been surrendered, and a cash fine has been paid, and, most important of all, the "purdah," of which the tribesmen were so proud, has been removed. It may confidently be said that the British prestige has been re-established there. The short march which General MacGregor's Brigade made into the Atmanzai country evoked no opposition, and terms were promptly complied with.

To enumerate the units in this short campaign would be impossible, but before closing these notes the work of the 20th Punjab Infantry under Colonel Woon deserves mention. This fine regiment, composed of Sikhs, Dogras, and Afridi Pathans, called forth admiration from every member of the force, and they deserved all the praise they received. At Shabkadr they had over thirty killed and wounded and they bore the brunt of the subsequent campaign. To show the pluck which pervades this regiment, at Jarobi, two men, one wounded in the thigh and the other with all the bones of his right food splintered by a Snider bullet, walked down a mile or more to where the doolies were situated. The regiment marched into Mohmund land as fit as could be; and they marched down three weeks later unharmed by a campaign which had brought them the hardest of work under trying conditions.

The work of Lieutenant Logan's Maxim detachment also deserves to be noticed. He has the mule equipment, and during the turning of the Badmanai Pass, Lieutenant Logan and his Maxim were always in action with the advanced-guard on the right flank; this position was attained only by an extremely

THE MOHMUND EXPEDITION 79

severe climb, and was maintained on a hillside without a semblance of pathway. In fact, one of the ammunition mules had a fall of forty feet. This shows that with an energetic officer a mule Maxim can accompany an advanced fighting line almost over any country. It has been impossible to estimate the enemy's losses, as the severest of the fighting was during actions which covered the withdrawal of the forces from some punitive expedition. Therefore the enemy's wounded remained in their possession. The casualties at the Badmanai Pass are estimated officially at about thirty. The total casualties in General Elles' Column were four killed and twenty-five wounded.

IX

Lower Mohmunds fined and punished—End of campaign within view—An account of the Mohmunds and their characteristics.

·Peshawar,
October 3rd.

Except for the collecting of Mr. Merk's fines and punishment of the Yakdand section, one may say that the Mohmund campaign is at an end. Though the march of General Elles' Division has been much put in the shade by the disturbing sequence of events to the Bajaur Column, yet in reality the last fifteen days have seen one of the best pushed-through advances into an unknown country that we have made on our North-west Frontier. The cause which brought about the campaign, as is well known, was the hostile demonstration which a collection of Mohmund tribesmen and others made against Shabkadr Fort and Shankarghar village, under the direction of one Hadda Mullah, a much-respected preacher who, a refugee from Afghanistan, had for many years resided in Jarobi, the most fertile valley in Upper Mohmund. What influenced this Mullah it is impossible to say. Probably when the disaffection which was propagated from the Swat-

THE MOHMUND EXPEDITION

Bonair country reached him he was ambitious enough to believe that by a single *coup* the Peshawar Vale might be raided, and that, the raid being successful, the tribesmen would be safe when they had re-crossed the rocky defiles and the rugged passes which curtain off the Mohmund country. Whatever his aspirations, he succeeded in accomplishing one of the most daring enterprises ever undertaken on the British frontier. The frontier was crossed, Sankarghar looted and burned, and the fort of Shabkadr with its garrison of Border Police invested; in fact, the attack was so far pressed home that men with axes tried to beat in the gates of the main way of the fortress. It seems certain that the sack of Peshawar bazaar and the capture of three thousand stand of arms that lie in the cantonments were the enticing baits which the Mullah held forth to his following; and when the first issues were so successful, it is possible that the wary hillmen might have been induced to march inwards but for the prompt arrival of our column.

The fight on the border sand-hills is history now—another addition to the list of engagements which have been settled upon that yellow strip. The issue of that battle—and it was a battle—must have been sufficient to prove to the tribesmen that Peshawar city and the three thousand stand of arms were beyond their reach, for though they magnified their successful attack into a victory, yet the many new grave cairns in the Gundab Defile show how heavily they lost; and the fact that they fled that night up into their mountain fastnesses gives evidence that they considered that their game was up. But there remained the vengeance for it, and the day had arrived when it became imperative for the Indian Government to show these border thieves that their so-called impassable defiles were but delusions. In the last thirty years possibly the Government has not received such a severe slap in the face as the raid on Shabkadr. But it was over a month before preparations for the advance of the avenging division could be made; and a doubt must have grown up in the hearts of the hillmen as they saw the forces gathering at the foot of their hills. Yet we have it from the Politicals that they believed in the impregnability of their passes to the end, and took our measures to be but a demonstration to impress them. The two brigades constituting the division concentrated with a month's supplies at Shabkadr on the 14th, and on the 15th commenced the memorable march to Gundab (Ganalai). The object of the advance may be classed under the following heads: First, to punish the Mohmunds for their raid, to disarm them if possible; in default to damage their interests by whatever means suitable; secondly, to prove to them that their passes were not impregnable; thirdly, to break up the armed gathering with which the Hadda Mullah was threatening our force in Bajaur-Swat; to supply that force with a certain addition in food, and to destroy Jarobi, the heart of the political unrest.

It was anticipated by the Political Officer, Mr. Merk, C.S.I., that of the six tribes of Mohmunds which, according to the Udny Commission, should come under the sphere of influence of the Indian

THE MOHMUND EXPEDITION 83

Government, the Tarakhzai alone would be amenable, and that the Baizais and Kwazais would resent our presence to the last. Not that the Tarakhzais and Halimzais, which constitute the Lower Mohmunds, were in any way less connected with the raid, but being a poorer people, nearer our influence, they would be more easily overcome, and a policy of conciliation with them meant a safe line of communication. How well this policy worked is shown by the fact that not once was the telegraph wire cut or the post stopped in Lower Mohmund, but as soon as the force debouched into Kamali and Upper Mohmund, followers were cut off and the post harassed. Whether the Mullah hoped for success or not is only a matter for conjecture, but there is evidence that he preached and promised success, and there is no doubt that the preparations made at Nawagai for the attack upon General Blood's force were meant to be the deciding issue of the campaign as far as the Upper Mohmunds were concerned. The Mullah here staked his all, and the fury of the rushes could only have been sustained by confidence of ultimate success. It was at Nawagai that the allies had been collected, and when they found that the rushing of a camp was a costly venture, these allies probably dropped away, short of commissariat and disheartened, so that the one thousand five hundred men who defended Badmanai were probably only the fighting men of the local sections.

As is the way with most of our frontier wars, one upstanding engagement settles whether the affair is capable of prompt political measures or will develop full military interest. The defence of Nawagai tended to the settlement of the Mohmund trouble, just as much as the fighting at Inayatkila has magnified the gravity of the situation in Swat-Bajaur and Bonair. Thus we have attained in fifteen to twenty days the objects of the Mohmund Campaign. The Lower Mohmunds have been fined and to a great measure disarmed. The Upper Mohmunds have had less consideration shown them. Wherever they have shown opposition, they have had their strongholds demolished and their grain stores tapped. Therefore Shabkadr has been avenged in the coin which the Pathan understands best—blood for blood. The Mullah's Valley—the Promised Land in a bleak country—has been destroyed, and the armed gatherings have been dispersed with loss by the actions of Nawagai, Badmanai Pass, Jarobi Valley, and Koda Khel, and, greatest of all, the tribesman has been shown how easily his much-vaunted fastnesses have been approached.

The strength of the Mohmunds as a race has been in their country rather than themselves. They seem a vacillating race, and the nature of the country —hot, arid, and enclosed—has kept them from attaining the fine physique which one finds in the Waziri and Afridi. They are good cultivators, and both their buildings and irrigation works show them to be industrious artisans, though it is probable that most of this manual labour is done by the women, who appear to be of much finer physique than the men. The difficulty of the country lies in the scarcity

THE MOHMUND EXPEDITION 85

of water, and but for a very few natural springs, not only cultivation but the natural wants of the people are dependent upon rainfall. The whole of the country is intersected with waterways; in fact, most of the so-called valleys are but the courses of mountain streams, which, after a rain, become raging torrents, the water remaining only a few hours, as a natural drainage carries it to the plains. Therefore, the country being dependent upon rainfall, its inhabitants must often be put to great straits by water famine, and as often as not a famine of cultivation as well. They store water by a series of cut tanks, and in a few places very deep wells cater to the supply. In the valleys there is very little cultivation, as they are generally simply the beds of the watercourses; the fields are, as a rule, carefully cut terraces on the less steep of the lower hill slopes; but even to the casual observer it is evident that the fertility of the country is most limited and that it would be absolutely insufficient to support the inhabitants.

The Mohmunds, therefore, to make both ends meet, levy dues on the commerce of Afghanistan and India. They have fixed and recognised rates on the Lalpura, Gundab, Alikandi, and other converging routes, and it seems that these dues are collected and paid with an honesty altogether out of keeping with the Pathan character. But even these tolls would hardly make ends meet if the Mohmunds were not, as other Pathans, professional thieves. At best they are a poor tribe, and very different except in perfidy to other frontier Pathans. The country to look at is bare and sterile, and you may go for miles without seeing a single tree. Being so enclosed with bare rocks rising to five or six thousand feet, it is always a hot climate in the summer months, as the hills shut out the cool breezes, while in the cold weather it maintains a muggy heat for the same reason, being free, of course, from the biting cold found on more open ranges. Excepting Jarobi Valley there was no part of the country that the force entered that one could call wooded, or that afforded a scenery pleasant to the eye. The villages are plentiful, and are all built on the usual defensible style common to the frontier.

The Mohmunds' masonry work is excellent, being chiefly shale slab-filling, though in places where water is more plentiful mud plaster and mortar are used. Like all Pathans, these men live in a constant state of blood feuds, and the country is covered with towers of refuge. These are generally circular, and a rope ladder hangs from the entrance, which is in the top storey. The fugitive hard pressed reaches the tower and enters, hauling the ladder after him. He then from the loopholes keeps his pursuers off. The curious part of this system of warfare is that, though a man may be besieged in one of these towers for days, yet no attempt at starvation is made, and his womenfolk may bring him bread and water. This curious system, I presume, originated in the fact that no Pathan will fire on a woman. If they killed the women as freely as they kill each other, the race would soon cease to exist. They have but little property, and of their possessions wood seems the most valuable : there being no trees in the country, wood has to be brought great distances. One cannot say that they are well armed, for they have neither the means to buy weapons or the pluck to steal them, which has so far advanced the Afridi, Orakzai, Bajaur, and Bonair sections.

At the same time there must be many hundreds of breech-loaders in their possession, and our wounded at Badmanai show that the Lee-Metford has come into their possession, as also the Dum-Dum bullet. But rifles are not plentiful, for the market value of a Lee-Metford is Rs. 900 and that of a Martini Rs. 600. The cattle of the country are small, almost *gainis;* this no doubt is due to long residence in a land destitute of water ; goats, sheep, and a gaunt species of fowl are about all the domestic animals which they possess. Their chief grain is barley, though near springs a stunted Indian corn was found. It was ripening as the force advanced, and was a big sweet grain, much bigger than that of the plains.

THE TIRAH EXPEDITION

"The general object of this expedition is to exact reparation for the unprovoked aggression of the Afridi and Orakzai tribes on the Peshawar and Kohat Borders, for the attacks on our frontier posts, and for the damage to life and property which had been inflicted on British subjects and those in the British service.

"It is believed that this object can best be attained by the invasion of Tirah, the summer home of the Afridis and Orakzais, which has never before been entered by a British force."

Gazette.

The Orakzais raided on the Samava from about the 14th of August; the Afridis in the Khyber from the 17th of the same month.

Malakhand and Chakdara were attacked by the Swat tribesmen on July the 27th. Shabkadr was burned by the Mohmund on the 7th of August.

X

The Amir's influence—Routes to the Tirah Valley—
Conflicting rumours.

PESHAWAR.
October 4th.

FEW except those who have intimate knowledge of the Peshawar frontier fully realise what the present Tirah Expedition means. Drawing a parallel with our average frontier expeditions, there is little to show the public that we are on the eve of a campaign which, even though it may be a short one, will probably be the most sanguinary that the frontier has seen for years. Leaving the Orakzai section alone, the Afridi clans themselves will prove an enemy obdurate enough. It must be borne in mind that from the extreme fertility and geographical position of this section of the frontier, the Afridis have become a wealthy clan, and that they have exercised this wealth in arming themselves with the latest pattern of breech-loading rifle. Moreover, a fighting nation by birth and instinct, a very large proportion have received military training in our own regiments. The chief tribes of the Afridis are the Kuki Khels, Kamba Khels, Kamrai Khels, Malikdin Khels, Sipah and Zakka Khels; they, of course, are divided and sub-divided up into many sections and subsections, which in peace time consider themselves as separate units, but which upon the nation being involved in war at once combine with their sections. Of the tribes enumerated above, the Kuki Khels and Zakka Khels are the strongest; but roughly speaking the whole fighting strength of the Afridis is nearly thirty thousand men, and of these fifty per cent. are armed with weapons of range and precision. This is irrespective of the Orakzais.

Reliable information is to hand that the Afridis intend fighting to the last, and now that their autumn harvests are in, they will have a free hand; and it is this point that one would press home, that fifty thousand fighting tribesmen of the stamina and instincts of the Afridi and Orakzai will mean heavy fighting before a British Agency can dictate terms from the Tirah Plateau, and it seems that this is the only place from which we can dictate terms which will carry sufficient weight to meet the situation. Once the tableland is occupied, the back of these frontier risings should be broken, especially when Sir Bindon Blood and his division have whipped their end of the frontier from Nawagai to farther Bonair. But this will not mean peace—and it will probably be years before fighting of a desultory kind dies out.

The attitude of the Amir with regard to the Afridis at present seems decided, though his Afridi agents were with him shortly before the attack on Lundi Kotal, and he must have had a knowledge of what was taking place, yet he has now finally washed his hands of the turbulent tribesmen who have given him such trouble, and whom he has never been strong enough to chastise. It seems that he denies their contention that it is a *jehad* by quoting a passage from the Koran which only admits a *jehad* to be possible between *Sultanats* (kingdoms), and that his answer to the Afridis is that they are nothing of this. Further information shows that a certain Mullah of

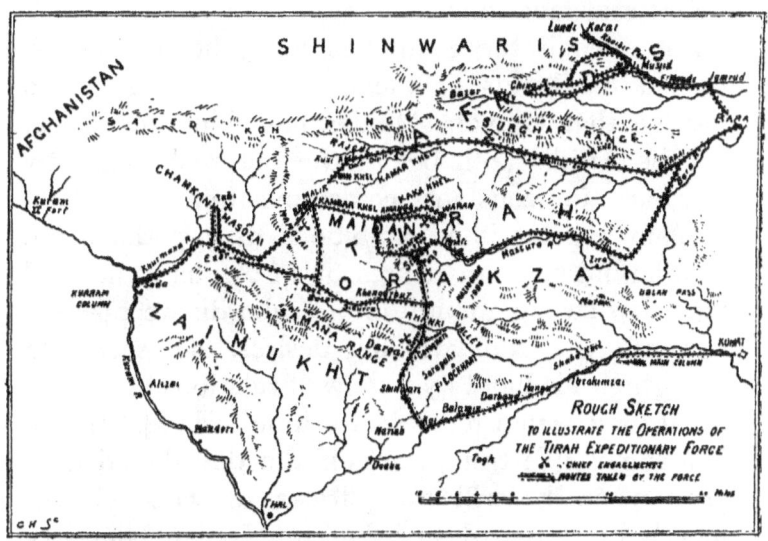

the Malikdin Khels has been made by that section a "Badshah," and that he has been recognised by some tribes.

But this being the case does not disprove his original implication with the outburst. If he had never countenanced the preaching of a holy war, his strange publication would have been a book without an object. No Oriental ever yet took so decided a step without some ulterior motive; and with true Oriental subtilty the more important passages of the work were veiled in a double meaning, so that the author can argue from either standpoint. If it suited the Amir to set the mechanism working, it evidently has not suited him to openly aid the working of the machine, though he possibly can find means to supply the necessary lubricants, even when expressing righteous indignation at the attitude of the frontier fanatics.

But even if the Amir has, for political reasons, washed his hands of them, it does not seem so positive that Ghulam Haider has done the same, and the Afridis both before the outbreak and now even are in constant communication with him. Ghulam Haider is an ambitious man, perhaps the most ambitious man at present in Afghanistan, and not being strong enough in his subordinate position to reach the standard he desires, he seeks to strengthen his hand by a show of religious sincerity; and it may be that he looks to these turbulent tribesmen as possible trump cards if the day should ever come when he will have tricks to win. Consequently he has no desire that the Indian boundary should move up to that of his own country. And this is what we presume will be the termination of the frontier policy. If there is another termination and, after a stubborn fight and a few months' occupation, our influence is withdrawn, why, we are only paving the way for a second expedition a few years hence. The plateau itself from all reports is a glorious spot suited before all others to be a base for operations upon our North-west frontier, and it adds to its virtues by being well suited as a sanitarium.

Native report says that no Indian hill station can

compare with it. The valleys are fertile in the extreme, fruit-trees grow and flourish, and its crops run into luxuriant growth. It is never subject to heavy rain, as it is out of the monsoon current. Snow falls heavily during the winter months, but it is a dry and healthy cold, and seeing what physique the Afridi Pathan has, it seems possible that these reports are true in the main. That the expense of opening out and retaining this "Garden of Eden" will be immense one can readily understand, but it can never equal the expenditure on the expeditionary forces which its retention will prevent; besides, Peshawar and Nowshera can be reduced if Tirah is firmly established.

But we have to arrive at Tirah yet, and it may be that many who start to march the short distance there, will never arrive, for the well-armed and staunch tribesman, choosing his own battle theatre, has chances against the invader which go far to minimise the latter's superiority in arms and system.

MOUTH OF KOHAT PASS,
October 9th.

There are several routes by which Tirah can be reached. But as there was only native information to rely upon, the choice of passes and entrances did not lie with the difficulty of approach. It seemed given that all were difficult, and all have proved to be so. Therefore it was a matter of the most suitable bases. There has been much argument as to the policy of moving so large a force as two divisions by one road and of forcing, by sheer fighting strength, the one route chosen. But it is an easy matter to say now, when the country has been traversed, that half a dozen columns could have operated with more success. It must be remembered that in the beginning not a soul was able to foretell what tactics the tribesmen would adopt. From the Samana history it certainly seemed that there was some cohesion amongst them, and that they were moving in large bodies. Thus a weaker column than a division might—and many strange things happen in war—have been absolutely enveloped and overpowered. We were playing a game in which we could not afford to play a false card at the commencement. As the choice of Kohat-Kushalghar as a base in preference to Peshawar, events have proved that great sagacity was shown in the choice. When it comes to lines of communication in a trying campaign, it is not expense which is the beacon guide: it is safety; and the political theory was that the Orakzais would soon repent of their show of fanaticism. And in this the political theory was right, and we were thus able to maintain the line of communications through a friendly country right up to the Ashanga Pass, the very doorway of the Afridi Tirah. Thus, when the Mohmund Field Force, part of the Malakhand Division, and the Reserve Brigades were broken up and the main Tirah Expeditionary force formed, the troops which had been using Peshawar as a base of operations were marched as three columns to Kohat over the Kohat Pass, which is Adam Khel country, a linked section of the Tirah Adam Khel Afridis.

The leading column of the three advancing on

THE TIRAH EXPEDITION

Kohat from Peshawar arrived at the foot of the Pass on the 9th October, the Gordons, Devons, and 2nd and 4th Gurkhas having marched through from Bara and Jamrud, and the remainder of the column, the Nabha Battalion and No. 8 Battery, having marched direct from Peshawar in two days. The whole force will cross in the morning and do the eighteen miles into Kohat. The troops doing the march from Bara to the pass halted on the 8th at the police post Metani, the native inspector of which was full of wild stories of the recent Afridi attack. He took all visitors to his post to the top of his small mud tower and pointed out the spot where the Afridi Lashkar descended into the plain with the object of attacking him, and then related how he sent round the fiery cross to the neighbouring villages, and made such a show that the Afridi army retired. As a matter of fact the utmost uncertainty is prevalent in camp, and the most conflicting rumours find circulation. Some foretell a six months' campaign, others are positive that ten days will see the important part of the business over, while vague reports of unconditional surrender of Orakzai or Afridi, or both, supplant each other; and the official news which the Politicals have sent in does not seem much better. They report that the many tribal Jirgahs which have met have agreed to submit certain conditions to the Politicals, but a conversation which was held with a native officer of an Afridi company points to a bitter resistance if we enter the country. He is of the opinion that the tribesmen will content themselves with night attacks and night firing, and this being the case one may safely look forward to a long and trying campaign.

The 1st Division, which General Symons is to command, is as good a body of troops as could have been brought together, both British and Native, and the two British regiments, the Devons and Gordons, which marched in together from Bara, in spite of the wretched situation of their last month's quarters, are as fine a body of men as any in the service. A new system has crept in with this campaign, and one which commends itself to all, that is, the supplying of each column with a couple of companies of Gurkhas to act as hill scouts or permanent advance-guard.

The three columns from Peshawar, which are to concentrate at Kohat, march over the Kohat Pass on the 10th, 11th, and 12th, and beyond that they join their own divisions no one here with the moving columns has any knowledge of the plan of campaign or of the date of moving into the enemy's country. We anticipate no opposition during the march to Kohat, for the Adam Khels have expressed a desire to remain friendly, and their country being situated as it is, there is little to induce the Jowaki Afridis to prove themselves antagonistic to the advance.

Possibly some young bloods of the other sections may come down, but it is not anticipated. The weather on the frontier still remains extraordinarily hot for the season of the year, and in spite of the light scale marching orders most of the force will be glad to be into the cooler regions of the hills. The health of the troops is good, but the water supply on this march is bad.

XI

Start of General Hamilton's Peshawar column—Order of advance of troops to the front—Stupendous task entailed in moving the army—Accident to General Ian Hamilton—Advance up the Dargai Ridge—Its position and surroundings.

KOHAT,
October 11th.

REVEILLE sounded at 3 A.M. at Imulchabutra, and in the light of a nearly full moon the leading Peshawar Column under General Hamilton marched into the mouth of the Kohat Pass, to cover the seventeen miles to Kohat. The Gurkha scouts went in front, followed by the Devons who supplied the advance-guard, the Gordons following, then the Nabha Battalion, with the 2nd and 4th Gurkhas supplying the rear-guard. The early part of the march was very fine, for the upward incline was found to be easy, and on either hand immense spurs and kotals stretched away, which in the white light of the moon made an imposing scene, but the grandeur was intensified when just as the first halt sounded up the valley the moon sank behind the crests on the left, plunging the defile-plain into darkness and lighting the summits on the left with a weird fantastic medley of light and shade. Then as the column advanced day broke, and in the growing light the regiments wound up a stony gorge. In places the road was good, but the path at times became intersected with nullahs, the beds of which were simple shingly waterways. As day advanced the valley broadened and proved to be well cultivated and populated. The villagers showed pleasant friendliness, and in one place a Khan had brought down tea and Pathan bread, and placed it for use on the roadway.

No opposition was experienced, and at 9.15 the column halted at the foot of the steep ascent to the Kotal proper. After an hour it proceeded, and from the Border Police post on the summit a lovely view of the Kohat Valley lay beneath us. Nestling in the dip of a green stretch lies the brown-baked frontier station, patched with a darker green than fields and surmounted by its imposing fort. The edges are fringed with the white streaks of the canvas of the many camps. Kohat is four miles from the summit of the kotal, and at that hour the road was blazing hot. But the men buckled to, and by 12.15 the leading regiments were in. Kohat presents the scene of a huge military mobilisation, and when one remembers that over thirty thousand troops have mobilised for this expedition, and that two-thirds of that force are now at Kohat, one can realise this more fully. General Lockhart has left with some portion of his Staff for Fort Lockhart, four marches away. It is from there that the general advance will take place, probably about the 19th or 20th instant.

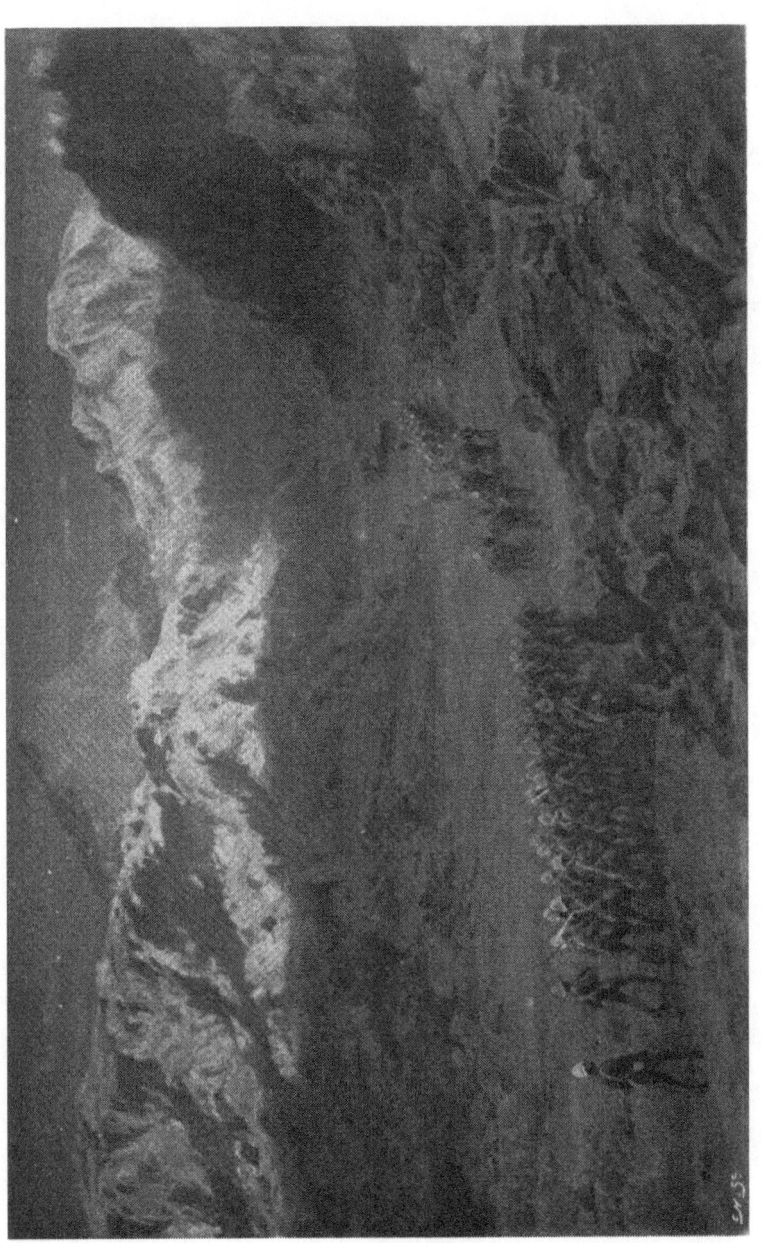

THE 1ST DEVONSHIRE REGIMENT ENTERING THE KOHAT PASS

At 3.30 A.M. October 10

THE TIRAH EXPEDITION

The order of advance of troops to the front from Kohat is as follows :—On the 11th a column under Colonel Dixon advances to Shinwari (four marches), consisting of the King's Own Scottish Borderers. On the 12th for the same destination, a column under Colonel Purdy, R.A., No. 8 Battery R.A., 1st Battalion Gordons, machine gun, and signalling party 16th Lancers. On the 14th the 1st Dorsets and No. 5 (Bombay) Mountain Battery, under Colonel Piercy. On the 17th the following troops proceed to Kai under General I. Hamilton (three marches): 1st Battalion Devons, 1st Battalion 1st Gurkhas, Kohat Mountain Battery, 28th Bombay Pioneers, Nabha Regiment, scouts of the 5th Gurkhas. On the 18th, under General Gaselee, the Yorkshire Regiment, the Royal West Surrey, and 2nd company of the 4th Gurkhas. No. 1 Mountain Battery, No. 3 Company Sappers proceed to Hangu. The 30th Punjab Infantry stand fast at Hangu, and the 3rd Sikhs and two guns No. 2 Derajat Battery move direct to Shinwari from Kurram.

KOHAT,
October 13th.

The reports from the front seem to show that the tribesmen have already started quarrelling among themselves. It appears that a deputation of Aka Khel were coming in to the Political Agency at Hangu, when they turned back without reaching their destination, having heard that the Ali Khel section of the Orakzais were advancing in force upon their villages to punish them for showing such vacillation as to have even friendly conversation with the invader. And a clan circular has gone round that the Adam Khels had similarly committed a breach of tribal faith, and that they should, therefore, in accordance with the determination arrived at in former Jirgahs, be treated as enemies to the cause of Pathan independence. All this tends to show that the want of cohesion among the enemy which the Politicals had anticipated would separate the Orakzais from the Afridis had commenced, and it at once strengthened the arguments in favour of the long lines of communications through the Khanhi-Mastura route.

KOHAT,
October 16th.

It is not until one has visited the base of one of our frontier expeditions that one realises what a stupendous affair the movement of an army in India is. If the many skilled tacticians of Europe who, we from time to time are told, have mapped out the invasion of this peninsula, could make one short flying visit to Kohat at the present moment, they would possibly pigeonhole their scheme of operations if they included a transport register on the same scale as ours. A few figures will give some idea of the immensity of it all. Before the Peshawar Columns arrived at Kohat at all there were over thirty thousand head of transport cattle engaged either at Kohat or engaged on the lines of communication between the Kurram and Kushalghar. To these have been added the new arrivals from

THE TIRAH EXPEDITION

India and the transport of the three strong columns which marched over the Kohat Pass from Peshawar, quite another twenty thousand head of transport. Thus, in round figures, we have thirty-odd thousand men carrying arms engaged between the Khyber and the Kurram, requiring fifty thousand head of transport. Allowing one man to every three animals, we find attached to the force seventeen thousand transport drivers, and with other followers the total of non-combatants must swell to that of the actual combatants. Therefore, in round numbers, one may safely say that there are sixty thousand men, with fifty thousand transport animals, to feed. In a country where the facility of rail might carry the supplies to within a few hundred yards of the fighting line this does not seem so enormous a business, but when your advanced base depôt is two long marches from the railway, and each day the force advances the chain extends, the transport of so large a force becomes an immense question.

Kohat at the present moment is a maze of transport. As you come in from the 1st Division camp, you meet every class of bullock vehicle, from the neat Government cart to the clumsy hold-all of the country, creaking their weary way to the front laden with compressed *bhusa*, beef tins, and the bulkier of the commissariat stores. Lines of lank camels, ragged, disconsolate-looking creatures, saunter at an even pace with the carts; mules jingle past, ponies and even tiny donkeys, one vast medley creeping up to the front, patient units in the country's vengeance. Every spare open green in Kohat is given up to something military—hospitals, field parks, regiments, transport lines, commissariat godowns. To-day one of these is here; to-morrow it has joined the wave which swells steadily on, and something else has taken its place. Such are the conditions of the movement of an army in India. And think what those European officers may, they will be able to do with no less if they are ever fated to commence their schemes, and they will be ill prepared to face the situation. One can only marvel what it was in years gone by, when subaltern officers marching to Kabul or against the Sikhs were allowed their fifteen to twenty camels, and when colonels carried their wives and drawing-room suites with them. No, it must be a nation rich in both specie and resource that will bring two hundred thousand head of transport cattle over our frontier passes to invade India.

An unfortunate accident happened yesterday. General Ian Hamilton's horse fell with him and rolled over his leg, breaking it. This, of course, makes the command of his brigade vacant. Immense sympathy is felt with General Hamilton, for apart from the painful accident, he loses a chance which may not occur again for many years.

General Reginald Hart, V.C., was given the vacant command of the 1st Brigade.

Ustazai Camp, midway between Hangu and Kohat.

It was a hot march in from Kohat, but the last few miles through a very pretty country. Ustazai is a Pathan township standing on a small conical

THE TIRAH EXPEDITION 105

hill, overlooking one of the prettiest valleys that I have yet seen in India. Woodland and crops, which make the river banks look like meadow, are an eye-rest from the continual blazing rock of Mohmund across to Kohat. Such a sight even tends to make one less sceptical about the reports one has heard of the beauties of Tirah.

There is no doubt now that the Afridis intend to do their best to impede the passage of the expeditionary force, as they have taken the field in front of the Shinwari position, and daily we have reports of their raiding parties swooping down and cutting up stragglers between Kohat and this. There is every indication that the Afridis mean a bitter opposition, and those who know them could not believe that they would ever have done anything else: they have their homes and their wives and children to protect.

The various stories which have circulated may be taken for what they are worth, and they are for the most part worthless, especially the rumour which has gained so much credence that the tribesmen were taking their families over the Safed Koh into the Shinwari country, and that they were going to give us an empty march through their country. True, they may have removed their families into the hills and fastnesses, but it would be hard to believe that eighty thousand families had removed into Shinwari over a difficult mountain pass, and that they were squatting quietly in a foreign country ruled by an un-aiding monarch. Commissariat difficulties alone for so large a host would render such an exodus impossible.

A few of the headmen and the more influential may have removed their households, but for the rest, we shall find them in Afridi land.

The march from Hangu to Kai was interesting, as on one's right lay the complete panorama of the centres of the stirring events which have so recently taken place at this end of the border. The whole ridge of the Samana lies before one, and it is possible to trace with the glass each spot of interest. Fort Lockhart, the much threatened; Saraghari, the scene of the tragic but magnificent end of a handful of Sikhs; Gulistan, so fiercely invested, with English ladies behind its mud ramparts; and the Changru Kotal, where the huge engine of our vengeance is slowly getting up steam. Apparently there is to be but little delay, and the 1st Division arrives at Kai, to find the 2nd Division pushing onwards on the 20th on the lightest possible marching scale. This is the latest in the camp to-night.

CAMP SHINWARI,
October 19th.

The day before yesterday orders came from Fort Lockhart for the division at Shinwari to make a reconnaisance in force towards the Khanki Valley, as the enemy had been seen moving on the frontal position above Changru, and had interfered with the road-making parties. The force moved out of camp at 4 A.M., the 4th Brigade under General Westmacott taking the right advance and the 3rd Brigade under General Kempster the left; the whole being under the orders of General Sir Power Palmer, com-

RUINS OF SARAGHARI POST

Destroyed by the Tribesmen—Defended by a detachment of the 36th Sikhs

manding the lines of communication. The objective of General Westmacott's force was the summit of the kotal which directly overlooks Shinwari, and which is a formidable hill about two thousand-odd feet above the level of the camp. No. 9 Mountain Battery and the Northamptons from Fort Lockhart were to concentrate with General Westmacott at 8 A.M. at the Mullan Tank. The Shinwari force was the first to arrive, and General Westmacott sent the 1st and 3rd Gurkhas as advance-guard down the reverse of Chagru Kotal. The 9th R.A. Mountain Battery and the Northamptons then arrived, and the force proceeded up towards the Dargai Ridge. What from the plain appears a simple ascent proved to be a steep, rugged, and almost impassable hillside. Road there was none, and the men toiled silently up paths and sheep tracks.

Dargai Sir is the crest of a hill upon which stands a village from which it takes its name. It is about a thousand to fifteen hundred feet higher than Changru Kotal, to which it lies at an angle of ninety degrees. On the near side it is almost a sheer precipice, and there is only one means of access to the kotal, which is up three steep waterways converging to the left of the position. From their point of connection, a slope under the perpendicular cliff which juts out sheer on the left has to be crossed. This was the death-trap where Major Jennings-Bramly fell, and it is only two hundred to two hundred and fifty yards' range from the cliff summit. Once crossed, the very steepness of the cliff itself affords cover from the summit, and a path winds round its base and zigzags up until men in single file can reach the ridge. The ridge dips to the cup plateau where the village lies, and then runs upwards two hundred feet to the peak of the Sir, making a frontal of the best part of a mile from the sheer cliff to the peak. On the far side the hill slopes away to the Khanki Valley with more or less of an easy gradient, so much so that it is terraced and possible of cultivation. But the near side is a terrible ascent, and the one path before the perpendicular cliff brings a space of about fifty yards under the concentrated fire of the whole summit of the cliff at two hundred yards' range, being a cross fire from two front flanks.

Almost as soon as the real advance commenced, the enemy opened fire, and No. 9 and No. 5 came into action, with the effect that the fire slackened.

The advance continued steadily, the road becoming worse rather than better, till in one place a kotal between two spurs had to be crossed with barely a foot of purchase way, and a sheer drop on either side. The steepness of the ascent saved the force considerably from the enemy's fire, until the last two hundred yards from the summit, over which there was no cover at all. The Borderers and Gurkhas had brought themselves up to this by sheer climbing power, and the Gurkhas were ordered to fix bayonets and carry the position, while the Borderers, who had behaved splendidly, covered their advance by "close up" volleys. Under this collected fire, the Gurkhas pushed up their way in company rushes.

FORT GULISTAN

Defended by Major Des Vœux and a Detachment of the 36th Sikhs

THE TIRAH EXPEDITION

As they neared the summit the enemy evacuated, the line of glittering steel being too much for them, and after a brief rest, as soon as the Borderers joined them, the Gurkhas pursued. But not for long, as the General, who had been with the advance-guard directing the operations throughout, recalled them. On gaining the crest it was found that a village lay in the cup plateau, and that sungars had been built all along the summit and also high up on a hill which covered the crest, about two hundred feet above the village. General Westmacott waited for two hours on the summit, and anticipating that General Kempster would not make his way up, began to withdraw his men, as large bodies of the enemy with thirteen standards had been seen moving to the left rear, these being the men presumably who later came into action with the 3rd Brigade. As the retirement from the crest commenced General Kempster arrived, and as the last two companies of General Westmacott's Brigade withdrew the Gordons re-occupied the crest. General Westmacott retired back into the camp, the only incident being that two Gurkhas were cut up in a friendly village on the way down.

But with General Kempster's Brigade it was different: the enemy, who evidently were encamped in the Khanki Valley, had moved up in force which gathered as the troops withdrew, and the Gordons became very hotly engaged as they covered the retreat, losing Major Jennings-Bramly, shot dead, and Lieutenant Pears (attached) wounded. It was not until late that the brigade was back in camp.

It is presumed that the original defenders of the ridge were the Orakzai piquets, and from the number of killed lying on the crest, it is evident that the Borderers and Gurkhas dealt heavily with them; but the final attack on General Kempster's rear-guard seems to have been made in such force that it is probable that the Afridi contingent had come up from the valley below at the sound of firing as stated above. The object of this reconnaissance in force was to find a suitable place for a second baggage road, and it was thought that the right column coming into action would draw the enemy from the left, and that the watchmen on the range would be caught between two fires and severely punished. The list of casualties you have already had.

Casualties.—British officers killed: Major Jennings-Bramly, Gordons; Lieutenant Pears, attached Gordons, wounded. Killed: rank and file, nine; wounded, fifty-two.

Camp Shinwari is a scene of the greatest military activity. The camp lies upon two adjacent hills and in the valley below, and has been put into as sound a state of defence as possible; that is, walls and zerebas have been built round all the extremities and the mouths of the valley have been faced with wire entanglements. With ten thousand men and their attendants lying here and with twenty days' stores for double that number, the place appears like a teeming city in the shadow of the hills.

As this first action at Dargai has caused much comment in both English and Indian Press, this may

CAMP AT SHINWARI

Showing Crest-line of Dargai Ridge and the Chagon Kotal

THE TIRAH EXPEDITION

be a suitable moment to study the position which led up to the stirring events of the 20th. The question has been raised that when the Dargai cleft had once been occupied why it was evacuated, necessitating a second action on the same ground, entailing the heavy loss of life in the attacking brigade. An examination of the situation is necessary. General Lockhart was at Fort Lockhart with a regiment belonging to the 4th Brigade. The 2nd Division was in camp at Shinwari at the foot of the Samana, fifteen to eighteen miles from Fort Lockhart, and the 1st Division was well on the march between Hangu and Shinwari, closing up upon the latter post. The choice of three routes lay with General Lockhart to make his advance into the Khanki Valley. The one was the Samana, down the Suk, through the Rabia Khel country; the next over the Changru Kotal, through the narrow valley winding at the foot of the Dargai Ridge (both these having been traversed by the Miranzai Expedition of 1891); the last in the direction of Norik, a few miles west of Dargai. It must be borne in mind that the enemy were known at this time to be in great force in the Khanki Valley, and it was General Lockhart's intention, if possible, to divide their gathering. For this reason the principal spy was told in greatest confidence that the most westernly route would be taken, it being known that the spies divulged all news to their fellow-countrymen. Already the two roads taken by the Miranzai Expedition were the routes which it was intended to use. It is no mean operation to force an Indian division and its endless tail of transport through fifteen miles of difficult defile, therefore, when a further road was reported which would act as an alternative pathway for the baggage, a reconnaissance was ordered on the 18th to ascertain if it really existed, and, if existing, if it was practicable for baggage. The reconnaissance had to be made in force, as the enemy were known to be in strength in the valley beyond. In a practically unknown country the exigencies of war are great, and it so transpired that it was found necessary to take the Dargai Ridge. Now it is easy enough to say, "Once taken, why not held?" But there are many military reasons which are hard to evade. In the first place, it would have taken a complete brigade to have held the position; for with the enemy in thousands in the valley, and the position being so easy of attack on the reverse, it would have been necessary to have had at least three regiments on the ridge. Then the picketing of seven or eight miles of road over the Changru Kotal to Camp Shinwari would have called for half a brigade to hold the communication securely. It had only been a reconnaissance which went forward, and no arrangements for a separation from Shinwari had been made, and there was not a drop of water available from Dargai to camp. And finally, and this is a most important point, if Dargai had remained held, the enemy would have seen through the crafty plan devised to hoodwink them, and instead of their forces being divided as they were on the 20th, watching both routes, the opposition against the general advance would have been

FORT LOCKHART

Principal Military Post on the Samana Range

THE TIRAH EXPEDITION

from their combined strength. As it was, when the force withdrew from Dargai, the tribesmen became more convinced that the western road required watching in strength. Again, as was said above, General Westmacott saw the enemy moving in such force in the valley towards his flank, that he feared he might have been cut off. Thus it seems clear that there was sound method in the message flashed from Fort Lockhart ordering the division back into camp.

XII

Storming of the Dargai Heights—Gallant charge of the Gordons—List of killed and wounded.

CAMP KARAPPA,
October 22nd.

ROUSE sounded on the 20th instant at 3.30 A.M., and an hour later the advance-guard of General Yeatman-Biggs's Division left Shinwari Camp under General Kempster and proceeded to wind its way up the Changru Pass; divisional headquarters marched out about daybreak. It is a long weary wind up over this kotal. The road is good enough, the Sappers having worked hard at it for the past ten days, yet it is but a narrow way for a whole division and three mountain batteries. The force toiled up to the Mulla Tank and then stretched over the broken summit of the kotal. This was at about 8.30 in the morning. The advanced-guard then sent back news that the crest of Dargai Sir was held by the enemy in force. Dargai Sir is the same precipitous mountain crest which was turned by General Westmacott on Monday, the 18th, and from which the Gordons retired under such a galling fire. The enemy could plainly be made out from the Changru Kotal, and they had with them a black

THE TIRAH EXPEDITION

standard, which denoted that some of them at least were Bar Khumber Khels. Moreover, on the far ridge of the opposite range could be seen huge masses of the enemy, with a dozen standards showing white against the sky line. General Kempster was ordered to dislodge the enemy and to occupy Dargai Sir. The 1st and 2nd Gurkhas, the Dorsets, and the Derbys were sent up in the above order, while the Gordons took up a position below the ridge in the village of Mamukila to cover the advance, if necessary, with long-range volleys. The position to be attacked was precisely the same as that which General Westmacott had taken with the 3rd Gurkhas and Borderers on the 18th.

As a position the Dargai Ridge should be almost impregnable, for it is only possible from the Changru Kotal by frontal attack, and being a sheer precipice the summit can only be reached by a steep zigzag path, up which two men can barely climb abreast. The approach is so steep that a covering infantry fire is almost impracticable without complete exposure to the defender; and though the Changru Kotal offers a splendid artillery position from which to shell the crest line, yet the natural shaping of the sheer bluff is such that the nine-pounder shell can make but little impression, and the cliff formation renders the effect of shrapnel almost abortive behind the natural cover. The tribesmen had also built magnificent sungars on its ridge with loopholes slanted to converge their fire upon the exposed forty to fifty yards of pathway. As the regiments told off to turn the position climbed up from the valley three mountain batteries were massed on Changru Kotal to shell the position. No. 8 on the left, No. 5 (Bombay) in the centre, and No. 1 (Kohat) on the right, came into action at 1700 yards, the latter battery having come through from Kai that night. On the Samana Suk behind, No. 9, which with the Northamptons had come through from Fort Lockhart, came into position at 2900 yards. The 3rd Sikhs remained as escort to the three batteries on the Changru Kotal. At 9.50 the enemy opened a long-range fire on the advanced-guard of the Gurkhas, as they pressed up the centre nullah of the three spurs converging to the bluff. The Gurkhas came steadily on, and at 600 yards opened with half-battalion volleys, lying along the centre ridge of the waterway. At ten o'clock precisely the guns opened fire, shelling the whole length of front where the enemy could be seen; as soon as firing commenced the tribesmen ceased to show themselves. By this the second line had joined the Gurkhas, and Gurkhas and Dorsets pressed up the nullahs to the point where they converged. Colonel Travers gave his men time to breathe, and then ordered a rush across the open to reach the cover, the Derbys covering. Until our men showed in the open we had no knowledge in what force the position was held. A thousand rifles at least must have been centred on that fatal spot, and though three companies of the Gurkhas managed to reach cover beneath the cliff, yet the path was strewn with the dead and dying; the tribesmen continuing their fire till the

DARGAI CLIFF

Scene of the Actions of October 18 and 20

last of the wounded ceased to move. In fact, we could see poor fellows fall, stagger to their knees and feet, and perhaps creep a few yards, to be shot again and again by the marksmen on the crest.

Captain Robinson, of the Gurkhas, got across with his men, and, though wounded, he returned to rejoin the main body, which had been checked by the severity of the fire only to fall mortally wounded as his goal was almost reached. Then the Dorsets essayed to join the three companies beyond. An officer and eighteen men rushed to cross the zone of death, and melted away before the murderous fire which the tribesmen opened upon them. The heavy artillery fire seemed to make no impression upon these men in their magnificent cover, and though Dorsets and Gurkhas faced the open, yet the head of each rush melted away as soon as the fatal spot was reached, and the path was blocked with dead and wounded, for once down a man could not move but to call a concentrated fire upon him. An officer whose men had been checked dropped with his wounded and lay with them. A wounded Gurkha tried to struggle to his feet; in a second he was down again, with three fatal bullets in him, and the officer's clothes were shot through by the same volley. Then it was, after these magnificent yet fruitless attempts to cross where the three companies of Gurkhas lay, that the helio flashed back that the position was impregnable, and that further attempts would be but a useless waste of life and men.

Matters were taking a serious turn, as it was twelve o'clock, and the enemy still held a position which might be termed the key of the Changru route into the Khanki Valley. General Yeatman-Biggs, watching the action from the position of the guns, realised what a check at this period of the

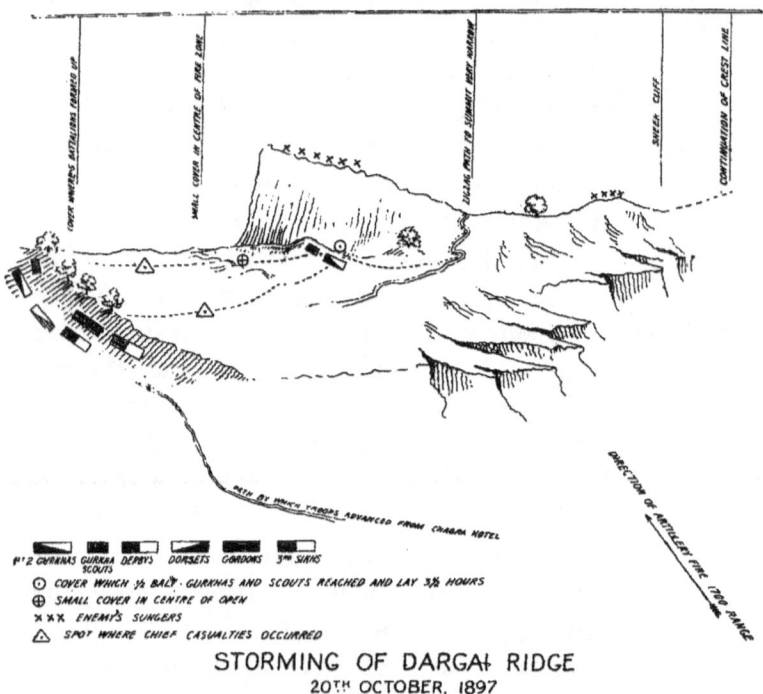

STORMING OF DARGAI RIDGE
20TH OCTOBER, 1897
SHOWING DISPOSITION OF REGIMENTS ENGAGED
BEFORE SUCCESSFUL ASSAULT

campaign would mean, and his orders were concise: he told General Kempster that the summit must be taken at any cost, and General Kempster went at once to the front, taking with him the Gordons from Mamu Kila and the 3rd Sikhs. It took the fresh troops the best part of an hour to climb up to the position, and then for a time was witnessed as grand

THE TIRAH EXPEDITION

yet as awful a sight as could be seen : five regiments of infantry, the pick and flower of our Empire, Highlanders, Lowlanders, Sikhs, and Gurkhas, standing massed in the nullah, the midday sun glittering on a field of naked bayonets.

General Kempster helioed up to the guns asking, when he gave the signal, for three minutes of concentrated artillery fire on the hill summit. Then the preparations for the assault were made. There were two ways to reach the cover where the three companies of Gurkhas had been lying now for three hours. The top ridge was absolutely a death passage. But a hundred yards below, where General Westmacott had fought his way up two days before, the fire zone was shorter, and it was determined to rush both paths at once. The fresh regiments were to take the lead. Colonel Mathias collected his men on the edge of the nullah and said, "Gordons, the General says that that position is to be taken at all costs. The Gordons are to do it!" The men received this with a low determined murmur: a murmur bred of the awful reality of the moment; bred with the sight of the motionless corpses of their comrades lying in the path of death before them; with the wounded groaning in their midst and the solitary little band of living hugging the bare face of the rock. Just a few short paces from them they massed on the limit of the cover—a quivering line of fierce, determined men. The signal was given, the guns boomed out their salvoes, and the cliff was crowned with a circle of bursting shrapnel; then the final order came—a momentary pause—and the officers of the Gordons dashed over the nullah. The pipes rolled out the slogan, and with tight-clenched teeth the Highlanders burst into the open. It was an awful two minutes. The length of the exposed zone was swept with a leaden stream, and the dust of the striking bullets half hid the advancing men. The head of the upper column melted away, but a few struggled on, and there were more to take the places of the fallen. Out over the cover came the kilted soldiers; the Sikhs, Dorsets, Derbys, Gurkhas, in spasmodic rushes as the firing slackened, and the cover halfway was won. A moment for breath, and the men were up again. Another terrible rush, another medley of struggling men and writhing figures, and the three companies of Gurkhas were reached.

When the tribesmen saw that the space was crossed, they left their sungars and streamed down the reverse slope of the hill. They had no wish to meet men who could brave such a fire hand to hand. Forming at the base of the perpendicular rock, the mixed troop caught their breath and then proceeded up the zigzag path which leads to the summit of the kotal.

The fighting for the day was practically over. But it had been a terrible place, as the bodies which strewed the fatal passage showed. Four officers had been killed, one mortally wounded, eight or nine wounded, while the total casualties were one hundred and ninety-four killed and wounded. Of these thirty were from the Gordons, and the majority of the remainder among the Dorsets and Gurkhas.

FRONT VIEW OF THE BLUFF OF THE DARGAI RIDGE

Held by the Enemy on October 18 and 20

THE TIRAH EXPEDITION

It is difficult to write temperately of the gallantry of the Gordons in leading the final assault, and of the little Gurkhas who first attempted the fatal rush. The story of the fight teems with incidents of personal bravery and self-sacrifice in the early phases of the engagement. Many a man sacrificed his life to save a wounded comrade. But most efforts of the kind were in vain. No single man could stand or live under such a fire as the short-range volleys which were poured in. The enemy, too, behaved with the greatest caution. No shot was wasted, and they invariably reserved their fire until the men were actually in the open.

As General Kempster climbed up to the summit of the crest the victorious Highlanders gave their General three ringing cheers. Now that the kotal was taken, it was determined to hold it permanently, and the 1st and 2nd Gurkhas and the Dorsets were left to bivouac on the summit of Dargai.

As the Gordons led down, the regiments they passed broke into cheers, and there is no doubt that each regiment engaged that day kept alive the prestige and heroic traditions of the British service. And another point: the Gordons volunteered and carried down the Gurkhas dead and wounded, as the little men had to crown the kotal for the night—an act of kindly consideration which every native regiment which was with the force appreciated. The heights were not taken until 3 P.M., and it was too late to push the baggage on down to the Khanki Valley, so the 1st Division halted as it was, the regiments bivouacked on the Changru Kotal, and the baggage was parked as it stood. It was a bleak cold night and every one more or less was in discomfort, as both food and water were scarce. During the earlier part of the day the enemy, who, as was said before, were in large masses on the hills to the left, came down with their standards and threatened our flank, but they only received their disheartened comrades in the plain below.

It is impossible to estimate the enemy's losses, as they had ample time to remove any of their dead and wounded; but on climbing to the summit the Gordons found blood marks in most of the sungars, and a distinct trail where the wounded had been carried down: still, after viewing the strength of their position and the natural cover which the crest supplied, it is impossible to think that their losses have been heavy, or in proportion to what it cost us to turn them out.

The rapidity with which the tribesmen made their movements was well demonstrated on this occasion. Although barely a quarter of an hour elapsed between the main rush and the hoisting of an officer's helmet on the actual summit, yet the enemy had got so far down the reverse slope—which is a gentle one, terraced fields in parts—that barely a dozen volleys were fired into them, and these were perforce long-range firing. Any one who saw the dust of the striking hail knew that they were on the crest of the bluff in strength, yet they seemed to have vanished. From Shinwari Camp a portion of the reverse was visible, and officers of the 1st Division report that as soon as the result of the assault was

AFTER THE BATTLE OF DARGAI
The Gordon Highlanders carrying down the wounded Gurkhas

THE TIRAH EXPEDITION

confirmed, they could make out streams of defenders vacating at a great pace, making down the slopes into the valley. They poured out in hundreds. When you saw their position, it was impossible to realise why, even though the explored zone was crossed, they did not cover the zigzag path to the actual crest line. Only two men could climb up abreast, and the advancing files could have been destroyed in detail by a dozen marksmen with breech-loaders. The only solution is that the defenders, having been heavily engaged for upwards of five hours, had practically exhausted their ammunition; for they could have no reserve, and were dependent upon the bandolier and pouch supply which they carried on their persons.

Our casualties for the day were:

	Officers.		Men.		
	Killed.	Wounded.	Killed.	Wounded.	Total.
Gordons	1	6	2	35	
Dorsets	0	1	9	39	
1st and 2nd Gurkhas	1	1	16	49	
3rd Sikhs	0	4	3	16	
Derbys	1	0	3	8	
	3	12	33	147	195

Several officers and men were wounded slightly, but, continuing to do duty, were not returned.

XIII

Determination of the tribesmen to fight—The story of the buried standard and its effect on the Afridis—Arrival of General Hart, V.C.—Persistent firing into camp throughout the night.

KHANKI VALLEY,
October 23rd.

IN my last letter it was shown how the Dargai Heights were taken and afterwards held by the Gurkhas and Dorsets for the night. The baggage of the 2nd Division was parked as it stood on the road up to the Changru, and the various regiments bivouacked on the ground they were on. It was a trying night, as they were short of food and water, and the cold was intense, especially as many regiments had not got their great-coats up. Fires were lit, and the men made the best of it, and there was no one who was not relieved when day broke. At ten o'clock General Westmacott's Brigade moved off down towards the Khanki Valley. The 15th Sikhs were advance-guard, followed by No. 5 Mountain Battery, two companies Sappers and Miners, the Gordon Highlanders, and in this order the force moved down the pass, the 21st Pioneers keeping parallel to the advance coming down a spur from the Samana, where they had been on picket duty during the night. The 1st and 2nd Gurkhas and Dorsets moved down on the left flank from Dargai, where, with the Derbys, as was said above, they had bivouacked for the night. It was a very bad road, and most severe on the transport; but no shot was fired, and the advanced-guard and leading regiments reached the bottom of the valley, and leaving Karappa behind, advanced along the bed of the Khanki River.

Two miles from Karappa the advanced-guard of Sikhs encountered a sharp fire from three villages with towers on the slopes, up from the valley. The enemy came out of the villages, and in some force demonstrated in the open ground north of the centre village and planted a red standard. General Westmacott ordered up the battery and opened on this group at about fifteen hundred yards, and extended the Sikhs, who advanced on the right-hand village, also sending one company to work up a spur on the right which commanded the villages. The enemy would not stay, but after the exchange of a few shots and the firing of half a dozen shell they cleared off. If cavalry had been up they probably would have been able to have cut the enemy off when they debouched into the open. The Sikhs succeeded in securing in the village the red standard of the enemy and a flash-light lamp, which must be part of the signalling equipment which the *lashkar* secured at Sharigari on the Samana. The camping ground chosen is the same knoll where the Miranzai Expedition camped in 1891.

The division came in slowly, as the road down

from Changru was in a terrible state, and but little of the baggage got in that night. But General Lockhart and Staff and the Northamptons came down from Fort Lockhart. Just before night fell there were many evidences of the enemy upon the hills on all three sides of camp, and a regiment and battery were moved up to the nearest ranges. But the enemy were satisfied with demonstrating, and added to the situation by mounting the helio, which they had also captured at Sharigari, on a high ridge which overlooked the camp. They energetically called up the camp with the rays of the setting sun. The three towers which General Westmacott had found occupied in the morning were destroyed by the Sappers and Miners. With so many of the enemy about, one could scarcely anticipate a peaceful night, and about 10 P.M. the enemy began to fire into camp, and heavily engaged an outlying Jindh piquet, but their energy flagged after one hour. The force has halted since the 21st to allow of the commissariat moving up, and the troops in camp have been employed foraging and placing the camp in a thorough state of defence.

CAMP, KHANKI VALLEY,
October 24th.

Early on the 23rd a reconnoitring party of the 3rd Gurkhas went out towards Sampagha, which is the pass from the Khanki Valley into the Mastura Valley. It is a long winding pass, and the local report had it that it was very heavily entrenched, the Afridi-Orakzai combination having determined

THE KHANKI VALLEY AND RIVER
Showing Karappa Camping Ground

to defend it to the last. Though it is one of the chief highroads between Tirah and the Khanki, no white man as yet had crossed it. They found the enemy occupying the heights, and a few shots were fired as the reconnaissance was withdrawn. One sepoy was slightly wounded. Foraging parties which were out during the day found the enemy lurking upon most of the spurs, but there was no serious attack, though a few men fired at short range. The head of the 1st Division moved in from Changru in the evening, and a large convoy of commissariat was streaming in all day. In the evening the enemy were seen in most of the neighbouring hills, and it was thought probable that they might make an attempt upon the camp. Just after nine a severer fire than usual was opened, and it was evident that the enemy was moving in the bed of the nullah which runs north-east of the camp. The Gordons, who held the north ridge above camp, were reinforced by two companies, when the enemy in force crept in among the rocks at the foot of the hill on their front. When the moving figures could be discerned they were received by a heavy fire, which extended to the outlying picket, due west, before which the enemy at one time collected. Morning showed that the tribesmen meant business, for among the few dead bodies which marked their line of advance in front of the Gordons' lines was found an Orakzai, who had eighty yards of string trailing behind him. Evidently the object of this pioneer was to sneak into camp, and if successful in finding a weak spot to signal to his main attacking body at the end of the string. The result of the fire during the night was that a native officer of the 21st Pioneers was mortally wounded (since dead), a man of the 1st Sikhs wounded, and a mule. The camp is by this so full of men and animals, and covers so large an area, that it is marvellous that there is not more loss from night firing.

This morning General Hart, V.C., arrived to take over command of the brigade vacated by General Hamilton. He has made a wonderful journey up from Belgaum to join his brigade. At two hours' notice General Hart left Belgaum on Monday night, took a special train after the ordinary trains disconnected, and arrived with Lieutenant Hart, his orderly officer, in camp at ten this morning, having come through direct from Kai, where his tonga ponies broke down last night.

There seems now to be no doubt that the tribesmen intend fighting tooth and nail to defend the approaches to Tirah, and the following story, which reads more like a chapter from "Kings" than anything else, has reached the Politicals. It appears that according to Afridi folklore about a century ago an influential Mullah buried a sealed earthen pot which contained his standard. It was buried with great ceremony, and the legend thereto attached was that at any time when the senate of tribe elders was at a loss how to act in a national question they were to unearth the pot. If the intentions of the majority were to prove successful, the standard would appear in all its pristine glory ; but if other-

THE TIRAH EXPEDITION

wise, eaten by decay. Mullah Said Akbar called a Jirgah, and with great pomp the pot was unearthed from its sacred resting-place. The standards of his tribe representatives were planted in a circle round it. Seven cows were beheaded, and a libation of their blood was poured upon the pot. The pot parted, the standard stood forth untarnished and unharmed by time, and by divine impulse the circle of surrounding flags dipped in salutation. This story has gone forth far and near among the tribes and has been received with such credulity that all sections are confident of success. The circulation of such a fable shows that Said Akbar at least is bent upon keeping the tribesmen up to the finest fighting pitch.

It is impossible in a single day to collect all the incidents of an event like the storming of Dargai. The story of the pipers of the Gordons must thrill all who read it. It appears that Lance-corporal Milne, if not the first, was among the first to leap into the zone of fire playing "The Cock o' the North," and that when shot through both legs he still played his regiment on in a sitting position. Four other pipers played across the fatal passage, three being wounded, one severely in the chest. In the rush of news individual names are passed over, but it should be recorded that when the three companies of Gurkhas led across the fatal spot early in the day, Lieutenant Tillard, in command of the 3rd Gurkhas attached to the 2nd, was the first man across. Though a turn of speed does not imply the boldest heart, yet all who saw Lieutenant Tillard,

I

speak of his action with the greatest enthusiasm, as he stopped and encouraged his men midway. And it was no place to stop in!

CAMP, KHANKI VALLEY,
October 25*th.*

Never before has the Khanki Valley presented a scene as at the present day. With the exception of one battalion and a battery the whole of the two divisions are encamped upon the two low hills which stand at the base of the slopes up to the Sampagha Pass, and as the stream of transport pours in daily, the wonder of the scene increases. What the transport difficulties for such a force are, none but those who can see the army of followers and appendages to the fighting strength, can realise, and small wonder that the progress of the force is slow with roads such as had to be crossed. At the present moment the totals in camp are: British troops 6400, Native troops 11,280, followers 17,000, animals 2400. In the morning a foraging party with an escort of a half-battalion of Devons, Derbys, 1st and 3rd Gurkhas, No. 1 (Kohat) Mountain Battery, and a half-battalion 3rd Sikhs, under Colonel Yule, went down the valley due west with fifty animals. They proceeded about four miles and found plenty of forage; they also captured a hundred-odd head of cattle, which were sent back to camp. Just as the force was forming up for the return to camp the enemy suddenly appeared, and with marvellous rapidity lined the neighbouring heights, so that the rear-guard came

CAMP AT KARAPPA—KHANKI VALLEY

under rifle fire at ranges from 1000 to 1200 yards simultaneously from both flanks. The Mountain Battery came into action, and each new battalion was judiciously withdrawn under the cover of its and the rearmost regiment's section volleys. But the tribesmen, who were chiefly Shekhan and Ali Khel Orakzai, were in their element. They had all the advantages of position, and they skirmished brilliantly and with such determination that they followed Colonel Yule's party back to camp.

General Hart later in the day went out with eight companies to support the withdrawal from the valley. The enemy still stuck to their heights, and at about 4.30 commenced firing into camp, which was the first time that they had been so bold as to trouble us in the daylight. Unfortunately their temerity met with some success, as the casualties in camp were considerable. Captain Badcock, D.S.O., Field Intelligence Officer Headquarters, was hit as he sat at dinner, and so seriously wounded that it was found necessary to amputate his arm this morning. The incidents of the day were numerous. During the brush with the enemy No. 1 (Kohat) Mountain Battery lost a gun, which burst as it was being discharged. The Derbys were again in a hot corner when it was their turn to cover the retirement, and lost one man killed and eight wounded. The total casualties, including followers, were over thirty, which is a big bill for an off-day. The senior officers must be keenly feeling the delay which the severity of the strain upon the transport is causing them, for there can be no doubt that the longer we stay here inactive, the more confident the tribesmen will become. Probably they have already interpreted our prolonged sojourn as due to the opposition which they have so far shown. Yesterday's harassing attack was more probably due to the success of the foraging party, for it must have gone to the hearts of the tribesmen to see their cattle and grain carried away before their very eyes; but this does not detract from the fact that the sojourn here is capable of construction to suit the war party among the tribesmen.

By this time every one is convinced of the severity of the campaign before us. Of recent years the conditions of frontier warfare have changed, and no matter the size of the force entering a frontier country, the tribesmen, armed with rifles of precision, have, if they stick to guerilla methods, an advantage which it is extremely hard to wrest from them. In fact, the strength in numbers of a force rather adds to the tribesmen's advantages. And in their own hills they are wonderful skirmishers. Their rapidity of concentration and dispersal is marvellous, and their aptitude in taking cover seems rather an instinct born than an art acquired. Consequently if the Afridi is bent upon maintaining his present tactics, and will defend no position long enough to allow of real punishment, it is impossible to say how long the operations may last. To exhaust his ammunition apparently will not be possible, or he would not use it as freely as he does at present, and if it is only night firing that he is going to content himself with, it may be months before the war party

A NATIVE MOUNTAIN BATTERY IN ACTION NEAR KARAPPA

THE TIRAH EXPEDITION

will be sick of the Feringhee presence. But it is now certain that it will be a campaign full of many vicissitudes.

Last night, though the firing into camp was more persistent while the light lasted, yet it was severe after dark, and two distinct attempts were made on the north-west ridge of the camps on the point of the Dorsets and 3rd Sikhs. Thus there was heavy firing early in the evening. A new departure was tried—thirty of the 3rd Gurkha scouts under Lieutenants Tillard and Benyon were sent out after dark to stalk a party of persistent night-firers, who had a commanding position on a ridge above the camp. The tough little Gurkhas climbed the hill and succeeded in getting quite close up beneath the enemy, leading on with the rifle flashes as guides. Just as the critical moment arrived the attempt was made on the camp, and a star shell fired from the northern battery disclosed the position of the Gurkha party to the enemy, who would not wait to try conclusions, but fled rapidly. The Gurkhas then retired upon the camp, but their adventures were not at an end, for they were witnesses of a pathetic tragedy. As they were skirting the nullah towards camp they heard a scuffle and a cry. Then as they neared, a voice was distinctly heard supplicating in Hindustani for mercy. The Gurkhas disturbed the butchers, but could not prevent the atrocity, and a flying volley was all the murderers had, though the morning showed that five native followers and one man of the Queen's had been killed. What they were doing out of camp at that hour must ever remain a secret, as they were all dead, but presumably they had fallen out sick during the day and were trying to work their way into camp.

The Gurkhas add an interesting little history. As they lay below the Afridi camp followers they distinctly heard words of command given in English —" Ready, present, fire," and a whistle was used. A pathetic story comes from the Derby's hospital. A sick man on the point of recovery was hit and mortally wounded by a chance shot. It may be interesting to conclude with some transport figures. There is now a train of seventy-one thousand eight hundred animals, made up as follows :

Two-Maund Animals.

Tirah Expedition	29,440
Peshawar Column	3,220
Kurram Valley	280
Rawal Pindi (Reserve B.)	460
Malakhand F.F.	2,950
Tochi	2,300
Kohat Garrison	180
Peshawar Garrison	500
Reserve	3,000
	42,330

Five-Maund Animals.

Tirah Expedition	13,370
Peshawar Column	980
Kurram Valley	2,390
Rawal Pindi (Reserve B.)	670
Malakhand F.F.	3,320
Tochi	4,200
Kohat Garrison	750
Peshawar Garrison	790
Reserve	3,000
	29,470

XIV

Advance up the Khanki Nullah—Description of the pass—
Defence of the pass.

MASTURA VALLEY,
October 30*th.*

THE two divisions marched out of Karappa on the morning of the 28th. Before daybreak the Northamptons and 36th Sikhs had been detached to crown an extremely high hill which covered the advance as far as Gundakhi. This hill was the succeeding spur to the one up which a Gurkha picket had been sent the night before to prevent the enemy from firing into camp. This picket had rather an unpleasant night, as upon arrival at the summit they found the enemy in force occupying the valley beneath them; but beyond a few of the more adventurous creeping up and putting in two volleys at short range in the dark, the Gurkhas were not molested. After the unpleasant experience at Karappa on the day of Colonel Yule's rear-guard skirmish, where the enemy, in open daylight, fired into camp from 1500 to 2000 yards, a more elaborate system of picketing was adopted. An experience, perhaps severe, was beginning to show the hand of these wild hillmen. And it was evident that the Afridi was very careful of his skin—so much so that it began to be patent that they never would show fight unless they had the advantage of altitude. It was found that upon arrival at a new camp there was rarely any annoyance at night, but that on the following night, after the positions of our pickets had been carefully noted in the day, the skulking camp-prowler crept in over dead ground and disported himself well out of harm's way. Thus after the bad night a new system of picketing was adopted. Stronger pickets were sent to the highest peaks within range, and the positions of the inlying piquets were constantly changed, so that a tribesman believing his original "landmarks" correct was apt to stumble upon a surprise in the presence of an unexpected picket post. The effect was marked, for after the rearrangement of postings the night disturbances practically ceased.

The covering party on Thursday morning was able to gain the necessary positions without opposition, their advance scaring off the few sentinels whom the enemy had left there. This enabled General Westmacott's Brigade and the 2nd Division's baggage to advance up the Khanki Nullah to the foot of the cutting which leads to the Sampagha Pass. General Symond's division went by another route, taking the spurs which stretched away on the left of the advance. Small parties of the enemy occupied these spurs, and there was some long-range firing while the force settled itself about Gandakhi, an easy three miles from Karappa. A few men of the Devons were hit, and a sergeant of the Yorks killed.

THE TIRAH EXPEDITION 137

In the afternoon a reconnaissance was pushed forward to find a suitable spot from which the artillery could shell the enemy's position in the morning. During this Colonel Sage, of the Gurkhas, was unfortunately wounded in the leg. The appearance of the pass was simple. It seemed a fair roadway, winding up to the summit of a ridge which extended continuously right and left. Tribesmen were seen upon nearly every crest, and groups could also be discerned building breastworks on the roadway. Some of them closed in also, and early in the evening a few men in camp were hit. The orders for the general advance on the pass in the morning were as follows:—General Hart was to supply regiments from his brigade to operate on both flanks of the advance. General Gaselee with his brigade was to make the main attack, with General Westmacott and General Kempster in close support. The attack was to be made by the pathway seen to lead out of the nullah which is the source of the Khanki River, and upon the banks of which the camp stood. The batteries of the two divisions massed under General Spragge were to occupy a knoll at the foot of the pass and support the advance with shell fire.

Before daybreak General Westmacott's Brigade marched down into the Khanki Nullah and waited the arrival of General Gaselee's Brigade. The latter advanced shortly after and formed in front of the 4th Brigade. The regiments lay in this order: The Queen's, the 2nd and 4th Gurkhas, the Yorks, the 3rd Sikhs; then the 4th Brigade, 36th Sikhs, the King's Own Scottish Borderers, the Northamptons (as they came down from the hill which they had occupied during the night, the 1-3rd Gurkhas moving as a rear-guard). No impedimenta were taken except water mules and reserve ammunition.

It was bitterly cold waiting in the dim light of early morning. Down in the stone-lined nullah the sight was weird and fantastic, as the grey figures of the men wound silently by to find their positions. The distant crest-lines stood out in the shadow marked by the fires of the enemy as they cooked their early meal. The batteries caused some delay in the darkness, they missed the track and came down into the river bed, and until they were in position the assaulting column was halted in the river bed. At daybreak the infantry advanced, but was again temporarily delayed, as the leading brigade in a labyrinth of nullahs mistook the path which leads up to the first slopes of the Sampagha. But this was speedily rectified, and the advance began.

A description of the pass here will aid in the narrative of the day's action. The pass from the nullah of the Khanki River to the summit of the kotal must be about four miles, the path winding in the first place up the prominence of a spur for about a mile, then dipping for a few hundred yards until it reached the second and more precipitous ridge up the side of which it wound. The summit of this ridge was sungared by the enemy, and some sheer rocks on its crest gave cover for sharpshooters. The real road wound behind this up a steep climb

THE TAKING OF THE SAMPAGHA PASS

Mountain Batteries in Action. October 29

THE TIRAH EXPEDITION

to the third ridge, but the whole of the path from the second to the third ridge was covered by the main crest of the range, which sloped steeply up, with occasional rocky eminences, each of which gave cover to the enemy's riflemen. The pass after the third ridge ran along the inside of a big hill, which likewise had a rocky crest until it reached the main kotal, from whence it dropped, more rapidly, between two high spurs; the spur on the right being an extremely difficult one, ending in a thickly wooded slope on the far side. The position lent itself exceptionally for defence, as the many rocky eminences and cliff-crest terminations covered the roadway all along, and would have been difficult to turn if held by a more determined enemy than the Pathan tribesmen.

At 6.35 A.M. the enemy fired the first shot on the extended flankers of the 2nd and 4th Gurkhas, and then fell rapidly back to their rear. The regiments in the first line worked steadily on, and at 7.30, when the tribesmen could be seen on a small plateau between the second and first ridges, the guns opened. A few shells were sufficient for the enemy's advanced post, and they scuttled back to the second ridge.* When the Gurkhas and Queen's reached the first ridge the enemy opened sharply from the sungars on the second, and the machine guns were brought up; but the tribesmen could not stand the excellent practice made by the batteries, and after the third

---

* It might be noted here that this must be the first time for many years that a British force has had six batteries in action, massed under a General Officer.

shell had burst in their position they streamed out, exposing themselves to long-range infantry fire. A battery, No. 5, then pushed up the pass as only a mountain battery can push, and came into action

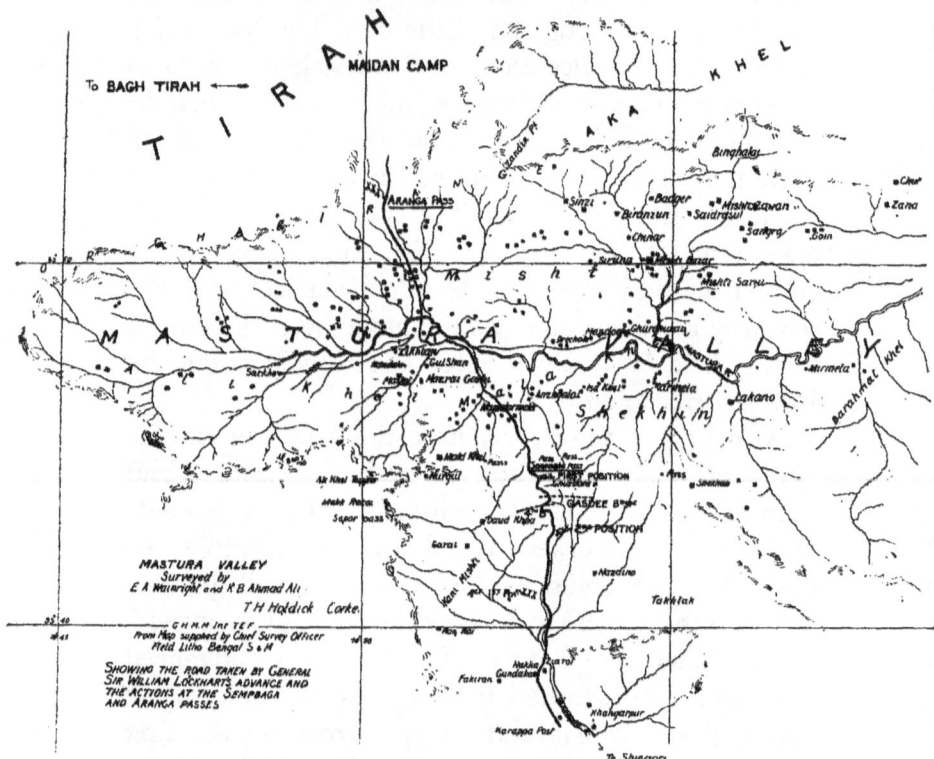

from the enemy's first position, while our front of attack lengthened as the regiments extended. The enemy's riflemen hung on the rocky crest of the second ridge, and the Queen's fixed bayonets and worked up as rapidly as the severity of the ascent would allow, losing here five men and an officer

THE FINAL ASSAULT ON THE SUMMIT OF
THE SAMPAGHA PASS

October 29

wounded (Major Handford Flood, who was slightly hit in the arm, but never left his battalion). The line of extended Gurkhas worked out to the left, seizing such points of vantage as the ridge crests afforded.

General Westmacott, as the front became broadened out, pushed on his two leading regiments, so that the sloping crest of the third position was reached by the Yorks and 36th Sikhs simultaneously. Here it was found the Queen's had advanced on to the right of the kotal, with the Gurkhas on their flank, and were driving back one party of the enemy, while others still held eminences on the left; in fact, they had so posted marksmen that the pathway was covered by men who knew the exact ranges, and No. 5 (Bombay) Mountain Battery lost Captain De-Butts as he was forcing his battery up. So accurate was the shooting of these unseen marksmen that on certain portions of the path it was impossible to show. General Westmacott extended the 36th Sikhs, and supporting them with the Borderers assaulted the cliffs which held these dangerous sharpshooters. It was a stiff climb, and three Sikhs and two Borderers dropped before the tribesmen considered it expedient to leave. On the right they took refuge in the wooded crest before mentioned. Once they menaced a small party of Gurkhas which had climbed to the spur beneath them. But a flank attack by two companies of the Queen's moving to the Gurkhas' support was more than they would wait for, and by 10.30 A.M. the Sampagha was won.

Plainly the defence of the pass was not what had been expected after the front which had been shown at Dargai, and now there is no doubt that, beautiful skirmishers and rifle-shots as the enemy are, they are very careful of their skins, and have no wish to expose themselves to punishment either by artillery fire or close-quarter fighting. When the covering heights had been crowned, the force—General Lockhart and Staff with it—proceeded down into the Mastura Valley. It was an easy descent, and the valley is much higher than the one just left. Already as the head of the force advanced, it was found that the tribesmen had deserted their homesteads, and countless blue columns in the valley showed that they had fired them as well.

The valley appears to be beautifully fertile, and is intersected by a spring-fed rivulet of pure water, quite the best that the force has yet procured. It is not closely wooded, yet there are many beautiful groves dotted about, and the autumn tints remind one a little of England. The villages, which are only a few hundred yards apart, betoken the easy circumstances in which the owners dwell; they are chiefly two-storeyed, though each is a little fortress in itself, in strict keeping with Pathan observances. The climate is lovely, but the men were feeling the cold, as but little of the baggage of the force had as yet been able to cross the pass; and there was very little food in camp. The men were glad to get the little Gurkhas to make them champaties from the coarse flour in the villages. The air was clear and bracing, and one seems inclined to believe the story

THE TIRAH EXPEDITION 143

of the Promised Land which lies beyond the pass in front of us. Suffice for the present, the best part of two divisions lies encamped in a lovely valley where the white man has never set foot before.

The following were our casualties at the Sampagha.—Wounded: Queen's, one officer and seven men; the 4th Gurkhas, two men; the Rocket Detachment, one man; the 36th Sikhs, four men (two mortally); the Borderers, two men; No. 1 Mountain Battery, three wounded; 30th Punjab Infantry, one; No. 5 Mountain Battery, one officer; 36th Sikhs, one man; and Queen's, one man.

XV

Events *en route* to the "Promised Land"—View of Tirah from the Arhanga Pass—Choice of the camping ground—Description of the mosque at Bagh—Daring attack on the baggage.

TIRAH PLATEAU,
November 2nd.

THIS is from the Promised Land, but the events which led up to the arrival here must be chronicled first. After the day of rest in the beautiful Mastura Valley, orders were issued for the 4th and 3rd Brigades to move at daybreak on the 31st, followed by the 2nd Brigade, the 1st being left to garrison Mastura Camp. It was a cold raw morning, and a cold wind was sweeping across the valley, as General Westmacott's Brigade, the Borderers leading, wound down the nullah towards the Arhanga, the last pass which separated the force from Tirah Maidan. The road to the pass lay, as do most Afridi Orakzai roads, up a nullah, which was flanked by low hills, culminating in a conical eminence which exactly fronted the pass. This hill, like most of the knolls in the valley, had a walled village on the summit. This consequently was the first position that the main attack proceeded to hold. The pass was a low kotal connecting higher ridges, in no way like the Sampagha, which was a series of ridges. On either flank of the Arhanga were higher peaks, the right ones being wooded. Halfway between the village on the knoll and the pass stood a square block-house which at the commencement of the advance was occupied by a sharpshooter.

General Westmacott's Brigade took up position in the centre village, while the guns massed on the ridge below, one battery following the King's Own Scottish Borderers up into the knoll. The man, or men if there were more in the block-house, seemed responsible for the casualties. Captain Searle, of the 36th Sikhs, was struck by a long dropping shot, and severely wounded in the thigh, as was also a gunner in the battery. Just before the guns opened, the sharpshooter got the range of General Yeatman-Biggs's flag, and several shots pitched into the group of Staff officers, one passing under the neck of the pony of a press correspondent, hit Captain Rigby, signalling officer, who was talking to the pressman, on the boot, luckily only taking off a piece of the sole. The battery then trained on to the block-house; the persistent riflemen evacuated, and it was shortly in flames. A few men could be seen on the summit of the hills, and the peaks were shelled.

Then General Gaselee's Brigade was detached to make a flank attack on the right, General Kempster's on the left. It was a stiff climb, but the enemy did not mean staying, and at ten minutes to ten the Yorkshires and Gurkhas were simultaneously on the top of the heights on the right, and half an

K

hour later General Westmacott's Brigade had made the main point of the day, and the last partition before Tirah was broken down. At 11 A.M. Sir William Lockhart and Staff were on the summit as well.

From the top of the Arhanga Pass down into Tirah is a rapid drop of nearly a thousand feet. The heights being crowned by General Gaselee's Brigade, General Westmacott's led into the valley, a mile down a rough ungrateful path, with a small hill running at right angles to the path. On the summit were a couple of block-house buildings; the southern slope was bare, but the north side, facing the valley, was thickly covered with fir and walnut.

The Borderers and Brigade Staff climbed to the top, and before them lay the full panorama of the Promised Land—the Valley of Tirah Maidan, the spot which, the Afridi was wont to boast, no infidel had ever gazed upon, and the valley which no king or army had ever invaded. It was a magnificent view: from the foot of the fir-grown slope stretched away a valley, to the west as far as eye could reach, to the east for miles, at least an area of a hundred square miles; broken here and there by undulations, ravines, nullahs, and waterways, stretching upwards towards the lower slopes of the Safed Koh. Every inch of it seemed cultivated, and on either hand it was one expanse of terraced fields, sprinkled with groves and coppices and dotted with countless habitations. The valley appears to be about eighteen miles by six, with two distinct stream beds intersecting it. The effect which

THE TIRAH EXPEDITION

most prominently strikes the new-comer is the number of houses in the valley : it is hard to find a hundred square yards which has not its fortified block-house, the reason for this being that the Afridi temperament will not allow of several families living in one fortified village. Thus each family builds a homestead for itself, and fortifies it against all comers. The houses are all two-storeyed, the foundation storey being soundly built of boulders and plaster, the upper storeys generally being wicker frameworks plastered heavily with mud, so as to be rifle-bullet proof. Inside the houses appear dark, stuffy, and dirty, and being generally smoke-begrimed, present an unwholesome appearance.

The valley at present is brown, as there are no crops in the ground, but the autumn tints upon the trees are beautiful and carry one back to the mother-country at once. One can well imagine that when the spring crops are in and the valley is green from end to end, this is the beautiful spot which has so inspired the Pathan poets. It is autumn now, and the walnut leaves are falling, the sign which, we are told, warns the Tirah Afridi to flit to the lower plateaux. It is hardly as wooded as one would have expected from reports, but groves are numerous, and it is a beautiful valley. One can hardly think that the dwellers in Tirah expected the force as soon as it has arrived, for the valley is stocked with supplies. They seemed to have removed little but their live stock : Indian corn, beans, barley, and other grains are to be found in abundance, while stocks of honey, potatoes, walnuts, and onions are being daily brought in. Beautiful valley though it is and fertile, it boasts of little in the way of roads, and there are but bridle paths from house to house, the only general way apparently being the nullah beds.

On arrival the leading brigade found the valley almost deserted: a few moving figures could be seen from the first hill, and the Borderers tried long shots. Then the brigade marched down, and the present camping ground was chosen. It is about the most level expanse in the whole valley. The Arhanga Pass, though not of great altitude, is very steep and has barely a track; consequently there has been another severe baggage check. In fact, on the 31st very few of the troops in Tirah got their baggage, besides which some enterprising Afridis attacked it after dusk and succeeded in carrying away some two hundred kits belonging to a Sikh regiment. The pass being on the valley side simply a waterway, it is hard to make a road rapidly, especially with a stream of baggage and troops constantly passing.

Bagh is the tribal centre and Afridi Parliament ground. It is a mosque situated about four miles farther up the valley than our present position. It was from this spot that the orders were issued to make war upon the British Government, and it was here that Said Akbar Mullah preached his *jehad*. The Borderers, 1st and 3rd Gurkhas, No. 8 Mountain Battery went out under Colonel Dixon, the chief of the Staff and Mr. King, Political Agent, accompanying the reconnaissance. As the party

AKBAR MULLAH'S MOSQUE

advanced under one of the flanking hills of the valley, long-range fire was opened on the main body from sungars on the top. A few men only having shown themselves, a company of the 1st and 3rd Gurkhas was detached under Lieutenant Champain to dislodge them. This party creeping up the hill suddenly came under fire from a lower sungar which was thought to be empty, and lost one killed and three wounded before they could make the cover of a village. Here they remained until a couple of shells dislodged about fifteen men who were in the sungar.

The reconnaissance then proceeded to cross the main nullah of the valley, and presently found Bagh. It is an insignificant-looking mosque, just an oblong block-house lying at the junction of three rivulets. It is shaded by a dozen to twenty trees, and lies under the lee of a bare hill. A few men were on this hill, and fired at the company of the Borderers told off to clear it, wounding Captain Maclaren slightly. The mosque, as was said above, is but a block-house, that is, it has two walled sides and two open; its mud roof is supported by twenty-one wooden pillars, a few of which are crudely carved. On the west wall is a niche for a lamp, and a small altar or pulpit with three steps. Some Korans were found here; the floor was strewn with some very soft grass, a grass which no one recognised, so which presumably is rare. The two walls had at some period been whitewashed and rudely decorated with some black pigment, but time had almost completely obliterated this. On the north side was a dark little retiring-room with a carved door and lintel; it was practically empty. The entrance to the mosque was a rough hole in the side of the plinth wall which was the foundation of the whole structure. The trees which shaded the temple were walnut and Himalayan oak. It is curious to note that the mosque did not lie due east and west, but was several points out. Its dimensions were eleven paces by eighteen.

Such was the spot where the Afridis and Orakzais resolved to wage war against the British Government. Before the reconnaissance withdrew, the gunners and Gurkhas ringed the trees of the grove. There was no sign of the enemy as the force withdrew.

It was thought when we practically walked over the Arhanga, and found the Tirah homesteads unburned like the Mastura Valley ones, that the tribesmen had thrown up the sponge, and that practically the object of the campaign had been attained. But yesterday has rather disabused us of this view. A foraging party of the 3rd Brigade moving up toward the Bara end of the valley found the tribesmen in great force occupied in removing grain and chattels from the villages. They showed such front that the small escort of the party withdrew, but not before an officer had been seriously wounded. The probable reason for the presence of these men is that they belonged to the Zakka Khel and Malikdin Lashkar which was watching Bara, expecting the direct movement from there, and that they had returned on hearing of the arrival of the

Saran Sur Peak Kotal into Waran Valley Path up Arhanga Pass

CAMP AT MAIDAN IN AFRIDI TIRAH

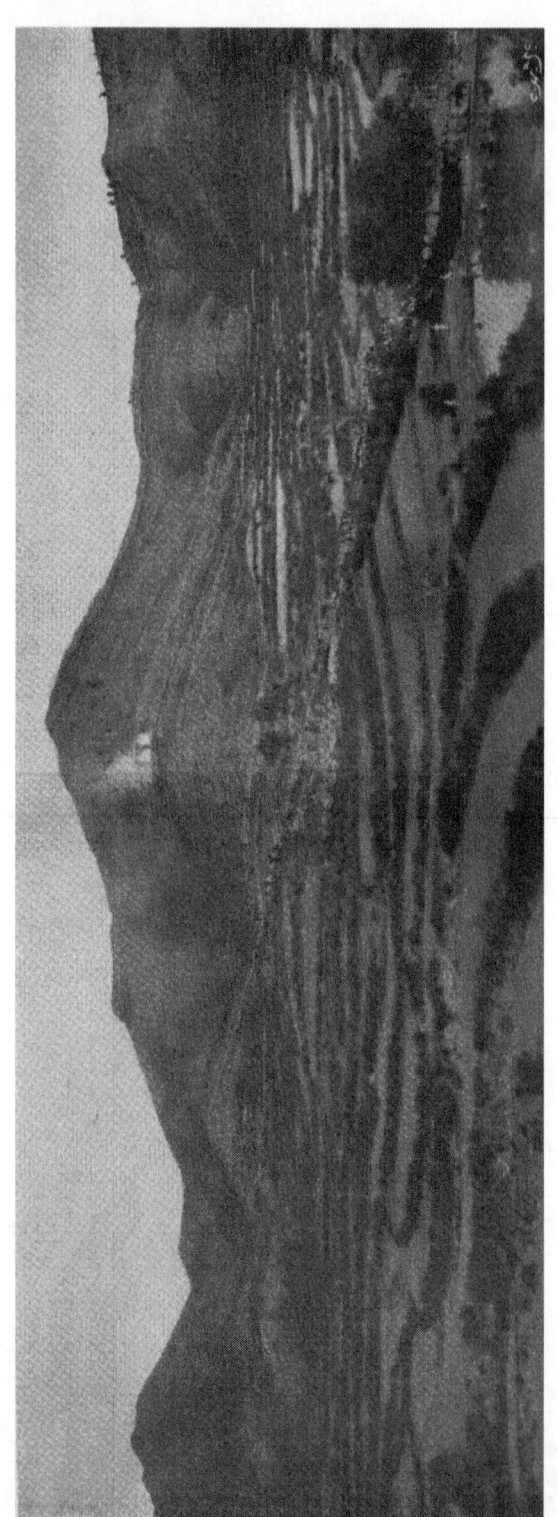

THE ARHANGA PASS
Block House fired by Shell-fire

THE TIRAH EXPEDITION

force in the valley. But the attack on the foraging party is not all; a party crept down the wooded slopes to the west of the 4th Brigade camp and attempted to rush an outlaying piquet of the 36th Sikhs, who were in one of the villages across the centre nullah. This attempt was abortive, as unwittingly the tribesmen exposed themselves to a flank fire from another picket of the 3rd Gurkhas also across the nullah.

But their further attempts were more daring and more successful. A strong party of swordsmen crept up to the villages which stand over the path leading from the pass to the camp, and as soon as it was dusk pounced upon the first weak line they met. It was baggage belonging to the Queen's, and they cut up the drivers of five mules and severely wounded one of the two soldiers who formed the guard of that section, a sword cut almost severing his wrist. They then disappeared until the treasure-chest guard of the Queen's passed. Carefully waiting until the main guard had passed, the swordsmen again dashed out, killed three of the adjacent guard and wounded several others, and there is no knowing to what extent they might not have pushed the raid if the Northampton rear-guard had not come up and driven them off; as it was they secured several thousand rupees.

Now that they have commenced this method of harassing warfare, one is inclined to believe that they are not so cowed as was thought; but that, having had a taste of a general action at Dargai, they came to the conclusion that opposing artillery fire was a useless waste of both life and ammunition. The Afridi has always been an adept at caravan raiding, and our lengthy line of communication over so bad a country must give them many an opportunity of following a method of warfare which is according to their natural bent. The posts from which they made their attacks last night are now in flames, and a few days should show if they are prepared to sacrifice their valley. There is an impression that the tribal gathering has in contemplation some big *coup;* that having got the force into their valley they never intend to let it return again. If they are building their hopes upon a night rush, they have a severe lesson to learn; for though they may cause many casualties, yet the assaulting of two divisions entrenched and armed with quick-firing weapons is a serious operation to undertake.

An interesting discovery was made in the Mastura Valley by a party of Gordons. They found a regular arsenal containing forges, anvils, and all the appliances for moulding bullets and refilling cartridges, also one hundred and fifty dynamite cartridges (Nobels), and innumerable tins of Curtis and Harvey's powder. They also found a large store of the old nickel Lee-Metford envelopment, from which the lead had been carefully extracted for bullet use.

It is very cold up in the valley, and this morning there was a quarter of an inch of ice on all standing water out of doors. From this you can gather what has been the hardship of those whose kit was blocked on the Arhanga.

CAMP AT MAIDAN TIRAH

XVI

Description of an Afridi homestead—Attack on a foraging post—Difficult position of Captain Rowcroft and two companies of the 15th Sikhs—General Westmacott punishes the Zakka Khel villages—The kotal of Saran Sur—Arrival of Sir William Lockhart and withdrawal from the summit commenced.

CAMP, TIRAH MAIDAN,
November 7th.

THE force still remains stationary on the Zakka Khel Maidan, and absolute uncertainty rules as to what our future movements will be. On the one hand, Jirgahs are reported to be coming in, while as a set-off against this the tribesmen carry on their harassing methods of warfare. Yesterday's chronicle gives a fair idea of the situation. The usual foraging party went out with an escort furnished by the 3rd Brigade. As soon as the units were sufficiently split up the marauding parties of the enemy who were in waiting pounced down upon the weaker parties, and the escort of 13th Sikhs and Madras Pioneers had a hot time. Several baggage animals were looted, and the Sikhs lost a native officer and a sepoy killed. Then as evening closed in a Jirgah arrived, and was lodged with the Gordons' outlying picket outside the camp. The arrival of the Jirgah seemed to be the signal for the severest camp firing that we have had since Karappa, which cost us an officer of the Northamptons killed, an officer of the 36th Sikhs wounded, and several casualties in men, followers, and animals. Not only this, but a party lay in wait for the tail of an expected convoy on the pass and fell into a pitfall, as they "took on," instead of a weak escort, a covering party of the 3rd Sikhs, two hundred strong, returning from the crest of the kotal.

This hardly looks like a desire for peaceful issues. It is all put down to the Zakka Khels, but it is open to argument if only this section is concerned, as the interests of the Zakka Khels are identical with those of the other Tirah Afridis; and the Zakka Khels can hardly be strong enough to stand alone against the popular feeling of the valley. As a matter of fact, I fancy that when the terms including partial disarmament are proposed, they will be politely rejected. The Afridi will then be in a position to be tardy over the making up of his mind. When it comes to their making a choice between their homesteads and their rifles, they will hesitate at sacrificing the former to the latter. Though their houses are well built, yet they are not of much monetary value, since wood abounds, and the rest is but the manual labour of the particular family clan. But a rifle is the apple of the Afridi's eye. To possess it he will sell to dishonour his wife or sister, and freely jeopardise his chances in Mahomed's Paradise. If one man or a few men ruled each Afridi section, it might be that common sense would make them use

THE TIRAH EXPEDITION 155

their influence; but ,with a people split up into countless numbers of family clans, each jealous of the other, ecah more or less nursing some blood feud against his neighbour, it is without the pale of probability that the work of disarmament will proceed smoothly. Undoubtedly they would return their recent acquisitions, the outcome of their raids upon the Khyber and Samana, and their recent successes on our convoy lines. But those weapons which they have purchased with money or had in their possession long, if of value, they will never readily surrender.

Before giving details gathered from the desultory fighting of the last few days, I will give a brief idea of the Afridi homestead. As was shown in a previous letter, their houses are double, often treble-storeyed, with the usual tower, the blood-feud citadel. attached. Each house is the domicile of the family clan, perhaps ten or fifteen; or of a well-dispositioned family, twenty to twenty-five persons living together. The houses are rudely but firmly built of mud, stone, and fir logs, third storeys invariably having walls of wicker smeared and coated with mud. Most have a courtyard facing south, with cattle outhouses. Apertures are few, and what there are, excepting entrances, are mere loop-holes; in fact, each homestead is constructed with a view to defence from rifle fire. In the centre of each building in the second storey is the guest-reception-room, reached by a ladder from the ground below, and absolutely cut off from communication with the rest of the building except by means of its one entrance.

This in itself is characteristic of the extreme suspicion in which these hill-rangers hold each other. The other portions of the houses are intricate, with dark passages dividing the house off into poky family quarters, dingy and dirty in the extreme. The Afridi apparently finds a use for everything, and the houses are stocked with quaint odds and ends. There is absolutely no sign of refinement in any household, though one might have expected something in the houses of such as have risen to high positions in our native army, and who have in a way been allowed an intercourse which their home rearing never warranted. As cultivators they seem of the first order, though their implements are cruder and more grotesque than those of the cultivators of Bengal. The soil of the Mastura and Tirah Valleys is of the richest, and is of far greater moisture-retaining property than that of the best of Bengal even. Wheat, Indian corn, and barley apparently grow freely, and in the lower terraces one finds rice even at this altitude. Undoubtedly it would be a productive land for tea-planting, and possibly in the future Tirah tea will be a magnificent enterprise.

We have now in camp ten days' rations for the whole force, and camel convoys are coming in daily, also heavy baggage; and as the weather is now delightful, except for the night firing into camp, the force is becoming very comfortable. The men are keeping wonderfully well, in spite of the cold at night, and except for some cases of dysentery the health of the force may be said to be excellent.

THE TIRAH EXPEDITION 157

Dysentery is worst among the followers. To-night, as a set-off against the enemy who skulk round camp, the pickets have been trebled.

And now to yesterday's history again. Captain Rowcroft was sent out with two companies of the 15th Sikhs in charge of the foraging party. The same route was taken as the 4th Brigade had taken on the previous day; that is, up the valley towards Bagh. As the different parties of foragers distributed themselves in the villages, the numbers of the escort remaining with Captain Rowcroft became very reduced, so that by the time he had got well up to the nullah he had only a Subadar and half a dozen sepoys with him. There seemed no harm in this, as the villages in front had been visited and sacked the preceding day. Suddenly Rowcroft saw a detached officer galloping at full speed down a nullah, and the enemy firing at him from above. In a minute the fire opened upon his own party, and the enemy, skirmishing admirably, were upon him. Rowcroft could have withdrawn all right, only unfortunately one of his party was shot so severely in both thighs that it took three men to carry him, and the rest, though the officer himself took the wounded man's rifle, were not sufficient to keep the enemy's fire down. They were now retiring down the terraces, and suddenly Rowcroft found that the wounded man had been abandoned. He detached a man to the rear for support, and proceeded forward again to the body to assure himself that the man was, as the carriers said, dead. He was, but the stop had allowed the enemy to close up, and the Subadar was shot. Luckily, a loose mule was found, and the Subadar placed on this, but not before he was wounded again, as well as the man tending him.

Hardly had the Subadar been despatched to join the convoy when the remaining wounded man was again wounded, and another sepoy as well. It was impossible then for four sound men to convey away their wounded and face an enemy as well. So choosing the best spot available, Rowcroft halted and determined to wait for help. It seemed a hopeless chance, as the Afridi party were now within two hundred yards' range, taking cover in the terraces. Luckily, their hearts were not stout enough to rush the little party, and they confined themselves to the rapid firing "out of cover and back" which is the Afridi speciality. Another Sikh was wounded, and the bullets were so splashing dust up into the survivors' eyes that they could scarcely see to make the answering fire, when the relieving party arrived and extricated them from a position which was within an ace of being a disaster. The enemy succeeded that day in carrying off over thirty forage mules, but secured no rifles or ammunition.

Tirah Maidan,
November 10th.

On the 8th General Westmacott took out his brigade to punish, as far as possible, the Zakka Khel villages for the continued night-firing which local information attributed to them. The brigade did its work thoroughly, and by evening the whole of the east of the valley was in flames. A few sharpshooters followed up the force, but the casualties were slight. The unfortunate occurrence of the day was the death of Captain Watson, Commissariat Officer of the 4th Brigade, who was struck dead as he stood in his go-down, by a chance shot, not half a dozen shots being fired into camp. There seems a strange fatality about this night firing: already out of many thousands in camp four officers have been hit. Captain Sullivan, of the 36th Sikhs, was shot when he had not been in camp ten minutes, having just arrived post haste from England.

For the 9th a reconnaissance was ordered to Saran Sur, the "Peak of peaks" in Pushtu, which commands the east of Maidan Valley, and the saddle of which is itself a pass on one of the roads to Peshawar. General Westmacott was entrusted with the command of the troops—four regiments, two batteries, and a company of Madras Sappers—making this reconnaissance, and was accompanied by General Lockhart and Staff. The Dorsets were sent out on the left flank, the Northamptons in the centre, and the 36th Sikhs on the right, the remaining 15th Sikhs in reserve as escort to the guns.

As this was a pathetically eventful day, it would be as well to make a careful study of the ground traversed. The foot of the hill to be scaled is perhaps a matter of three short miles from camp, but the intervening ground presents an extraordinarily broken surface. In fact it is a series of hummocks each topped with a house and growing in altitude until they reach a conical hill at the base of the

Saran Sur. Interwinding among these hummocks is a waterway cutting—a very deep, and in places narrow, ravine. Its bed is a watercourse covered with boulders, and, as the ravine leads eastwards and the hummocks increase in altitude, its sheer edges may be anything from seventy to a hundred feet from the water-bed. Moreover—and this must be borne in mind, as it plays the most important part in the coming narrative—this main nullah is intersected on both sides by feeding nullahs at almost every hundred yards, these being the drainage channels from the high grounds already referred to.

There can be no doubt that this nullah is a common roadway to and from Saran Sur Pass to Maidan proper, as all the Pathan pathways from the houses lead down to it. Between the conical hill and the Saran Sur proper is another ravine, part of the drainage to the main, and then commences a severe ascent. The ascent on this side finds two spurs: one on the left, wooded in parts, especially towards the summit; the other bare, over which the path winds. A thousand feet up on the bare hill is a knoll upon which stands a solitary tree. There is a dip and a ridge beyond, over which the pass, an admirable roadway, winds. Yet another ridge, and a thousand feet up is a sheer rugged cliff-summit with a slope on its north and east sides, which is the end of the wooded spur, but which on the west is a sheer cliff, very like the Dargai cliff, and along the base of which, a hundred feet below, runs the pathway. The south of the cliff terminates in the saddle —the kotal—which itself leads into another peak.

The reverse side is wooded, as are the spurs which lead down from the final peak. From over the kotal one sees a ridged valley, more wooded than the present one, cup-shaped, and bounded by hills of like altitude. The Kotal of Saran Sur must be 8000 feet.

Such was the place that Sir William Lockhart wished to reconnoitre. General Westmacott's force left camp at 7.30, and the disposition was as stated. A mile from camp desultory shots were fired by solitary marksmen of the enemy, men who were evidently posted as watchmen, and who took advantage of the nature of the ground and the succeeding hill crests to harass the advance. The guns took up the following positions: one battery in the last plain-plateau of the valley, the other with the 36th Sikhs on the conical hill at the base of the actual ascent. That any force advancing on the pass was expected by the enemy to come up the nullah was shown by the fact that, facing the termination of the nullah, were a series of well-built sungars, and from here two or three men armed with Lee-Metfords fired sharply into such of the Northamptons as took that route, but the main body skirted by way of the foot of the conical hill. Those in the nullah had two men wounded by these Lee-Metford skirmishers before the road on the hillside was reached. At this point General Westmacott was much concerned about the advance of the Dorsets on the left. They seemed to be engaged in the same desultory firing as the Northamptons, but to be making no progress up the left spur, which covered the Northampton advance. In fact, so anxious had the General grown, that all his Staff officers, except the brigade signalling officer, had been despatched by this time to direct the Dorsets to the intended line. A little before ten o'clock the Northamptons, with the guns and Sikhs covering them from the rear, commenced the ascent of Saran Sur, not knowing in the least in what force the enemy might be in front of them. There was a stiff climb of a thousand feet, and then the brow of the first knoll was reached. A man showed above it, and immediately a dozen bullets whizzed around him.

General Westmacott, who was up with the second line, ordered a halt that the men might recover their breath and fix bayonets. The men topped the crest and rushed to the next cover, which was the knoll where stood the solitary tree. The enemies' Lee-Metford party knew the range of this tree, and the advanced section lying behind it suddenly found themselves under magazine fire—this possibly being the first time that a magazine has been discharged against British troops. There was no alternative but to push on, and as the crest was breasted an open kotal had to be crossed, which was partly the roadway up. The men crossed it at the double, and though a considerable fire played on them there was no casualty, and the next crest gave cover. A section volleyed into the summit of the cliff, which was now only five hundred yards distant; but it was evident that the opposition was simply from well-armed outposts, who fell back to succeeding favourable positions as the force steadily advanced.

The advance-guard was now at the foot of the sheer cliff, yet there was no signs of the Dorsets on the left, a very ugly country and with cover almost up to the summit of the kotal. The General had no alternative but to trust that the Dorsets were working up through the cover, and to cover his left as well as he could from the weak companies of the advance-guard regiment. He detached five companies of the Northamptons to work round the north ascent of the cliff, which was an incline, and took the remaining three companies along the pass at the foot of the cliff, advancing parallel with the men on the summit. The sharpshooters were on the far right peak, and again opened with a magazine discharge; but a return fire sent them down the opposite slope, and at a few minutes past eleven the whole summit was in our possession, and the last of the visible enemy driven over the reverse. That they were in the vicinity was evident, as they could be heard calling to each other in the woods, but they had ceased active hostility, and were well driven away. The guns had fired about twenty rounds at the summit as the Northamptons advanced.

By 11.15 A.M. the 36th Sikhs and the Sappers had arrived; the intelligence officers were busy sketching the country, and Lieutenant Coke, the signalling officer, was searching for connection with the Bara Column. It was evident that the Saran Sur was the retreat of the Maidan Zakka Khels, for

one found on every side evidence of encampments,
—fire-stained walls and smoky caves, cattle litter,
bags of grain, and many hurriedly-deserted camp
fires. In fact, the summit because of the litter had
the appearance of mule lines. Several curious
things were picked up—an infantry drill manual and
some Jeypur mule kit. It was certain that the
tribesmen had been taken by surprise and had left
hurriedly. For this reason General Westmacott
was anxious to return to camp, as it was probable
that the fighting men had left to escort their families
and cattle, with the object of returning as soon as
they were bestowed in a place of safety, and the
calling heard in the pine forest was probably their
means of collecting.

The sketches having been made, and General
Westmacott, anticipating that Sir William Lockhart
had seen all he wished without making the whole
ascent, ordered his retirement to commence at 12.15,
the Sapper Company leading down. A quarter of
an hour later the 36th Sikhs were sent down to hold
the first cover-way point—the knoll with the
solitary tree. Sir William Lockhart then intimated
that he was coming up, and the rest of the troops
stood fast. Sir William arrived, and the real withdrawal from the summit commenced just before two
o'clock, when the Staff had got well down the hill.
The picket on the right fell back at a double and
joined the companies at the tree, retiring from the
kotal down the pass at the foot of the cliff. The
five companies had orders to withdraw as soon as
the three were clear.

THE TIRAH EXPEDITION 165

And now comes the point of the day's history. G Company of the Northamptons was placed within

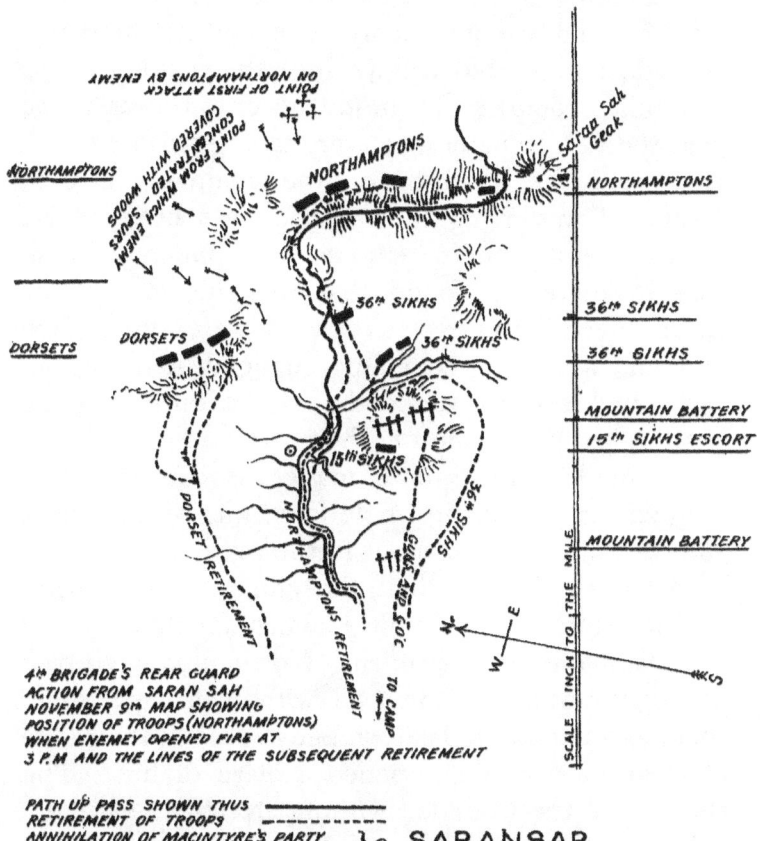

range of the wooded slopes, which should have been cleared by the Dorsets if they had come up the spur as intended. Suddenly G Company on the cliff was fired into, so directly and so cleverly that they could not discover their opponents for some time. As the fire enfiladed them they had casualties at once and men fell so fast that they signalled to the officer commanding A Company to help them. This officer could see no enemy, and was not fired into himself, but he fired volleys into the woods to help the other company by moral effect. It was found that the G Company men were falling so fast that it exhausted the strength of the company, already weak. Transferring the wounded was heavy work, as it took six men to remove one. General Westmacott, therefore, found that with his main body down the hill the Northamptons were still on the summit, with one company engaged and encumbered with several wounded. He at once sent the 36th Sikhs to reinforce them, and this regiment, understanding its errand, made the second ascent magnificently, and the whole force was withdrawn to the base of the hill without further casualty.

But it was evident that the enemy were in force, and were practising cunning tactics, for they allowed four companies of the retiring Northamptons to pass the open zone into the road without firing a shot; then, as soon as the last company reached the fringe of clear ground, they opened a blaze of fire. The carriage of the wounded without stretchers naturally delayed the retirement, and it was almost dusk when the foot of the hill was reached. But the enemy had taken every advantage which time, mobility, and their knowledge of the country gave them, and the moment the guns were withdrawn from the conical hill they began to creep up the nullahs and ravines, their numbers increasing

THE NORTHAMPTONS RETURNING DOWN
THE NULLAH

After the Assault on the Saran Sur Kotal

every minute. A reference back to the description of the country lying between the conical hill and the camp will show the least military reader the difficult position in which the Northampton rear-guard found themselves, and the advantages which such a country gave to an enemy consisting of, perhaps, the finest guerilla skirmishers in the world. Hampered with their wounded, and in rough formation from the descent of the hill, suddenly fired into from an almost invisible enemy, there was little they could do but choose the nullah to retire by. For a time it afforded cover, and it would have been impossible to have carried wounded up and down the many intersecting ravines. And men were falling thick, for each knot carrying or supporting a wounded comrade became a target at once. Matters grew very serious, for the enemy, creeping up the water cuttings and crowning the hummocks, grew bolder as the darkness crept on. The 36th Sikhs did yeoman service on the left flank, but the Dorsets themselves became severely engaged.

The Northamptons stuck to it, and slowly withdrew their wounded, though while so doing the number of casualties was doubled. Major Fraser cleared them from the nullah as best he could, and the main body of the rear companies joined the Sikhs, where General Westmacott stood till the last wounded man was between him and the camp. But one of those unfortunate things had occurred which must occur in war. A party of Northamptons with Second Lieutenant Macintyre and Colour-sergeant Luck had turned a corner of a nullah and were cut, off. The details will never be known, for it was not until the return to camp that it was found that they were missing. It is feared that they sacrificed themselves, as did many a stout soldier this day, in their devotion to their wounded comrades. Luck especially had shown earlier in the day the finest devotion. All that is known comes through one of the party whom Lieutenant Macintyre despatched over the brow of the nullah for help. He faced a volley which ruined the lock of his rifle and pierced his clothes, and eventually stumbled across a small group of the Dorsets. His story was that the enemy were upon the party at short range as he left. If they had left their wounded and followed him they might have saved themselves. One can but picture the awful situation of the officer boy and his handful, surrounded by an enemy wound up to the fierce ferocity of their devil nature, afraid to rush in to tackle the handful with their backs against the rock-side of the nullah at close quarters, but shooting them from the vantage ground which they held. The bodies were found in the morning, and in every case a bullet wound had forestalled the savage Pathans' knife, grim testimony of how the little party died.

But this is painful history. To return. By 7.30 General Westmacott came in with his rear-guard. It had been a terrible business, but it must in no wise be construed into a hopeless rout. There was nothing of this; even in the nullah the Northamptons behaved splendidly, and the fact that every man of their wounded was brought in shows how steadily they behaved under a trying fire. General Westmacott did all that was possible, but the delay caused by the wounded on the cliff and the inability to bring them down found the rear-guard at dusk in a country as difficult as any in the world over which to extricate a rear-guard encumbered with wounded, in the face of an enemy as active as goats, and who mass at will in inconceivable numbers. In the morning the brigade again went out and succeeded in recovering the bodies of the dead. Most had bad sword cuts on them, but there were no signs of disgusting mutilation. The Dorsets, who had apparently lost themselves early in the day, were considerably engaged on the left flank, and though reinforced by the headquarters of the 15th Sikhs, lost some men. The impression in camp is that if it had not been for the skilful handling of the retirement by General Westmacott our losses would have been much severer.

XVII

Rapid movements hampered by wounded—Political outlook —Terms of surrender—Zakka Khels, the "Thieves of the thieves."

MAIDAN,
November 12th.

YESTERDAY Sir William Lockhart with General Gaselee's Brigade made a second reconnaissance to the top of Saran Sur. The troops out were the 2nd and 3rd and 2nd and 4th Gurkhas, and three batteries of artillery, the 2nd and 3rd with their scouts being lent to General Gaselee for the day. The ascent was made under the same circumstances as on the 9th. A few well-armed watchmen held commanding positions along the nullah, and fell back up the pass from point to point as the force advanced. But at no time in the day did they show in much force. The reconnaissance was made, and the withdrawal commenced earlier than on the preceding occasion. The 3rd Gurkha scouts covered the withdrawal, the regiment itself being in position at the solitary tree on the knoll, on the right-hand spur leading down to the conical hill which is so conspicuous a feature in the landscape. The scouts by pre-arrangement retired so rapidly that the few

THE TIRAH EXPEDITION

enemy in position to follow came after them, thinking to repeat the advantage they had over the Northamptons, hampered with eleven wounded, on the first occasion. But they came into a cross fire from the little Gurkhas at the tree and suffered severely; so much so, indeed, that they were very cautious in following up for the rest of the day.

This is a peculiarity of this kind of warfare: all experience on the Indian frontier shows that while an undisciplined enemy presses forward a rear-guard advantage with great determination, yet his persistency is short-lived, and, if he is checked with any severity at the onset, he never perseveres. There is no doubt that the enemy considered yesterday's reconnaissance throughout to be a ruse, and they never showed in any force. Yet the retirement took four and a half hours; a significant fact, for from precisely the same position General Westmacott's retirement took only an hour longer, and he was harassed throughout by a persistent enemy and hampered with heavy casualties and insufficient transporting arrangements for them.

In this warfare it is the wounded who are the cause of disaster. A wounded man at once means six men out of the fighting line, four to carry the casualty and one to carry the rifles of the carrying party. Five casualties at once reduce a company to so small a number that they become insufficient to keep the enemy's fire down, and then follows one of these deplorable incidents in which our frontier fighting is so prolific. The losses which the Northamptons incurred were solely due to their wounded, and a wounded man at once becomes a group and a mark for the enemy's marksmen. If, as would have been the case in a European war, the Northamptons could have left their wounded with the knowledge that nothing worse would have happened to them than their becoming prisoners of war, their losses would not have exceeded a dozen, and the deplorable incident of the party annihilated in the nullah would never have occurred. It was solicitude for their wounded which cost this party their lives, and the incidents of devotion on the part of the Northamptons, officers and men, are too numerous to give in detail; but on one occasion three of the four men who went out to bring in a wounded comrade were shot as they were on the point of succeeding.

And now to the political outlook. The whole of the Orakzai Jirgahs are in, and to-day Sir William Lockhart had an interview with them, and Sir Richard Udney read them the terms which the Government of India have imposed. These are:—the restitution of all stolen property, disarmament to the extent of five hundred rifles, a fine of Rs. 30,000, and the cost of rebuilding the Samana Posts. The Jirgah has fourteen days in which to comply. The Khumber Khels, Malikdin Khels of this valley, and the Aka Khels of the Bara Valley have sent representatives, but our terms to them have not transpired.

The position in the valley seems to rest with the Zakka Khels, who at the present seem very well placed. The Khumber Khels and Malikdin, who migrate to British territory for the cold weather, have their families at the top of the Rajgul hills, and the exposure is beginning to tell upon them as the weather grows colder, but the Zakka Khels have sent their goods and chattels and *penates* off to their usual winter quarters in the Bara Valley, where they are perfectly happy, while the young men remain here under the Saran Sur pine-trees and grow fat on loot. They have secured already over twenty Lee-Metfords, a hundred head of transport animals with their attendant kit, and a quantity of Dum-Dum ammunition, while all we have done in the way of reprisal is to burn their summer residences and seize such forage as they have left behind. No wonder they are still defiant. But the last few days we have succeeded in causing them some loss of life, and this may influence them. Yet at present they show no signs of desisting, and as I write, the foraging party of the day is engaged with them.

No connection with the Bara Column was obtained yesterday. The casualties were about five, including one man of the Queen's and Lieutenant Wright slightly wounded.

The health of the force is excellent. The wire was left untouched last night for the first time for a week.

TIRAH MAIDAN,
November 14th.

I have not written for a day or two because there has been little but the humdrum of occupation-camp life to chronicle, and what news there is, is more conjecture than anything else. We have arrived at what one may term the "development" stage of the campaign, the hinge upon which most events in the near future must turn. Since the unfortunate rearguard action of the Northamptons, the most important event probably has been Sir William Lockhart's reception of the Orakzai Jirgah on the afternoon of the 12th. It was an impressive sight, seeing the hundred-odd elders of these turbulent tribes winding their way up to headquarters, escorted by a party of stalwart Gordons—a comparison in Highlanders, East and West. For the most part these elders were shaggy-looking ruffians, meet representatives of the race of border thieves to which they belong. They stalked into camp with an independent air, and it was impossible not to notice the keen glances which they threw to right and left. Most of them were venerable old gentlemen, whose flowing beards and aristocratic bearing carried one back to the biblical pictures of one's youth—yet probably upon each of their records, innocent looking though they were, hung a dozen men's lives. They marched solemnly into camp and circled round the Union Jack in front of General Lockhart's tent; presently Sir William and his Staff arrived, and Sir Richard Udney addressed them in their own guttural language. It was an impressive scene. The terms and details you already know. It seems that the Orakzais took kindly to them, but found difficulty in settling the distribution of the fines among their sections.

Certainly there seems a more peaceful aspect in this valley, insomuch that the Malikdin and Khumber Khel Afridis have intimated a desire to trade, and to-day the experiment is being tried. It is the sections included under the tribal denomination of Zakka Khels that seem determined to repel all peaceful approach. They are "the Thieves of the Thieves," and the other clans hate and fear them almost as much as they hate the white invader. In fact, it is the fear of the Zakka Khels which at present is keeping the other Maidan tribes so much aloof. On the 13th General Kempster's Brigade was detached to cross into the country of the Ziya-ud-din Khel section of the Zakka Khel country, and its mission is to punish the villages within reach.

This and the friendly attitude of the Maidan clans may do something to coerce the Zakka Khels, for, well placed as they are, with their winter retreat to Bazaar, they would fare badly if the Khumber and Malikdin Khels saw fit to submit completely, and then, seeing a promise of a division of the Zakka Khel Maidan, threw in their lot with the invader and aided in the circumvention of their truculent neighbours and brother clan. Such perfidy is not foreign or impossible to the Afridi Pathan, more especially when his stiff neck has been considerably bent by the presence of two divisions in his country.

Disturbing news comes from the Mastura Valley this morning. It appears that a foraging party, the escort of which consisted of a company of Derbys, two companies of the Devons, two of the 2-1st Gurkhas, a troop of the 18th Bengal Lancers, and a detachment of Jindh Infantry, the whole under Major Smith-Dorrien, came in contact with the Orakzai villagers, who, under the pending conditions of the Jirgah negotiations, thought themselves exempted from foraging. In spite of remonstrance the foraging was carried out, and as soon as the mules were loaded up the enemy opened fire. General Hart himself viewed the action and speaks enthusiastically of the way Major Smith-Dorrien carried on the withdrawal to camp. The enemy must have suffered considerably; our losses were Major Bowman, Derbys, and Major Money, 18th Bengal Lancers, wounded, and four men of the British force. It is a regrettable incident that this friction occurred, as it may hinder the peace negotiations; but Mr. Donald, Political Officer, has left Maidan for Mastura to-day to do his best to arrange more amicable relations in the future.

The health of the force in Maidan still keeps wonderfully good, the Principal Medical Officer's returns showing in the British lists a percentage of sick below cantonment average, while followers and natives, who were expectd to suffer severely, show a better percentage than British troops.

XVIII

General Hart's brigade at Mastura engaged in more hostilities—Good news from General Kempster's detached brigade—Story of the Bagh mosque—Military opinion with regard to the future—The " dwelling of the saintly mouthpiece of the Prophet "—Heavy day near Camp Maidan.

CAMP TIRAH
November 15*th.*

IT is settled now that we move on the 17th to Western Maidan, that is, into the Khumber Khel, Malikdin country. This, I take it, is the first move back towards India. Apparently the route by way of Saran Sur, through the heart of the Zakka Khel country, has been abandoned, and part of the force will pass through the Datoi Gorge, and go round through the Rajgul Valley to the Bara Valley, while the line of communications contract to Karappa when the Mastura Orakzais have complied with the terms. Nothing has been given out officially, but it is known that, much as Sir William Lockhart would like to retain the country and occupy it permanently, yet it is not to be, and the next best move seems to be, rather than the winter occupation of Maidan, the occupation of the Waran, Bara, and Karappa Valleys, with the promise of an early return in the spring, about sowing time, if the terms dictated are not complied with. At the present moment General Hart's Brigade at Mastura is to be engaged in more hostilities than the main portion of the force in Maidan. Whether this means that the Orakzais do not intend complying with the terms which their Jirgah received, or no, it is impossible yet to say. Of course, if the Afridis and Orakzais continue hostile throughout, the plans which I have mapped above will not hold, and a force may have to be hutted for a winter campaign in the valleys. But, taken all round, it seems that a blow struck in the spring, just about sowing time, would be the severest punishment possible. It cannot be that the Afridis, warlike though they are supposed to be, desire a continued struggle, and the majority are of the opinion that, though we must still expect desultory fighting, yet the pacific termination of the campaign is within reach.

The west end of camp last night was persistently fired into by some unusually daring desperadoes, and it seems probable that the members of the Jirgah, having located General Lockhart's camp, gave the marksmen the cue as to which end of the camp was most vulnerable. The enemy last night must have crept to within a hundred and fifty yards of the camp and got inside the picket.

The news from General Kempster's detached Brigade in the Ziya-ud-din country is satisfactory. They have not experienced much opposition, and the smoke from over the kotal shows that the Zakka Khels of that section are being well punished.

There is but little news in camp, so a reference to

the note book is all that remains. It is interesting to note that on the 9th, during the advance to Saran Sur, a Sikh quoit was found in a mosque. It had been broken into four, and was smeared with blood. Another tragic memento of Saragarhi!

The way in which the Northamptons stuck to their wounded, during their rear-guard experience in the nullah, is full of incidents of devotion and self-sacrifice. The tilts of the doolies made excellent marks for the sharpshooting skirmishers, and many a casualty occurred among the men told off to escort the doolies. On one occasion a wounded man dropped in an exposed spot, and four men at once returned to carry him in. Three of the four were hit as they brought their comrade back. Another wounded man, shot through the chest, marched into camp, with his rifle and accoutrements, a matter of four miles. Lieutenant Trent, who was wounded, tells a simple yet soul-stirring story of one of his men. Two were bringing him home, and, being tired, put him down for a moment. They were still in the fighting line, and, as the dust of a bullet smirched over the party, Lieutenant Trent said, "For goodness sake don't leave me here!" The answer came simply as the men hoisted him again, "All right, sir; a British soldier will never desert a wounded comrade!" And this was the sentiment which cost young Macintyre and his party their lives. His party had not the men left to carry on their wounded, so they stayed with them to the end.

The story of the Bagh mosque is quaint, and

gives an insight into the character of the Afridi. Mosques apparently grow best over the bones of a Mullah. The Malikdins had not the necessary handy, so they slew the priestly architect of the building, and Bagh flourished above his mutilated body.

I have, so far, eschewed politics, but I must give expression to the consensus of the military opinion up here with regard to the future. There is but one course open, say the soldiers, that will meet the end, and that is the permanent occupation of Tirah Valley. It may sound a staggering proposition at first, but in reality there is little against it and everything to commend it. To begin with, with a decent tonga road built over the forty miles to Peshawar, it is only twelve hours from a railway base, and it will have the advantage of an alternative route viâ the Khanki Valley. It brings us into direct contact with our frontier, and it must be remembered that now that we have built the roads, we cannot afford an independent State between us and our Afghan frontier of tribesmen liable to be hostile to us. Thirdly, it is most admirably suited to be a military cantonment from a climatic point of view. The first objection will be that warlike tribes such as the Orakzais and Afridis would never brook this. At first probably they would not, but warlike races have before now been brought to realise the uselessness of prolonged opposition, and history would in time repeat itself; moreover, we have in this and the Mastura Valley every evidence that the Afridi is a skilled cultivator, as skilled in the knowledge of tillage as he is in the art of war. This in itself argues in favour of

THE TIRAH EXPEDITION

their becoming reconciled to our presence when the first indignation has worn through. The next question is that of expense. No doubt the establishment of cantonments and the planting of a strong division in Tirah would be expensive, as in all probability two or three regiments would have to be added to the frontier force. But for the moment waive penny wise and pound foolish objections, and place in the balance the incalculable expenditure which expeditions such as the Malakhand, Mohmund, and present Tirah expeditions have incurred: they bear no comparison. You will find that the amount expended on the frontier wars would have kept a full division in Tirah for years; and yet if we fall back to our original position upon the Samana the same expenditure may re-occur within the next decade even, or a greater one if complications develop as there is every reason to believe that they might.

MAIDAN TIRAH,
November 18th.

The 3rd Brigade left Camp Maidan on the 13th, and taking all due military precautions crossed the kotal below Saran Sur, and reached a good camping ground a short distance from the Sheri Khel villages, the last of the baggage arriving in safety by 10.30 P.M. Except for a few long-range shots there was no opposition, and the brigade encamped quietly for the night, the 36th Sikhs being left to hold the kotal dividing the valley from Maidan. On the 19th regiments went out foraging in the Aka Khel villages, the 36th Sikhs destroying the defences in the Ziya-ud-din Zakka Khel territory. The 4th Company Bombay Sappers went to Said Akbar Mullah's homestead, and though tribesmen were hanging about on the crests, they responded to a flag of truce and expressed indifference to what was taking place.

The Mullah's house was found to be a fine stone-built dwelling with a double storey, and infinitely superior in finish and substantiality of architecture to other houses in the valley. To it was attached a mosque, a roomy building of the same class as the mosque at Bagh, but larger and better built; it led down to a tank, a luxury in these hills. The entrance to the mosque was adorned with three coloured balls hanging from the roof, and inside were found sundry articles of interest: a small wooden preaching stool, a curiously contrived lamp-stand, which was capable of mechanical elevation, and the usual Korans. In the house many interesting documents were found, some of extreme political importance, chief of which was a letter purporting to have come from the Amir; letters under the signature of Golam Haider, and an inflammatory epistle from the Hadda Mullah of Jarobi, which, if not so important as the others, showed how well up these priests are in the political situation of India, and even Europe, and how they are able to construct from an outline of facts a history to suit their own machinations. This letter from Mohmund land, the gist of which you have had by telegram, shows that it is not only a forward policy that is responsible for the late upheaval on the frontier. The letters purporting to have been written by the Amir are possibly fabrications, but I have no doubt that in due course we shall hear more of them.

The dwelling of this saintly mouthpiece of the Prophet was destroyed and the force returned to camp with plenty of forage, and passed a quiet night, being in no way molested. On the following day all animals were again sent out with grain-bags. This day proved to be more eventful. In the first place the tribesmen seemed more numerous. A party of Gurkhas approached some apparently friendly Aka Khels in a village with a flag of truce, which the enemy suddenly fired upon from short range, killing one sepoy and wounding another. The Gurkhas were able to punish them for their treachery before they made their way to the hills, and a wounded man was picked up. He was found to be an Aka Khel, and he gave the following history. " That he was quietly at work in his fields when a party of Zakka Khels came by and forced him to accompany them, which he had done for fear of a worse fate, as the Zakka Khels had told him that they intended violence against his clan if they turned friendly to the invader now that Allah had given them into their hands." Though all the forage animals were loaded up, yet the pickets were continually engaged all day, and a company of the Gordons were so menaced that they had to be reinforced. They lost two men wounded. The Dorsets, too, were smartly engaged, so they tried the Gurkha scouts' ruse of pretended flight, and with similar success, severely checking the pursuing enemy. It was evident that the tribesmen were gathering and that the Aka Khels' friendship was on the balance point; so every precaution was taken by General Kempster against a surprise at night. The expected attack opened with a couple of heavy volleys into camp about 8 P.M. The Dorsets' front was chosen, and simultaneously with a discharge of star shells from No. 5 Bombay Mountain Battery they returned the fire, with evident effect, as the attack dwindled

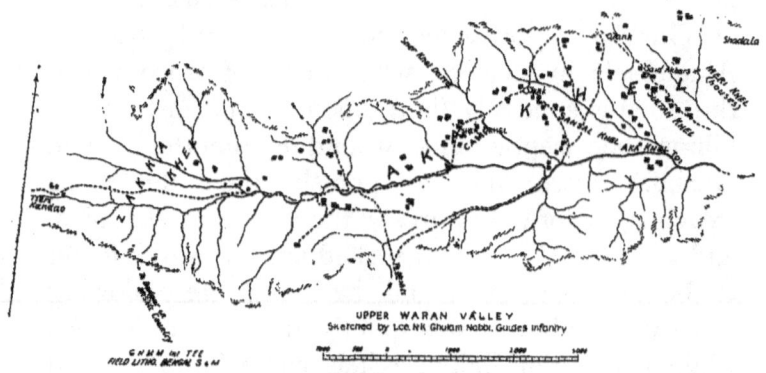

at once to solitary shots, which died away as the moon rose.

The 16th was destined to be a heavy day. The brigade was to return to Camp Maidan. General Kempster made the following dispositions. The 1st and 2nd Gurkhas were to cover the retirement from camp, the 15th Sikhs, under Colonel Abbott, to hold the kotal as the 36th withdrew to camp. Everything proceeded admirably. The baggage-tail was well over the kotal by twelve o'clock and into Camp Maidan by 3 P.M. But in the meanwhile the Gurkhas had been engaged in a rear-guard action, which, if not actually severe, might at any time have developed seriously if Colonel Travers had not handled his men admirably. As it was it cost the regiment an officer and three men killed and three wounded. Consequently the regiment was later in reaching the kotal than was anticipated, and it arrived a little past three so done up that, instead of continuing to cover the retirement, it passed through the 15th Sikhs without relieving them, and they remained to cover the rear of the retiring force.

At 4 P.M. Colonel Abbott's disposition on the kotal was as follows:—He had two companies under Lieutenants Carey and Gordon south of the ridge, two companies north, two companies under Captain Lewarne and Lieutenant Vivian on the fringe of the wooded spur of Saran Sur, one on the ridge proper, where Colonel Abbott himself was, one in rear under Captain Rowcroft, and one in rear 800 yards distant, covering the retirement of the Gurkhas. Suddenly the enemy showed in great force on the wooded spur, and conceiving that they were opposed only by a weak rear-guard, they suddenly debouched from the fir cover and two hundred charged down upon Lewarne's two companies. The Sikhs were well placed, and stolidly stood their ground, though so close did the enemy come that it looked as if it must become a *mêlée*. The solid front of the Kalsa Regiment was more than the Pathan could stand: the ragged line wavered and then swept back, leaving the ground strewn with their dead. It was but a few paces to the fir wood fringe, but the grim Sikhs had taken part payment for their brother soldiers' loan on Saraghari Hill. To show how close the enemy came, each officer had emptied his revolver.

The action was now general all along the kotal, and Colonel Abbott had been wounded. Ammunition, too, was running short. The senior officer felt that in the face of so many of the enemy and with his fifteen or sixteen wounded he could not descend into the ravine-cut valley without support, so he signalled his position. Colonel Haughten, with part of the 36th, was sent to reinforce the 15th, and two companies of the Dorsets were also detached for the same purpose. Thus supported, the whole rear-guard withdrew slowly from the kotal. When they reached the terraces which face the valley it was already dusk, and Colonel Haughten found himself hampered with wounded, in a ravine country exactly similar to that in which the Northamptons had been so severely handled a week before. Moreover, the enemy were round his front and flanks, increasing in numbers as they crept up the nullahs, gaining in confidence and daring as the night closed in, believing that they had in front of them two regiments demoralised and short of ammunition. In fact, they were already taking up positions in houses at short range, and men were dropping fast.

Colonel Haughten stood a moment, cool and collected, a foot taller than his tallest sepoy. He had made his disposition. He knew enough of rear-

THE ATTACK ON GENERAL KEMPSTER'S REAR-GUARD
The 15th Sikhs meeting the rush of Afridis

guard actions, and he knew what the two miles to camp in such a country meant. The enemy were gathering in a block of buildings on the nullah fifty yards away. "We will take those houses and stay the night there; so fix bayonets!" There was a momentary pause, men fell out to guard the wounded, then the three companies of the 15th taking the right block, the two companies of the 36th with their Colonel at their head taking the left, the line swept up. They were into the buildings before the Pathans were aware that they had a forward action upon them. Those that delayed were bayonetted; the rest fled precipitately into the darkness. But the loopholed fire had been terrible, and Captain Lewarne and five men had been shot dead and one wounded. Major Des Vœux on the right, having rushed his first clump of buildings, found them untenable, so with the mixed company of men which were with him he rushed a second one on the far side of the nullah.

This proved to be one small square building with a tiny outhouse five or six yards from its only door. Des Vœux at once set to work to "sungar" up the apertures between the walls of the buildings. The roof of the house had been burned and the charred and still smoking logs lay about. The men rolled these and what substantial litter there was into the gaps, and the breastwork was barely two feet high when the enemy returned to the attack; right up to the sungar they came, but they luckily fired high in their excitement, and one volley from the Sikhs swept them back again. The Sikhs were under complete control and retained their fire. So much so that the enemy believed that they were short of ammunition, and could be heard exhorting each other to make a further rush. Then they turned in the darkness and abused the defenders, saying that it was Saraghari over again—and called Gul Badsah, Major Des Vœux's faithful Orakzai, by name.

Des Vœux thought it expedient that the enemy should know that they were not out of ammunition, so when the breastwork was complete, he divided out the pouch-ammunition and found that he had over forty rounds per man. A sentry was posted at each face with orders to fire a shot at intervals, and but for casual firing they were not further disturbed.

To return to Colonel Haughten. His men found themselves in a very good position in a square house, with its roof likewise burned, on the summit of a knoll of terraces, a deep nullah on two flanks and lesser water-cutting on another. They built a sungar on the less protected flank beside a clump of trees.

Just as they were settling themselves, suddenly up from their very centre sprang half a dozen of the enemy, who were lying low, and dashed through the ranks. Lieutenant Munn passed his sword through one, and a sepoy bayonetted another; but it shows how close these men can lie in cover. Munn's sword remained in the man's body, but was recovered later. As the wounded were brought in more casualties occurred, for the enemy were firing in from all sides.

Lieutenant Munn himself was wounded in the wrist after having shown himself an efficient officer in a trying situation. It was bitterly cold, but it was found that the floor of the house was still hot from the burning of the roof, and the wounded, and such of the Dorsets as were there, lay on this for warmth. After the moon rose Colonel Haughten's post was not much troubled.

The Dorsets' is a sad history. Those of the two supporting companies who attached themselves to the Sikhs were safe, as far as the common safety went, but a half-company under two attached officers, Lieutenants Hale and Crooke, evidently tried to push their way home, instead of occupying the house they had taken or attaching themselves to the Sikhs. They were evidently massacred, like Lieutenant Macintyre's party of the Northamptons, as their dead bodies were found in a nullah in the morning. A party of the 36th Sikhs under Lieutenant Pratt became detached, and though only a havildar and eight men, they entrenched themselves in a deserted house, and had a perfectly peaceful night.

Another party of Dorsets came in. This was Private Vicory, of Dargai fame, and two associates. They have not a very clear narrative, but they say they heard a party moving in a nullah, and challenged it. A voice answered "Friend!" and then they were rushed. A Pathan wrenched Vicory's rifle from him, but he took it back and plunged it into his assailant; a swordsman then cut at him but cut short, only wounding his foot, and this man he rolled over with his rifle butt. These men got back to camp, and Vicory's rifle bears tragical evidence of the struggle, as Pathan blood was oozing from the magazine. This brave fellow's wound is not a serious one.

On the early morning of the 17th General Gaselee's Brigade went out to aid the belated regiments. They came in safely, and the dead and wounded with them; but it had been an anxious night in camp, for the flashes had been distinctly visible until a late hour, and it was depressing to hear the regimental calls sounding at stated intervals to guide stragglers to the camp.

It seems probable that, although our losses on the 16th were extremely heavy, yet the enemy was dealt a severe lesson in proportion to our casualties. Lieutenant Vivian, the surviving British officer of the companies that rushed on the fir-clad spur, maintains that over fifty of the enemy must have succumbed on that occasion; not so many, perhaps, in their advance, but in their disordered scramble back to cover. It being night it is impossible to estimate what were the enemy's losses in Colonel Haughten's action, but even if they were not considerable the moral effect of a rear-guard turning upon the tribesmen and bayonetting them must bear good fruit, and one can understand that the poor fellows isolated in the nullah sold their lives dearly. The camp from end to end is filled with admiration for Colonel Haughten's cool and collected enterprise, and for the stout front shown by the officers and men who obeyed him during that trying night. There are other incidents from Western Maidan which occurred upon this eventful day (16th). General Westmacott fought a skilful covering action, and treachery was attempted in the valley, but the details must wait for another letter.

XIX

Treacherous attack on Major O'Sullivan and officers prospecting for camping ground—Bodies of missing Dorsets found—Tribal representatives of the Khumber Khels, Aka Khels, Malikdin Khels and Kamrai Khels received by Sir William Lockhart and Sir Richard Udney.

CAMP BAGH, MAIDAN,
November 20*th*.

THE serious nature of the events which happened on the 16th prevented me in my last letter from dwelling upon what took place on that date to the force other than the 3rd Brigade. As a matter of fact, the morning in Western Tirah was of extreme interest. For the last three days the Malikdin and Khumber Khels had shown a disposition to be friendly, that is, their armed parties had held converse with the officers in charge of our foraging parties, and even some attempt at an amicable grain traffic had been made. But though this turn of affairs seemed reassuring, General Westmacott, when the 4th Brigade was ordered out on the 16th, issued orders that no armed parties of tribesmen were to be allowed within range, and no one was to be conversed with unless he came unarmed and protected by a flag of truce. On previous days it had been noticed that though the men who had come down into the valley had shown no actual hostility, yet they had invariably taken up good military positions.

On that day Major O'Sullivan, Deputy-Assistant Quartermaster-General, Army Headquarters, Major B. Logan Hume, and Captains Rigby and Holdane had pushed forward to prospect the present camping ground, and an attempt at open treachery was made. Major O'Sullivan was with the horses and the other three officers stood a little way off, when a group of apparently friendly and unarmed tribesmen came sauntering along down towards them. Major O'Sullivan's suspicions were aroused, as the enemy, instead of coming direct, were making a sweep which would have eventually cut the little party of officers off. Accordingly, Major O'Sullivan whistled to the others to double in when the tribesmen where about three hundred yards away. At the sound of the whistle the latter anticipated that their game was up, and immediately poured in a volley at the horses. Luckily the shots went high; the three officers doubling in were received with a second volley, which was also high. The party made for the cover of a neighbouring house, and their situation would have been serious had a company of the 1st and 3rd Gurkhas not been in the nullah below. They speedily extricated the officers from what was a severe situation.

A similar ruse was attempted with a Gurkha flanking company, but owing to General Westmacott's military precautions it also was rendered abortive. There is no doubt that a *coup* was anticipated, and that the tribesmen played the game of "friendlies" for a couple of days with the object of giving us another practical exhibition of Pathan perfidy. It would have suited their book exactly to have secured four officers alive to play off as hostages against our political procedure. After hostilities commenced, firing became general, and the 4th Brigade fought a pretty rear-guard action back into camp. The Borderers in the centre, the 1st and 3rd Gurkhas on the right of retirement, the Jindh Infantry on the left, and No. 5 (Bombay) Mountain Battery covering from the hogsback of picket hill, with the Northampton as escort. The brigade, with its animals fully laden with forage, was back into camp by 3 P.M. The enemy showed a determined front, and were seen in greater numbers than they had shown in since Dargai. In fact, in places they boldly descended into the plain. Our losses were one killed and five wounded.

On the 17th General Gaselee, with two regiments and a battery, went out to bring in the portion of the 3rd Brigade which had been benighted, as detailed in my last letter. The bodies of the missing Dorsets were found in a nullah, evidently a similar sad history to that of the Northamptons a week previously. They were ill-advised, poor fellows, that they ever left the 36th Sikhs, or finding themselves separated did not attempt to hold some village block-house. Probably they would have escaped unnoticed, as did Lieutenant Pratt and his eight sepoys of the 36th. But straggling along in that mazework of nullahs, tired and stumbling in their heavy boots, it was impossible for them to escape the wary hillman, who moves in his grass shoes as silently as a cat. The poor fellows no doubt sold their lives dearly, but it was heavy odds against their ever reaching camp in safety.

Camp Bagh,
November 21st.

One can well realise why the Afridis have called this end of their valley Bagh. For though we have a winter view at present, it is a beautiful spot. Terraces stretch upwards to the slopes of the rocky hills gradually and gently, so that one can imagine, in spring time when the wheat crop is a few inches high, one long rolling slope of green up to the rocky cliffs—a slope the monotony of which is broken by hundreds of towers peeping out from amid the peach and walnut blossoms of the groves which surround each homestead. No wonder the Afridi from the hilltops, with his children and wife perishing with the increasing cold, is stirred to that violent ferocity which marks his attacks upon our stragglers when he sees the smoke of his homestead tending to hide the sun's rays with murky cloud, and his courtyards given over to the defiling hands of the infidel soldier and the more detested follower.

But it must be done: we have given them their chance, and loth as every soldier is to destroy peaceful homesteads, there is no alternative. The Afridi will not come down to take his punishment in the plain, neither does he seem anxious to bow his stiff neck and sue for forgiveness for his unprovoked attacks upon the frontier posts. He is content to confine himself to a barbarous system of opposition—to night prowling and convoy stalking; and the only alternative that remains with the General in the field is to brand the fair valley with fire and sword. So the smoke of the burning houses casts a haze over the midday sun, and the axe is being laid to the roots of the beautiful groves. And it rests with the Afridi himself to stay the hand of the avenger.

Sir William Lockhart and Sir Richard Udney to-day received the tribal representatives of the Khumber Khels, Aka Khels, Malikdin Khels, and Kamrai Khels, and announced to them the punishment which he has resolved to inflict: Eight hundred serviceable rifles, 50,000 rupees in cash, and the restitution of all property stolen during the recent outbreak. They are given one week in which to comply. The ranks of these tribal elders held many a man who drew a pension for his military services, and one had five medals upon his breast, including service in Burma and Egypt. Whether they will comply or not is impossible to say, but the sections represented, with the exception of the Aka Khels, must be heartily tired of our presence. They have no retiring ground but the Afghan frontier and the hill crests and slopes of the Safed Koh. Their women and children must be suffering every privation, and their valley is becoming daily more and more impoverished. Moreover, they have the promise of a return of the force in the early spring, when the young crops will be in the ground, and being cultivators *par excellence*, the prospect for them is a poor one.

But the Zakka Khels being guerilla robbers by profession, the sword, and only the sword, can ever appeal to them. And from their knowledge of the country and their mountaineering training, the sword will never reach them unless we coerce the other tribes to drive them upon us.

Now that it is settled that Tirah is not to be permanently occupied, the pity of it all is probably brought home. We are destroying the most beautiful vale in India. Can it be that the tribesmen, if we leave them to their own devices, will ever be upon the same friendly terms with us? It will take many years, more years than one cares to think of, for the Afridi to live down the memory of the last two months. And as he recovers from the blow, and waxes strong again, he will never feel towards us as he has felt hitherto. Never again can we hope to see bands of Zakka Khel boys falling in as a mission wends its way to Kabul, falling in and saluting in correct military attitude, proud in the connection of their fathers with our service. From the day that the first shot flattened against Lundi Kotal's rampart there have been only two courses open: A settlement on the spot by military occupation of the Khyber, or invasion with ultimate occupation. The first opportunity was not taken, and half measures now will mark the alternative. Already it has cost us several millions sterling, and six hundred and thirty-five casualities in combatants alone, to occupy Tirah, and perhaps will cost many more before* Peshawar is reached and the force withdrawn. Military experts and others, who know the disposition of these wild hillmen, say that the time will come when the operations will have to be repeated, probably with external complications which are absent now ; therefore, as I have said all along, we are reconstructing our rampart on a plinth of sand.

On arrival at Bagh on the 18th, General Symons found the enemy occupying the surrounding slopes and spurs in great force, and General Gaselee's Brigade had to fight quite a smart action before the Pathan sharpshooters could be induced to keep a more respectful distance. The brunt of the day's work fell on the Yorkshires, 2nd and 4th Gurkhas, and No. 2 (Derajh) Mountain Battery, the latter once having a remarkably hot time of it, the riflemen having closed in up to two hundred and fifty to three hundred yards—two gunners were mortally wounded and all the officers had marvellous escapes. Captain Parker had a bullet through the slack of his breeches between the legs, the lobe of Lieutenant Brett's ear was carried away, and the third officer having laid a gun stepped aside, a gunner took his place, and within ten seconds of the change was shot through the chest by a Dum-Dum bullet. The Yorkshires' losses were the heaviest, and camp was pitched under a harassing fire which swelled the day's casualties to twenty-two wounded and seven killed, exclusive of followers.

* Casualty list to January 1st, 1898, exceeded fourteen hundred combatants.

THE TIRAH EXPEDITION

The Gurkha scouts reported that they had found the enemy in great force in the valley opposite to one of the eminences which they had occupied. The political opinion is that, being Thursday, there had been a large gathering to attend Friday's prayers at the celebrated Bagh mosque, and probably, owing to the situation, the gathering had been much larger than usual. The time must have arrived for the Afridis to be anxious to come to some uniform plan of action with regard to us. Finding us in possession of the sacred Bagh, they probably sought to retaliate before holding a parliament.

On the night of the 19th they prowled about the environs of the camp in the early part of the evening, but since the Gurkhas have been sent to permanently occupy the highest peaks within easy range, they have shown less activity at night. They evidently hate to feel that they have an enemy above them. There was a casualty on the march in on the 19th in the Borderers. Yesterday the Northamptons lost three men in the skirmish on the Arhanga, and we had one Gurkha killed crowning the heights opposite Bagh. This, with the sowar with the convoy, brings the total casualties up to six hundred and thirty-five to date.

XX

Advance into the river bed below Bagh—Yeoman service of the little Gurkha scouts—Sharp fighting with the enemy—Arrival of the force at Datoi—Anxiety on account of the baggage not arriving—Sir William Lockhart's determination to return to Bagh—Retirement from Datoi continued.

BAGH, MAIDAN,
November 24th.

THE 22nd was the date which Sir William Lockhart chose to make his reconnaissance to Datoi and the Rajgul Valley. Native report, which was the only information upon which to work, said that Datoi was about six miles away, and that it was an easy route into the Bara Valley; but Sir William Lockhart was careful to take a strong brigade under General Westmacott when going into this unknown country. The road was known to lie down a defile, commanded by high ridges and peaks, so the following disposition was made by General Westmacott on the morning of the advance. The Yorkshire Regiment was told off to hold the peaks commanding the right of the advance, the 1st and 2nd Gurkhas to do similar work on the left. The 3rd Gurkhas were the advance-guard of the column, followed by the 28th Bombay Pioneers, two companies Bombay

Sappers and Miners, the Borderers, and the baggage, the rear-guard being furnished by Colonel Haughten and the 36th Sikhs. The whole corps of Gurkha scouts were kept to be used as flankers as occasion called for them. Sir William Lockhart and Staff marched at the head of the baggage.

The advance into the river bed below Bagh took place at 9 A.M., though the flanking regiments had been out since daybreak. The first two miles of the road lay by a broad reach of the river which gathers its first force at Bagh. Either bank was steep, and there were numerous villages on the slopes above. There were evidences of the enemy at once: within a mile of camp the 3rd Gurkhas were engaged with stray riflemen, and a mile farther the main body caught them up as they were unable to proceed without support. The reach began to narrow here, and the spurs leading up into the hills were dotted with towers in the lower slopes. No. 5 Mountain Battery was called up, and with two companies of the Borderers was ordered up on to a conical hill, but before the guns came into action the flanking regiments had secured the necessary covering positions, and the advance continued.

The road, or semblance of a road, was fast being lost in the river bed, and in places the men were already wading knee deep. At all times a trying advance, this river-bed passage became worse as the decline set in, and the rivulet became a torrent. But the men plodded cheerily on, tripping over boulders and stepping into pools until there wasn't a man but was wet to the waist. As the force proceeded the river bed grew narrower and narrower, until three miles from camp the last habitation was passed, and the path led into a gorge, and a gorge of the most appalling aspect. The torrent became more rapid, and the path vanished into a deep cutting with sheer banks of a hundred feet which led to steep slopes covered thickly with holly scrub, dark and forbidding-looking, for, though it was midday, no sun found its way down this narrow slit in the mountain-side. Already we were able to feel what an advantage an enemy on those hillsides would have, for a shot was fired from above from barely a hundred yards, and a Pioneer mortally wounded.

But the little Gurkha scouts were doing yeoman service. They toiled along on either flank, over precipitous crests and along rough jutting crags, and where in places the sky-line opened out we could hear the patter of their rifles as they turned the skulking sharpshooter out. So rapid was the decline in parts that the river bed became impassable, and rough footpaths hugged its banks. At the second of these General Lockhart's orderly, as he topped a point, was shot dead, falling with three bullets in him, fired at almost point-blank range. The path then took us down into the river again into a second forbidding gulch; in fact, the gorge seemed interminable, and there were few who did not feel misgivings as they toiled along. By this time General Westmacott had used up all his scouts and Gurkha advance-guard in clearing the ridges and spurs above the gorge. So the Bombay Pioneers were pushed forward as advance-guard, the Borderers closing up to their support. On either flank the Gurkhas were constantly engaged, and it was to their smart scouting that the brigade owed its small bill of casualties. Yet we had tastes of what the hillside marksman could do.

The last few hundred yards of the deepest gorge were enfiladed by a party of tribesmen with Martinis, and they knew the range below them almost to a foot. As a company of the Borderers was ordered to close up they opened with deadly effect. The water was churned up around the leading files, then a man fell struggling in the stream; the doctor and a comrade turned to help him up, for a Martini bullet had broken his leg; the man helping was shot a second later, and then again as a stretcher was brought back a couple more of the sturdy Borderers were hit. This was within a few yards of where General Lockhart and his Staff were standing watching the advance-guard being reinforced. It was no place to stay in, for the marksmen were reaching down the ravine and the bullets splashed the stream up into the very faces of the Staff. A section of the bodyguard, the 3rd Sikhs, was detached to turn them out, and then the zone which the sungared hillmen covered was rushed by all who had been "bailed up" by their fire, and a few minutes later the Sikhs had turned them out. Beyond the gorge began to widen out and a lower knoll gave a position for the guns to unlimber.

In the meantime General Westmacott had pressed on with the Pioneers, and as the gorge widened out into a river reach the Bara Valley was seen beyond

—it was but a second reach and barely five hundred yards across; the hills again rose up, while the gorge itself terminated in high-peaked and hollyjungled hills on either hand. The enemy were in position both beyond the Bara stream and upon the hills to the right, and it looked as if the Pioneers were to have an evil time as they advanced across the open space of river beds; but No. 5 came into rapid action from their rear, and topped the hills with bursting shell. General Westmacott extended the advance-guard, and, personally leading his old regiment, took them across the open to the foot of the positions which they had to hold. It was a hot few minutes, but the Pioneers pushed through with five or six casualties. The enemy moved higher up, Datoi was reached, and the Borderers, Staff, and battery pushed up to complete the day, while the little 3rd Gurkhas clambered down from the flanking spurs, having left strong pickets on the peaks behind them.

It was about four o'clock when the Bara River was first forded by our men. It can scarcely be said that Datoi was a valley; it was but a river reach about five hundred yards across. To the north the hills rose up again with more gradual precipitousness than in the gorge just passed; to the west stretched the reach, narrowing until, three miles away, a gorge into the Rajgul Valley could be seen; beyond, the hills faded away to the snows of the Safed Koh; to the east the reach seemed to widen, and it appeared that the first few miles of the Bara Valley were open, with low slopes leading up to the higher hills. But our reconnaissance goes no farther.

Now that the force had arrived at Datoi the first question was a camping ground. General Westmacott determined to encamp on both sides of the nullah; so the Borderers and Pioneers took up their position in houses on the right bank of the Bara stream, the Gurkhas holding a very strong position which jutted out at the junction of the two reaches, and which had a tower at its point. All the summits were then strongly picketed, and two companies of Gurkhas were placed in the houses farther up the reach towards Rajgul; but though the advance-guard and the main troops were in, there was no sign of the baggage, and as night fell it was evident that it was not coming through.

It cannot be said that there was no anxiety felt on account of this baggage. It was placed in a terribly tight place—the gorge which has already been described. But the rear-guard was the 36th Sikhs, and there was a baggage-guard of several companies as well. With Colonel Haughten there we could rest assured that the best precautions would be taken; but it was a terrible defile. As it was, the troops that were through were in the greatest discomfort, wet to the waist, with only what food they had on their persons. The most part of them were detached on picket duty on bleak wind-driven peaks, the others were able to make fires and dry their clothes; it was bitterly cold, and with seventeen degrees of frost, no blankets, and no food, it is hard to be comfortable. But officers and men shared alike:

General Lockhart himself slept with his feet to a fire beneath a tree. As far as the enemy were concerned it was a quiet night, but the morning broke to an anxious day, for ever as the sun got higher there was no sign of baggage turning the point out of the nullah. From the picket posts the enemy, too, were seen to be moving up, and the situation was not pleasant, for the men could not keep up so many strong advanced pickets on empty stomachs and without food.

The Bombay Pioneers and two Sapper companies were detached to re-enter the gorge to make the road more practicable over the worst bits, and to entrench themselves if attacked. Helio communication also was secured about ten o'clock with Bagh Camp through the Yorks, who held the highest ridges above the pass, and at eleven the baggage began to appear, with the excellent news that they had been unmolested during the night. About noon the pickets both north and east of camp signalled that the enemy were moving up in force upon their positions, and almost at once they became engaged. Apparently the tribesmen had imagined that because the Pioneers had returned with their baggage a general retirement was about to take place; at any rate, they pressed on to the pickets with severity, and it was found that by mistake one of the most important peaks had had its picket withdrawn. The guns came into action, and Colonel Dixon with two companies of the Borderers proceeded to retake a commanding ridge which the tribesmen had occupied. The enemy stood so persistently that it came almost to close-quarter fighting before they were driven out, the officers dropping them with their revolvers. At this time, so severe had been the call upon the only two regiments in camp, that the Pioneers and Sappers had been detached to strengthen and supply pickets, so that there were barely a hundred combatants in camp; but at about five o'clock the rear of the baggage came in, and with it the 36th Sikhs and the details of baggage-guards from the other regiments. The pickets were engaged until nightfall, when with the darkness firing ceased, to be reopened by some skulking camp-firers later in the night. They crept close up to the 36th's camp and wounded a sentry and another man. But a couple of star shells scared them off.

Having seen the defile and the entrance into the Bara Valley, Sir William Lockhart determined to return to Bagh the following day (24th). General Westmacott consequently made the following disposition: All baggage was to be loaded up before daybreak; at daybreak the 3rd Gurkhas and scouts, under Colonel Pulley, were to commence their covering climb on either side of the ravine—half the outlying pickets were to bring down the bedding of the whole, leaving the other half to cover their retirement; three companies of the Borderers under Colonel Dixon were to move off as an advance-guard into the nullah, followed by the wounded on stretchers with a guard of the Borderers; No. 5 Mountain Battery to take up the same position from which it had covered the final arrival of the Pioneers at Datoi, the baggage to lead off just as its location suited rapid movement.

These concise orders were carried out without a hitch, and the movement may be placed on record as a military achievement, as the tribesmen, evidently collected in anticipation of attacking our rear-guard, were clearly given the slip. By eight o'clock the last of the baggage was within reach of the nullah, and the helio flashing to the pickets: down they came like hares, so that by 8.30 General Westmacott had his outlying pickets in and his rear-guard of the 36th Sikhs well into the nullah reach. To show how well it was done, the 36th were past the first bend in the nullah before a shot was fired, and the whole of the advance-guard, the wounded, and the Headquarters Staff reached the Pioneers and Sappers, who had had a quiet night without a shot being fired. When the tribesmen realised that the force had started, they closed up rapidly and a rear-guard action soon developed, which I will chronicle in to-morrow's letter.

CAMP BAGH, TIRAH,
November 26th.

To continue the history of the retirement from Datoi. Such great expedition was shown, as was said before, that the main portion of the baggage was well into the gorge and the flanking heights fairly crowned before the Afridis quite realised what was taking place. As soon as they saw that the force was being withdrawn they hastened down to carry out the movement they so well understood, namely, that of harrying a rear-guard, and when the 36th Sikhs were in the gorge, with the flanking parties withdrawing parallel, the hillmen waxed extremely bold. They took up the positions which they knew so well, and a well-directed fire churned up the stream about the rearmost baggage. It was impossible that the Sikhs should not suffer, and in the narrowest portion of that awful gorge they fell rapidly, indeed, at one moment it seemed that they were cut off, for they applied for help, and General Westmacott detached a company of the Borderers from baggage-guard to support them.

But retribution was at hand. A batch of hospital ponies had been sent back to bring up some of the wounded Sikhs: they were retiring by the torrent bed while the two rearmost companies of the 36th were taking the rough riverside path. Bold in the face of their superior position, a party of lank Pathans dashed forward up the very nullah to seize the loot, and the mule drivers fled shrieking. Colonel Haughten from above saw his opportunity. The marauders had not seen the few files which formed his rearmost guard. He detached Captain Venour and a couple of sections. Grimly the stolid Sikhs dropped down into the river bed, and they stood between the enemy and their only way of escape. Too late the situation dawned upon the hillmen—Sikhs in front of them, grim defenders of Gulistan behind them, the sheer sides of the gorge on either hand. They tried to save themselves among the boulders of the stream bed, but the bayonet did its work, and there was not a man among that rear-guard who did not think of Saragarhi. Seven bodies were rolled against the rock slabs, a few wounded broke through the line, the Sikhs drove in the captured ponies, and the retirement continued. Captain Venour was slightly wounded, but the price had been paid. This sudden reversing of the situation seemed to paralyse the tribesmen for a time, and the worst of the gorge was safely passed. Though they followed the rear-guard up almost to within three miles of Bagh, they never persevered again. It was a most masterly retirement, and the whole force is enthusiastic over General Westmacott's handling of his small force, and the magnificent work of Colonel Haughten and the 36th. This is the fifth rear-guard action which the 36th have been called upon to fight during the last month, and on each occasion they have quitted themselves like men. Five officers have been wounded and over a hundred men killed and wounded in this regiment since the first attack was made on the Samana range. The reconnaissance to Datoi from Tirah Maidan deserves to be historical not only on account of the hardships which the men so cheerily endured, but on account of the magnificent way both advance and retirement were conducted, the gorge being the worst that any frontier soldier has seen in our frontier wars. The return of casualties for the three days is as follows:

Lieut. Blair Surg.-Capt. Prall Major des Vœux

THE DEFENDERS OF GULISTAN

	Officers.		Rank and File.		
	Killed.	Wounded.	Killed.	Wounded.	Total.
Borderers . . .	0	0	1	6	
3rd Gurkhas . .	0	0	1	3	
No. 5 (Bombay) M.B.	0	0	0	1	
36th Sikhs . . .	0	1	2	15	
Bombay Pioneers .	0	0	1	5	
Yorks . . .	1	0	0	2	
	1	1	5	32	39

Total 6 killed, 33 wounded.

While enthusiastic over the troops of the main body, the work done by the Yorks and 1st and 2nd Gurkhas must not be forgotten. In crowning the flanking heights they often had to fight their detached skirmishes, and two British officers of the Yorks fell while leading their men with great gallantry.

XXI

Advancement of Colonel Collins and half of the Queen's into the Massuzai Valley—Magnificent sight of a burning valley—Bravery of Sir Pertab Singh—Advancement upon Esor.

DARGAI,
November 29th.

THE reconnaissance to Datoi was in fulfilment of General Lockhart's promise to the Orakzai and Afridi Jirgahs that he would visit every valley of their country, whether as friend or foe being a matter of the tribesmen's own making. The present movement of a brigade and headquarters over the Kahudhara Pass is also part of this punishment programme. But this time a concentration with Colonel Hill and the Kurram Movable Column was the objective. General Lockhart intended to cross by the Lozakka Pass, after having traversed the whole of the western end of the Khumber Khel Maidan. Then as the Massuzai and Mamuzai countries, Gar and Samil, were reached, to coerce and punish until, in the vicinity of Esor, he could concentrate with the Kurram Column. Then, in concert with that force, operate against the Chamkannis of Tabi, who were quite the most recalcitrant tribe on that part of the border, and who had mainly been responsible for the rear-guard action of the Kurram Column when it made its first reconnaissance to Esor, and in the annihilation of the Kuparthala picket in the Karmana defile. The country to be traversed was absolutely new ground until the force reached the Khanki Bazar and the Ali Sherzai country. Except in the coming to conclusions with the Chamkannis, it was not anticipated that there would be much fighting; but the movement of a brigade in such an enclosed, cramped country went far to show the tribesmen what was possible even in such conditions. The pass lies at the end of the Tirah Valley almost due west from Bagh. Native information gave it to be about six miles from Bagh Camp. As the country to be traversed looked a difficult one, General Gaselee, with a strong brigade, was detached on the 26th to work his way up to the pass headquarters, with the newly arrived wing of the Scottish Fusiliers and three companies of the Yorks to follow on the 28th. As for the first two days the operations of the advance and rear-guard were separate, it would be better, perhaps, to keep the accounts apart.

On the 26th General Gaselee advanced four and a half miles up the valley, and found it heavy going. Moreover, a number of sharpshooters had posted themselves in the villages, which are very thick at this end of the valley; and most of the day was spent in dislodging them and turning them out of the first spurs which cover the approach to the pass. These spurs were generally thickly wooded with fir,

Indian and Holm oak; and persistent marksmen gave much trouble. A group of the enemy, believed to be a Jirgah, suddenly opened fire on the 1-4th Gurkhas, and then dispersed up a spur. A company of the Queen's, under Lieutenant Engledue, stormed the crag and got to close quarters with the enemy with the loss of only one man. Finding it impossible to make the summit that night, General Gaselee chose an open spot to camp in; the marksmen closed in with the evening and fired into camp persistently, but did little damage. The casualties of the first day were one man of the Yorks killed, three Gurkhas killed and five wounded, two of whom were scouts.

At dawn on the 27th General Gaselee pushed forward the Gurkha scouts and the 3rd Sikhs to take and occupy a long, deeply-wooded spur, on the left of the main advance, and after having posted a picket to work round to the kotal. It chanced that the road taken was not the Lozakka Pass, but the Kahudhara, which is a weird path leading into the valley from which it takes its name, a valley parallel to the Lozakka defile, with only a rugged spur between them. By 9 A.M. this flanking party had reached the kotal, and General Gaselee, seeing that resistance would be slight, sent word back for the baggage to push up. The 3rd Sikhs had one killed in the advance, and it was no easy matter for the baggage to work upwards. The first part of the pass was a bouldered waterway, which tried to the utmost the pony transport, already suffering from the exposure of an intensely cold campaign. After three miles of this a ragged and scarpy path wound up the steep ascent towards the kotal; it was more than the baggage animals could stand, and of necessity the baggage had to be parked in the best situations that the officers could find.

General Gaselee had in the meantime pushed on half of the Queen's, a battery, and a company of Sappers and Miners into the Massuzai Valley, under Colonel Collins, remaining himself on the kotal with the 4th Gurkhas and 3rd Sikhs to direct the operations of crossing the baggage. It was a quiet night on the kotal, but a very severe one, as the men had nothing in the way of food and only what clothing they had brought up on their backs. Though the cold was intense at that altitude, there was a plentiful supply of firewood, and the little Gurkha riflemen had soon the whole length of the occupied ridge a blaze of fires. Down in the river-bed the baggage was in worse plight; much of it had no water, and a keen gusty wind blew down the nullah. Moreover, the enemy made one determined attempt to rush the baggage. Luckily, they stumbled upon a picket of the Queen's, and were roughly handled; but they succeeded in shooting two drabies before they desisted. The party which had advanced into the Massuzai Valley under Colonel Collins had nothing in the way of food except what the countryside supplied them with, which was little; rations, however, were sent down to them the first thing in the morning. The time was then spent in roadmaking, for it was evident that in its then state the baggage would never have got across.

General Lockhart left camp early on the morning of the 27th, hoping to be able to reach the head of the pass that day, but the helio which came back from the front showed that this would be impossible; so a camp was chosen on the side of a bluff about three miles from the pass. Just as the marksmen had harassed General Gaselee's advance by firing from the villages, so did sharpshooters pester the passage of the rear-guard; and so, to keep to his promise, General Lockhart ordered the villages that we passed to be destroyed. It was a very fertile and thickly populated end of the Maidan Valley, and as the rear-guard left it became a mass of flame, the dry fir rafters burning freely. It was the territory of the Bar Khumber Khel, men who it was believed were friendly. A theory was put forward that, knowing the conditions of Sir William Lockhart's proclamation, members of other sections who had been punished, jealous of the Khumber Khels' attitude towards us, had come and fired upon us simply to get punishment inflicted upon the Khumbers. Of course, it is impossible in war to discriminate, and the Khumber Khel, if not themselves implicated, should have been strong enough to have prevented others using them as a scapegoat. As it was, that day the Scottish Fusiliers and Yorks lost two killed and two wounded, and on the preceding day the advance-guard, as already detailed, had nine casualties. This was enough, and the penalty was meted out in full. It seems evident that something of the kind was anticipated, for during the march on various dwellings papers were found attached in prominent places in which hopes were expressed that the Kampani Bahadur would spare the dwelling as it belonged to such and such a native officer in such and such a regiment.

One of the most magnificent sights that one could wish to see was the destruction of that valley by "fire and sword" as the evening waned into night. The camp was ringed with a wall of fire—byres, outhouses, homesteads, and fortresses one mass of rolling flame, until the very camp was almost as light as day. Then the actual fury of the fire subsided, and the wooden structures of the houses and the uprights of the towers stood in outline glowing in the pitchy darkness: a warning to the skulking camp prowler who sneaks up to within the limit of his range to shoot the sleeping soldier and the harmless camp follower. It was a quiet night, and with earliest dawn headquarters pressed on to make the summit of the kotal.

Esor,
December 1st.

Sir William Lockhart and Staff remained in the summit of the Kahu Kotal until about 3 P.M., and then descended behind the 4th Gurkhas down the reverse spot to a path, three miles down, where the valley opened out a little. Here there were some habitations of recent build; in fact, as some were in course of construction, it seemed that it must be a new colony from the Khumber Khel country, for they are known to have established themselves on the side of the Massuzai Valley. The path down, though steep, was infinitely superior to the path of ascent. On arrival at the valley it was found that the Queen's and the 3rd Sikhs had pushed on four miles farther down to Dargai, where the gorge opens out into the Massuzai Valley. There seemed little hope of the baggage arriving that night, so everybody did their best to make themselves comfortable in the lofts and upper storeys of the houses. Hay and Indian corn-straw was plentiful, and it was evident that the villagers had been taken by surprise and had made a hurried flight, for food was found by the advance-guard actually simmering on the fire. But the Sappers had worked hard on the Maidan side of the pass, and by the greatest effort most of the advance column and headquarters baggage was got into camp by midnight. The little dip, nestling between two huge wooded spurs, as darkness crept on, formed a scene as impressive as it was weird. As the transport hurried in cold, tired, and harried, animals and men were packed away in the scant space which the few field terraces allowed; the very stone slabs in the centre of the stream which caused the hollow were covered with weary drivers and their animals, and as night closed in each group lit its fire to cook what little food was available. The whole valley became a sea of flickering fires, stretching far up into the woods upon the hillside, throwing out weird and fantastic shadows in a thousand nooks and corners.

With the earliest dawn the baggage recommenced to stream down from the pass head, and as soon as it was light headquarters followed the 4th Gurkhas down the river bed to the Dargai Camp. The valley closed into a gorge which marked the bed of a torrent, not a severe gorge from a military view, as it was flanked by spurs which lent themselves especially as picket posts. The scenery improved as the force advanced, and in places the forest-lined spurs were quite as beautiful as anything in Kashmir. The impression at once conveyed was that the Massuzai Valley is far more picturesque than anything in Maidan. Some of the trees are truly magnificent, with a girth of several feet. About midday the gorge and river each opened out into the Massuzai Valley proper, and we came upon the cluster of houses which mark Dargai. Camp again had to be formed on both sides of the valley, but it was an ideal spot for a camp, as the hills especially lent themselves as picket posts. It is worthy of notice that this camp of Dargai is the first village that we have yet come upon during the campaign in which we found the villagers waiting to receive us; but it must not be confused with the now historic bluff above Changru Kotal—Dargai is a common name upon the frontier. The Massuzais of this section, the Samil, came forward and expressed themselves willing to pay their share of the fines inflicted and to receive us with every show of friendliness. They also guaranteed to picket the hills.

While Sir Richard Udney was fixing the period by which the rifles were to be surrendered, Colonel Spurgin with the rear column was engaged severely on the pass behind. The burning of the Khumber Khel villages of West Maidan as punishment for molesting and resisting our advance in Massuzai, had evidently thoroughly upset that section, and they continued to hang upon the rear-guard's flanks and rear with exceptional persistency. The rear-guard, two companies Yorks and three companies of Scots Fusiliers, with the Derajat Battery, literally had to fight every inch of its way up to the summit of the kotal, and under most difficult circumstances, as the closeness of the fir-covered spurs prevented successful covering movements, and the Khumber Khel skirmishers were able to creep up to close range before they were discovered.

The rear-guard, especially the Yorks, behaved with great coolness, and at one time one company was almost mixed with the enemy, for these hill-men were bold enough to conceive the idea that they might be able to cut off and seize the guns, which object they deliberately attempted, and might have been accomplished if it had not been for the stubborn front shown by a company of Yorks, who, though not gun escort, finding the battery in peril, came manfully to their assistance. The enemy were kept at arms' length, the tail of the baggage was over the kotal by 5 P.M., and by the greatest effort every one was into Dargai, rear-guard included, by 1 A.M. The casualties for the day were two officers wounded, four men killed and eleven wounded. It is impossible to speak without enthusiasm with regard to the second column. For three days they were engaged in that most trying of situations—a desultory rear-guard action, they had but little food, and were forced to camp just as they stood in the most exposed places, the thermometer at night often registering over fifteen degrees of frost.

During the night of the 29th half a dozen shots were fired into camp, evidently by some of the more adventurous of the Khumber Khels who had followed the rear-guard down, two of the 3rd Sikh bodyguard being hit. Sir Pertab Singh of Jodhpur, who was accompanying the force as Extra Aide-de-camp to Sir William Lockhart, was also hit in the hand as he lay asleep. The veteran Prince at first informed no one of his wound, not wishing to bring himself into prominence; but insufficient dressing necessitated the requisition of a surgeon, though it was not until three days after the event that it was declared. Every one in the force was impressed with the veteran nobleman's endurance. He alone of all the Princes attached to the force remained until the operations were brought to a close. In the morning the headmen of Dargai were summoned to explain, also to give the reason why they had failed to pay in the tale of rifles which they had promised. They prevaricated again, and the torch was applied to the first of their homesteads; the effect was magical, and in a quarter of an hour the majority of the rifles were forthcoming and the fine paid in Afghan coin.

At daylight the force had commenced to advance upon Esor, where the junction with the Kurram Movable Column was to take place. In fact, a reconnaissance which General Gaselee had made on the 29th with two companies of the 3rd Sikhs had found helio connection with Colonel Hill's Column. The road from Dargai to Esor is a fairly good one, and for the country an excellent one, so headquarters and the main column were in by 2 P.M., and Sir William Lockhart and Colonel Hill met. Colonel Spurgin with the second column remained behind at Dargai, as Mr. White King, Political Officer, had to settle up with the tribal Jirgahs, and the rear-guard had certainly earned a rest.

Tirah is a beautiful country, but the Massuzai Valley from Dargai to Esor is better; it is not so flat a valley, being undulating and broken with hillocks, but it is infinitely better wooded and watered, and the soil appears richer. The inhabitants are fewer and the villages far between; the Massuzais must be admirable agriculturists, for the main feed of water has been ducted all over the valley, so that one finds stretches of paddy swamp, and even at this season of the year plateau upon plateau of green wheatland breaking upon the eye like meadow land. The houses, too, are more substantially built, and the Khan of Esor's house, where Sir William Lockhart is now residing, is built of solid fitted stone, and decorated with more care and finish than any Pathan house that we have yet seen, except Said Akbar's. Esor is a plateau tableland in the centre of the valley with the two streams winding beside it. Low hills surround it, with further valleys before the bigger ranges are reached, and its slopes are carpeted green with the growing wheat crops. To the south-west lies the Karmana defile, marking the spot where the Kapurthala picket was annihilated.

XXII

The Chamkannis resist—Retirement of Colonel Hill and the left column—Bravery of the scouts and the difficulties they overcame—Good work done by the Gurkha scouts—The return to Bagh camp.

CAMP ESOR,
December 2nd.

TWO columns went out yesterday, one under General Gaselee to collect the fines from the Gar Massuzais, the other to punish the Chamkannis. The former column had but little to do, and returned to camp about four o'clock. But with the other column it was different. To start from the beginning. The Chamkannis are about the most turbulent and recalcitrant tribe on the border, and their chief means of subsidence is by raiding across our border. They are extremely warlike and hardy, and think nothing of marching from Tabi, their stronghold, to Sadda in one day. Within the year they looted, before the frontier outbreak, over a thousand head of cattle from our border in one night, and got clear away with them. They are not a strong section, but they make up for their numerical weakness by audacity and enterprise, and their villages, as the reconnaissance of the last two days has shown, are situated in a valley more difficult of approach than any this side of Tirah. The Chamkannis were in the main responsible for the disaster to the Kapurthala picket last month, and secured the majority of the Sikhs' rifles.

Colonel Hill, with the 5th and 4th Gurkhas, three hundred dismounted sowars of the Central India Horse, and 6th B.C., the Kapurthala Regiment, 12th Bengal Infantry, No. 1 (Kohat) Battery, and Lucas and Bruce's scouts, set out on the 1st to destroy the villages of this nest of banditti. When well away from Esor Camp, it was found that the Chamkanni Valley was bordered on the east by a rugged chain of hills, there being two routes of access to the valley beyond, on the left a waterway gorge known as the Awaldhara, farther on the right a kotal reached by a gradual ascent of about two thousand feet. Colonel Hill detached a column, consisting of the 5th Gurkhas, the scouts, the 12th Kapurthala Infantry, and dismounted cavalry, under Colonel Gordon, to work its way into the valley by way of the river gorge; while he himself, with the rest of the force and guns, proceeded to ascend by the kotal route, the object being a concentration at the foot of the valley about eleven o'clock. The main column had crowned the kotal by a quarter-past ten, the covering spurs were picketed by the 4th Gurkhas, the guns were placed in position over the reverse of the crest, and the destroying of the few block-houses in the vicinity was proceeded with.

It was found that the Chamkanni Valley was an inclined plane, lying east and west, rising rapidly

THE TIRAH EXPEDITION 225

up to huge ranges in the west, about eight square miles in area, cultivated, well built over, with the large village of Tabi, the capital, in the centre, and skirted with bluff spurs, precipitous cliffs, and rugged peaks, the majority of which were wooded. This girdle of impossible rock gave to the place its natural strength, for riflemen climbing up to the precipitous peaks and spurs have the whole of the valley in easy range, for at the bottom of the plane runs the river which passes through the Awaldhara Gorge into the Massuzai Valley. The gorge becomes a defile as it reaches the valley, and it was through this that Colonel Gordon's column had to come. Colonel Hill was waiting for the head of the column to appear in the valley, when the enemy opened at long ranges from two opposite spurs, shooting a trumpeter of the 6th Bengal Cavalry attached to the Staff. The guns were laid on these spurs and the fire kept down; it then transpired that something was delaying the column in the gorge, and it was almost an hour before the 5th Gurkhas got through.

It appears that the enemy had allowed the advance-guard of the regiment past a certain spot, but had suddenly opened on the second company of the 12th Bengal Cavalry and wounded a man. It is not clear what caused the further delay, but the whole force was not through the defile until too late to complete the destruction of the valley, or to prevent young Battye, of the 6th Bengal Cavalry, being shot dead, and a party of hospital mules and officers' ponies being cut up. A few of the nearest houses had been burned by a party of the 4th

P

Gurkhas when Colonel Hill ordered the retirement and the left column to join him and return by the kotal. The enemy, recognising the "retire" on the bugle, pressed the rear with spirit, and, though they showed a marked dread of the guns, they had infinite knowledge of the country, and harassed the column severely as it returned to camp. The losses for the day were Lieutenant Battye, 6th Bengal Cavalry, killed; Lieutenant Pennington, 12th Bengal Cavalry, slightly, Lieutenant Villiers Stewart, 5th Gurkhas, dangerously wounded; rank and file: killed, six, wounded, sixteen; total, twenty-seven. On the right the Massuzais had been seen massed on various peaks, but they were but casual sightseers, and they made no attempt to take an active part on either side. A few shots were fired into camp that night. The time has not come for criticism, but, viewing the day with the experience of the recent campaigns, one could not help thinking that if the troops of the Kurram Movable Column had been engaged in one or another of the Tirah rear-guard actions, their losses would not have been so severe, neither would they have been so free in sounding the retire on the bugle, when every tribesman is acquainted with the significance of the call. But Sir William Lockhart had come to punish the Chamkannis, and punished they had to be, so the breaking-up of the Esor concentration was deferred a day, and Colonel Hill despatched on December 2nd with a changed force. He started with the scouts under Captain Lucas, and the 4th and 5th Gurkhas, the 3rd Sikhs, part of the Queen's, and the Kohat Battery. With

THE ATTACK ON THE CHAMKANNI TRIBE

THE TIRAH EXPEDITION 227

such a force a general might have gone to the world's end. They were over the kotal by 9 A.M., and the 5th Gurkhas, with Lucas's scouts leading, were sent to hold the hills on the left. The Chamkannis had evidently anticipated a second visit, for they were in force upon the left and had run up new sungars upon several of the spurs.

The brunt of the day fell upon the scouts, the finest hill soldiers in the world. Lucas breasted them up an almost precipitous scarp, the steepness of which, with their own adeptness for taking cover, alone saved them from the fire above. So severe was the climb that the men literally had to hand each other up. At the top of this climb Lucas found his eighty men confronted by three spurs, with dips between, each spur sungared and held, and the spot his men were taking cover in under a fire from three sides. In the face of it, it would only have been wasting valuable lives to have made a brilliant dash for the first of the three sungars; so Lucas gave his men breathing time until he saw the head of the leading company of the 5th on his left. Then was his time: half the opposing fire was detached by the arrival of support. Lucas told off half his company to sweep the sungar with a stream of independent fire, whether the enemy were visible or not, and then threw himself in the front of forty little black faces and forty gleaming bayonets. The Chamkannis showed more front than has any Yagistan upon this border yet, for they stood up and met the charge with a volley and then bared their knives to receive it. But the covering fire destroyed their composure and their aim. They waited till fifty and then thirty yards remained, when their spirits failed them and they raced for the next sungar behind them. Lucas repeated his tactics three times, but they left many dead and wounded behind them, and then when the little scouts had turned or literally driven them over the brow of the hill, they shot them at longer ranges as they streamed along the terraced fields below. It was a magnificent piece of work, and though a dozen of the little hillmen had bullets through their clothes, yet not a man was touched, and twenty to thirty of the tribesmen lay stretched or struggling on the ground. Would that the Kapurthala Sikhs had been there to see!

It is impossible to overpraise the Gurkha scout service or of its officers, Lucas, Bruce, and Tillard. The 5th Gurkha scouts came up ninety-two strong. They have been thirty-six times engaged in the campaign, have killed over their own strength of the enemy, and have lost one man killed and two wounded, and this does not extend to the many nights which they have spent stalking camp prowlers.

But back to the narrative. When the Gurkhas had cleared the left, the guns broke up the other gatherings that were visible and the 3rd Sikhs proceeded to demolish the villages. Over sixty villages were destroyed in the valley before the force commenced to withdraw. The withdrawal was simple, because the tribesmen made no show this day of following up the rear-guard. They had been punished in their own coin and they did not seem to understand. But it is significant that they made no attempt to repeat their spirited forward policy of the preceding day. The day's casualties were: Major Eden Vanstittart, 5th Gurkhas, slightly wounded; two Gurkhas killed, one wounded; two of the 3rd Sikhs wounded. General Sir William Lockhart and General Gaselee's Brigade leave the Kurram Column to-morrow, returning viâ the Khanki Valley to Bagh Tirah.

On the 5th the march back to Bagh recommenced, the 30th P.I. returning to Karappa, the 2nd being attached to Gaselee's Brigade. The march took the force up the actual source of the Khanki River. Leaving the Tasmak Pass into the Mastura Valley on the right, the river bed was followed up into the gorge which ends in the Singakh Pass into the Adam Khel Maidan. There was no sign of an enemy, and after a severe climb the head of the column dropped down and encamped for the night on the Bagh side slopes of the pass. The Adam Khels, knowing what they stood to lose in the Jowarki country, came in at once, surrendering their allotted fine; further, so anxious were they to save their dwellings, that they themselves picketed many of the adjacent heights to keep away any Malakdin or Khumber Khel prowlers that might be about. From the pall of smoke which overhung Bagh Valley, it was evident that General Yeatman-Biggs was carrying out punitive measures against the Maidan tribes which still remained recalcitrant.

On the 6th the force returned to Bagh Camp,

having been met on the way in by the K.O.S. Borderers, under Colonel Dixon. Bagh looked much deserted, as all superfluous and heavy kit had moved down to Karappa, and the force was prepared for the final evacuation of Tirah. And from the unsettled appearance of the weather it seemed expedient that the passage of the Datoi defile should be made without delay, for there was every evidence of the near approach of snow. No time was lost, and the orders for the breaking up of Bagh camp were published for the following day, the 7th.

The concentration at Esor broke up on the 3rd, the Kurram Column returning through the Karmana to Sadda, General Gaselee's Brigade marching back to where Colonel Spurgin's Column was in camp at Dargai. This column had, since its arrival in the Massuzai country, found the tribes were absolutely peaceful, and a general trafficking in small supplies and obsolete arms was taking place between the men and the villagers. The combined column had now to make its way down into the Khanki Valley. Therefore on the day that General Gaselee left Esor the Spurgin Column marched forward to the foot of the Massuzai Kotal into the country of the Ali Sherzai Khels. Sir William Lockhart and Staff pushed on and joined Colonel Spurgin's Column, but the brigade halted in the rear column's camping ground. When the foot of the Massuzai Kotal was reached, Spurgin's Column got helio communication with Fort Lockhart on the Samana. Thus the news of the force in the morning went .

round by Sadda, and in the evening across the Samana Suk.

On December 4th the Massuzai Kotal was crossed, and the whole force marched into Khanki Bazaar, being joined there by the 2nd and 30th P.I., who came out with two days' supplies from Karappa. A one-day halt was made at Karappa, and the inhabitants of the big walled villages having a short tale to their surrendered rifles, a tower was blown up to show them that Sir William had no time for dalliance: as a result, a batch of rifles were immediately surrendered, including two Lee-Metfords.

But little of interest had occurred in Bagh Camp while the 2nd Brigade had been away in the Orakzai valleys. The political situation had in no way improved, the Khumber Khels, Malikdin and Kuki Khels, in open Jirgah, saying that they could not possibly comply with the terms imposed within the prescribed period; the Zakka, Aka, and Sipah Khels had no truck with the Politicals at all. Thus it was evident that the force proceeding down the Bara Valley could expect to be roughly treated.

Therefore the evacuation of Tirah Maidan was arranged, and the force prepared to leave, having practically laid it waste with fire and sword from end to end, having unearthed and consumed the grain and fodder supply of the country, uprooted and ringed the walnut groves, prevented the autumn tillage of the soil, and having caused the inhabitants to live the life of fugitives, upon exposed, bleak, and bitterly cold hilltops. So much for the military occupation of Tirah; now to the evacuation.

XXIII

Evacuation of Maidan commenced—Attack by the enemy on Colonel Pulley's regiment—Borderers dislodge the enemy from the hillside—Discomfort of the troops in camp—Strange scenes in camp—Order of advance from Datoi—General engagement of all troops.

BARKAI,
December 16th.

THE actual evacuation of Maidan began on the 7th instant, though the valley was not clear of the invader until the 9th. The 1st Division was to march down the Mastura Valley, revisit the Waran, and come out below Barkai. General Lockhart with the 2nd Division would again face the Datoi defile and push down to India by what is known as the Bara River route, both forces being due to join the Peshawar Column on or about December 14th. The history of General Symonds' march must stand in abeyance for the present, for though a very creditable military achievement to all concerned, it was a peaceful undertaking, and is lost beside the terrible tale of hardship, exposure, and conflict which rendered Lockhart's march from Tirah to India one of the severest military marches of the century. There is no doubt that the move from Bagh was

THE TIRAH EXPEDITION   233

made not a day too soon: clouds were gathering, the wind was blowing fitfully from the north, and there was every evidence of the approach of snow, a foot of which would have made the Bara route impossible.

General Westmacott was again entrusted with the clearing of the Datoi defile, and it was hoped that the division, now reduced to the lightest possible marching scale, might be able to push its way through in forty-eight hours. Opposition in the actual defile was not anticipated, as, in spite of the devastation of Malikdin Khel Maidan, this tribe has shown a disposition to be amicable so as to save the remainder of their villages in the vicinity of the defile. The Kuki Khels, who hold the junction land at Datoi itself and the Rajgul Valley, also seemed to have tired of hostilities. The Malikdin Khels were, therefore, told to pass the word along the pass which was to save their villages from destruction. But in spite of their assurances there were few who left the camp that morning to face the defile who did not feel that the undertaking of the campaign was about to commence.

The leading brigade advanced in the following disposition: Colonel Pulley with the 3rd Gurkhas furnished the advance-guard, the K.O.S. Borderers in advance of the main body, with a half-battalion of the Scots Fusiliers and the Dorsets behind them. Then the baggage of the brigade and Headquarters Staff, the rear of the leading columns brought up by Colonel Haughten with the 36th Sikhs. General Kempster's Brigade to follow in as close order as possible after having detached portions of 1st and 2nd Gurkhas and 2nd Punjab Infantry and in the flanking of the whole force. The Malikdin Khels were staunch to their word, for the head of the column sighted the Datoi tower and the defile was passed without a shot being fired. This minimised the difficulties of the passage, but even then it was bad enough, and there was no alternative but for troops, baggage, and followers to wade through the torrent for almost two-thirds of the way. However matters grew more serious when the mouth of the defile was reached. The opening out of the gorge has been described in a previous letter, and it will be remembered that when the Bara stream is joined the junction expands into a reach about five hundred yards wide, commanded on every side by spurs and peaks, and the mouth of the gorge especially commanded by a high hill, or rather succession of hills, directly opposite.

The flanking of the advance through the defile had used up the whole of Colonel Pulley's regiment and the company of Gurkha scouts attached, so the Borderers under Colonel Dixon were with General Westmacott and had become the advance-guard. Everything seemed peaceful, and the regiment in extended order was halfway across the Bara River reach when suddenly a fire was opened upon them from the opposite hill, almost exactly under the same conditions as it had been opened on the 28th Pioneers on November 22. The enemy were in force, but their shooting was wild, and the Borderers made the cover of the far bank without casualty. From the trying experience of his former visit, General Westmacott knew the best positions over which to distribute his fighting line. Colonel Dixon was ordered to take and hold the opposite hills, and was supported by a company of Dorsets and Scots Fusiliers; No. 5 (Bombay) came into action on the tower crest at the mouth of the defile, and what was left of the little Gurkhas hurried away to picket the spurs on the left of the Rajgul portion of the stream. Colonel Dixon knew that it would be impossible to take the main position with a frontal attack without enormous loss of life, so he detached Captain Macfarlane with two companies of Borderers, supported by a company each of Fusiliers and Dorsets, to turn the sangers from the right flank, while Captain Sellar with another company of Borderers climbed up and demonstrated on the front.

The Borderers from their previous heavy experience knew the ground, and, working beautifully on the hillside, steadily dislodged the enemy, so that by 3 P.M. the whole of the original picket crests were held and the baggage streaming into camp, the first shot having been fired at 11.30 A.M. Though the camp was adequately protected, the enemy were by no means driven off, and the Borderers' pickets were heavily engaged on the peaks to the north right into the night; but the camping ground had been taken at the small cost of one Borderer and three native combatants wounded, which, considering the force the enemy were in, must be considered exceptional and due solely to the magnificent hill skirmishing of the Borderers in a country they knew.

It is impossible to appreciate the movement made by the tribesmen on this occasion. Why they should have chosen to commence hostilities when the 4th Brigade was through the defile and in a military position which gave it an advantage over them is impossible to understand. In the Datoi Gorge a similar number of rifles to those which opened on the Borderers in the river reach could have obstructed the advance for an immeasurable time, since the defile was such that artillery could not have come into action except under exposure to an annihilating fire. A determined body of riflemen could have found commanding positions which it would have taxed the strength of the whole division to have turned unsupported by artillery, and loss of life in the defile must have been phenomenal. Every soldier of frontier and Afghan experience in the force considers the Datoi defile to be the most difficult military position of its kind that a British division has ever crossed. But the enemy never held it, and the baggage streamed through all night unmolested. It may be that the Malikdin Khels prevented opposition, or it may be that the movement of General Gazelee's Brigade to the Arhanga detained the fighting sections there, and it is also possible that Sir William Lockhart's decision in starting a day earlier than had been originally determined found them unprepared. Whatever the reason, the result was, perhaps, the most fortunate circumstance of the campaign. It was a serious

THE TIRAH EXPEDITION 237

enough matter a few days later, when in the more open Bara Nullah the force was so hardly pressed, within a few days' march of the Peshawar Column, that one shudders to think what the results would have been if, with its communications cut behind, and two marches through a terrible country in front, there had been heavy business before Datoi. As events proved, the evacuation of Maidan Tirah was made with but a small margin to spare. On the day following the withdrawal of General Kempster's rear-guard it rained in the Bara Valley, and that meant snow in Maidan. Thus it may be that the pacific bearing of the Malikdin Khels in aiding the passage through the defile meant that they too saw signs of the near approach of snow, and fearing that opposition would retard our evacuation of the country, did all in their power to see the force away, lest their wives and families should be exposed to the rigours of the high altitudes which they had taken up as refuge camps.

If the 7th had been a hard day, the night was worse for the troops of the advance brigade. The various parties which had been detached to take the spurs and crests commanding the camp went up there wet to the waist, and there they had to stay for the night. It was not a peaceful night for any, but Captain Macfarlane's picket passed the severest time. It has been told how this company of the Borderers dislodged the enemy by flank attack, but the tribesmen had only retired to a corresponding spur. Captain Macfarlane and his men had to crawl into the sungar, for to show on the crest was to be a mark to fifty rifles on the corresponding brow. The men climbed in and did what they could to strengthen the breastworks, and as they did so the enemy increased in force, the fire opening from other spurs. Midway between the two positions lay a couple of Pathan corpses, probably killed by a shell from Money's Battery, and time after time the tribesmen stole up behind the scrub bushes to attempt to carry them away; the Borderers also made an attempt to secure these dead, but both had to desist, as no man could face the open where they lay.

The night closed in, and with it rose the moon. Taking advantage of the shadow of the scrub jungle the enemy crept up, and so completely did they cover the sungar that two sentries who showed themselves for a second were shot dead. So close to the breastwork did they creep that they threw large stones into the barricade trusting to induce some one to show, and for hours they could be heard whispering and even cursing their opponents. A helmet placed upon a rifle-muzzle was riddled, and when at last the morning broke and supports had driven the enemy farther back, the tree behind the post was found to be stripped of its bark and lower leaves by the bullets which had struck it. The political opinion is that in the evening the Kuki Khels were joined by a number of Shinwaris from across the Afghan border, a matter of a couple of miles from the camp, and that the pickets were attacked so furiously in the hope that being held by British troops more Lee-Metfords might be secured. It is certain now that on the first occasion that Datoi was visited the Kuki Khels were joined by Shinwaris, as the spy who took the proclamation was present at the funeral of fourteen men whom the Borderers had killed, half of whom were transborder Shinwari.

The baggage continued to stream in up the defile until three o'clock in the morning, but, though the pickets were engaged all round the camp, the baggage came in unmolested. The rear-guard of the leading brigade was in camp about 10 A.M. on the 8th, followed by the head of the 4th Brigade, and it was evident that there would be no chance of Kempster's rear-guard being in all day.

On the morning of the 8th General Lockhart had intended to advance up the Rajgul Valley to complete the punishment of the Kuki Khels, but, with so many picket posts to be held, it was impossible, as there was not a sufficient force in camp; in fact, so heavy was the work on the men that several night pickets on relief had to be sent out again to support the day pickets.

The camp that morning was a wonderful sight. On either side of the nullah the field terraces were filling up, fed by the constant stream of transport which came struggling round the tower point out of the defile; animals and men worn, tired, and chilled to the bone. Among the fir-trees, on a slope above the camp, a party of Gurkhas were trying to dislodge a solitary Lee-Metford marksman who had found the range of the camp, and a smart fire ran along the crests as they turned him out. Below them another party of little marauders were dismantling the homestead of some local Khan, while below them, again, the men of a British regiment just in were busy drying their nether garments before a line of fires. Immediately below, the transport were in and picketed, and the little animals, ragged and bear-coated, were, after a twenty-four hours' fast, ravenously attacking the forage which a long train of mules had just brought in from up the valley.

So cold was it that the very transport animals were stamping to keep warm. Men of all denominations were flocking here and there to find wood for fires: outhouses, byres, mosques, and even graves were dismantled in the rush for fuel. Staff officers were hurrying backwards and forwards, wet to the waist, as half a dozen streams had to be waded before an order could be transmitted by hand across the river, and a section of mountain artillery was hurrying out to support a Sikh picket in difficulties. Thrusting the baggage aside, the big gun mules splashed up the river bed, guns and carriages clanking and rattling, as they covered the boulders at a slashing trot. Through a glass the Sikhs could be seen, and the constant firing was evidence of the work upon which they were engaged. The grim, stolid defenders of Gulistan were slowly turning the hated Pathan out of some position, and at one's very feet, in spite of the fact that they had slept in a watercourse all night, another party of the same great regiment were cheerily throwing up earthworks in the rice fields for night protection. The stream of baggage stopped for a moment, and two dust-stained Borderers cleared the way for the party, carrying down the corpses of the two men killed on picket the previous night. It was all stern reality here, and, as the first round from the guns then opened and the reverberating sound was thrown back and back again, one felt what an awful thing was war. Yet how callous were the rest! Around us fifty followers were cooking their first meal for many hours, and, warming by the fire, were fast forgetting the privations of the night. Even the stern reality would not move them, for the Lee-Metford marksman was in position again, and the "spit" of a Dum-Dum bullet was among the crowd. Then one of the poor wretches was hit; two men joined us to help him to a hospital which was being pitched in the neighbourhood, but the rest went on with their meal. It was nothing to them apparently that the Gurkhas above were still stalking the solitary rifleman. They took it as it came: *Kismet.*

Shortly after the 36th Sikhs, who had done rearguard to the brigade, arrived in camp. They were ordered to send a company to occupy a peak about two miles up the valley which covered the advance into the Rajgul defile. Lieutenant Van Someren went out in charge, and No. 5 Mountain Battery took up a position near the Gurkhas' camp to cover their advance. With their poshteens on their backs prepared for another dismal night, the Sikhs began the ascent of the spur; it was a rocky climb, but with excellent cover, as it was bushed with stunted holm oak throughout. When Van Someren was halfway up the enemy opened, and he then found that they were entrenched on the top in much greater force than had been anticipated. He flagged down for reinforcement, and General Westmacott, who was watching the operations from the position the guns had taken up, ordered up a company of the 3rd Gurkhas to support, and also a company of the 36th from camp to work along the picket ridge.

Lieutenant West took the Gurkhas up, and in an hour they had reached the Sikhs; in the meanwhile the defences on the summit had been heavily shelled by No. 5, and the Gurkha scouts turned out to occupy a parallel ridge in support of the main attack. West and Van Someren then advanced to the assault, Gurkhas and Sikhs covering each other with alternate independent firing, and by 4.30 in the afternoon they were into the position. It was a pretty skirmish to watch, and conducted with extreme coolness by the two subalterns in command, so much so that General Westmacott later complimented them both. One killed and three wounded were the casualties.

On December 9th, while the tail of General Kempster's Brigade, still unmolested, was coming through the Datoi defile, General Westmacott took a portion of his brigade to destroy the Rajgul Valley. The morning of the 9th showed how well the force was out of Maidan Tirah, for it had rained at Datoi during the night and the hills were white with snow a few hundred feet above us. It had probably snowed in Maidan. A defile led into the Rajgul Valley, while the valley itself was very like the reach at Datoi; it was thickly wooded on the left, with low rolling spurs of bare hills on the right. The pecu-

THE TIRAH EXPEDITION 243

liarity of the valley, which is the source of the Bara, is that it only boasts, practically speaking, one village, which is built after the Waziristan fashion in one huge block. General Westmacott took with him 100 rifles 3rd Gurkhas, 200 2nd P.I., 400 Bombay Pioneers, 150 Borderers, 200 36th Sikhs, a company of Scots Fusiliers as gun escort, and No. 5 and No. 8 Mountain Batteries. General Lockhart accompanied the force. There was a little opposition, and the Bombay Pioneers when told off to destroy the big village had some smart skirmishing with a few of the villagers who were covering the retreat of their womenkind and cattle. The village was completely gutted, the towers blown up, and the force returned to camp about 3 P.M. The tail of General Kempster's Brigade was then almost in, and by 5 P.M. the Gordon Highlanders, his rearguard, were into camp, and the whole force had made the Datoi defile passage without a hostile shot being fired. So far from molesting the rear-guard, as the force evacuated Bagh Camp, all sorts and conditions of tribesmen swarmed into camp to pick up what odds and ends remained, and they repeatedly had to be swept aside at the bayonet's point, taking the whole with great good humour. A Kamrai Jirgah was in on the 9th, and it was hoped that Colonel Warburton would be able to arrange as peaceful a passage down the Bara Nullah through their country as he had through the Malikdin. But a chapter of great events was at hand.

Immediately upon leaving Datoi the Bara Valley opens out and broadens until it is nearly a mile across, the river running in several streams. As the force retired, the right was commanded by immense wooded hills—hills that were almost cliffs down to the river bed. Not parallel ridges along which flanking parties could march, but succeeding peaks, which had in turn to be ascended and held, and in many cases with tribesmen to be dislodged. The left was a totally different country: in the first place, as a rule, the valley allows of cultivation, and the riverway terraced up until the low hills commenced; then the heights stretched away as bare spurs and uninviting hills until the rocky mountains which border the valley were reached. The breadth of the valley varied: at times it was as much as a mile across, but, mostly, the limit lay within a few hundred yards, and in several places it was little but a defile; never once could it be said that the river bed was out of rifle-range from either flank.

The order of the advance from Datoi on the 10th was: the 4th Brigade advance-guard, the 3rd bringing up the rear. From the moment the outlying pickets fell in from Datoi on the 10th till Barkai was reached on the 14th, it may be said that it was a general engagement, not only on the rearguard, but all down the line of advance of both brigades from front to rear. General Westmacott's Brigade led out in the following order: 36th Sikhs and 3rd Gurkhas advance-guard, and furnishing flanking detachments as well, 21st Pioneers with Sappers and Miners, the King's Own Scottish Borderers main body, with No. 5 (Bombay)

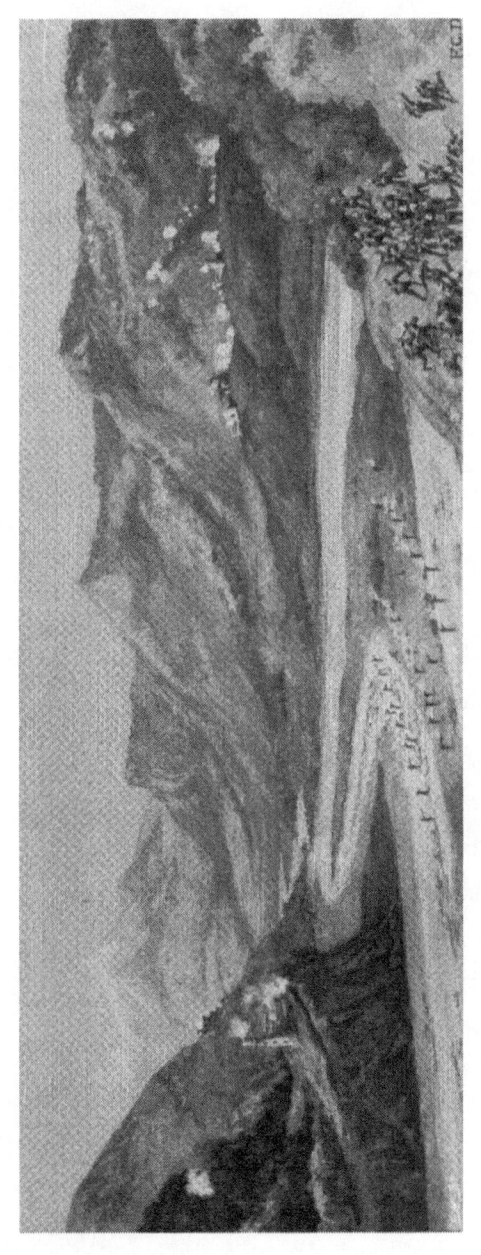

GENERAL WESTMACOTT'S BRIGADE DRAWING OUT THE ENEMY

THE TIRAH EXPEDITION 245

Mountain Battery and the Northamptons as rearguard. As soon as camp was struck the baggage moved in a broad front along the river bed, for the most part in the water, as the nature of the soil made the fields impossible for transport. The advance-guard led out of camp at 7.30 P.M., and at 8 both the 36th Sikh and Gurkha flanking parties were engaged in dislodging the enemy as they gathered on the hills and spurs. But the serious opposition to the advance-guard did not take place until about five and a half miles of the valley had been traversed. Here the river turns to the right, and the front of the advance was exposed to a fire from a heavily-fortified village which stood nestling at the base of a spur upon an extensively-terraced plateau. There were no less than ten towers in this village, and it seemed that the enemy had organised a stand. The Sikhs were extended and, with the battery shelling the commanding spur, skirmished up the terraces to the plateau. The towers were extremely skilfully situated, but the terraces gave the extended skirmishers excellent cover, and, after a brisk fusillade, the enemy evacuated and the village was taken. But this had caused a temporary check on the baggage, and, while the advance-guard was engaged, two riflemen armed with Lee-Metfords crept down to short range and fired into the baggage train. It was impossible to see them, and the startling crack of their weapons and sickening spit of the Dum-Dum bullet was all there was to discover them by on their first appearance. Before a party of Gurkhas could turn them out they had wounded three combatants, killed a follower, and wounded four others and two mules.

A mile farther brought the head of the column to the camping place, which was a strong village built into the river cliff on the left. The 36th Sikhs and part of the Gurkhas cleared the left, when suddenly the enemy opened a hot cross-fire from the right, where several towers and houses stood out among the trees. The 28th Bombay Pioneers and the rest of the Gurkhas became heavily engaged, clearing these villages and turning the enemy out of the wooded spurs above them, and, while camp was being formed in a dip between two spurs, a general engagement was taking place on every side, while skulkers were firing into the baggage from points which the outlying pickets had not reached. It was a wonderful panorama, for on every side you could see a battle being fought by the best skirmishers in the world.

Behind the camp the 36th Sikhs were scattered like a fan over the low-lying crest, creeping steadily outwards, while on the opposite plateau of the ravine the little Gurkhas were skirmishing among the houses, so close that, as the bullets fell among them, you could see the dust they raised. Stealthily, with the cover-taking instinct which is theirs by nature, they crept on, now behind a wall, now under the ledge of a terrace, until it was time to reach the dead ground on the left of the spur which was their object—across they go in spasmodic rushes, and though the enemy's fire raises a cloud of dust yet no man is down—and;

THE ENEMY OPENING FIRE ON THE ADVANCED GUARD FROM VILLAGES, TOWERS, AND WALLS

once they reach the spur, the Pathan falls back; he will not face an advancing Gurkha on a hillside. The camp pickets had taken their positions early in the afternoon, and there was time for a foraging party to go out. It secured its forage, but the escort became engaged among the houses and lost two men.

General Kempster's Brigade had not been able to reach the camp of the 4th Brigade, so it remained behind, and camped three miles higher up the nullah. As the Datoi pickets fell in, the enemy closed upon them, and they had their rear-guard harassed from the moment it left camp; in fact, a man of the Dorsets was shot as the regiment was waiting its turn to move off from camp. The total casualties for the day were seventeen, ten in the leading brigade and seven with the rear-guard. It had been a cold, overcast day, and it developed into a worse night, for about ten o'clock it commenced to rain, and in the dip where the camp lay baggage and troops were soon in a morass; a bitterly cold wind also rose just before daybreak. The enemy were prowling about all night, and at one time they crept close up to the Pioneers' camp, but they attempted no rush, and after a heavy fusillade drew off, having shot three men and several animals from the river bed. The camp was in the Sipah country, and it is interesting to note that the buildings of this section were the most solid and best-constructed that the force had found anywhere in the whole Afridi-Orakzai country. The towers were magnificent, being absolutely built in the hillside.

XXIV

The troops meet with no opposition on the march through the Zakka Khel country—The baggage take the wrong road, which causes a grave delay—Serious position of Major Downman and his soldiers—Captain Uniacke's bold conduct in attacking a village—Anxiety in the Sher Khel camp—Search party sent out—Block of General Westmacott's column in the river-bed—Afridis' coup in attacking the column—The march of Lockhart's 2nd Division a great military achievement—General Lockhart's order to G.O.C.

THE morning of the 11th dawned cold and miserable; it was sleeting hard, and the hilltops a few hundred feet above camp were wrapt in snow. The river, too, had swelled greatly. It was a miserable day, and, blue with cold, the advance-guard waded out into the river bed. General Westmacott moved his force out in the same formation, and the 3rd Gurkhas were engaged as the valley narrowed into a defile before making the right-angled bend to the right which brought us into the Zakka Khel section of the Bara Valley. Then there was a complete surprise, for the whole of the leading brigade marched through the Zakka Khel country with practically no opposition except from occasional invisible marksmen with Lee-Metfords. It is difficult to account for this strange action on the part of the tribesmen. It may be that the snow on the hilltops deterred them, or it may be that they anti-

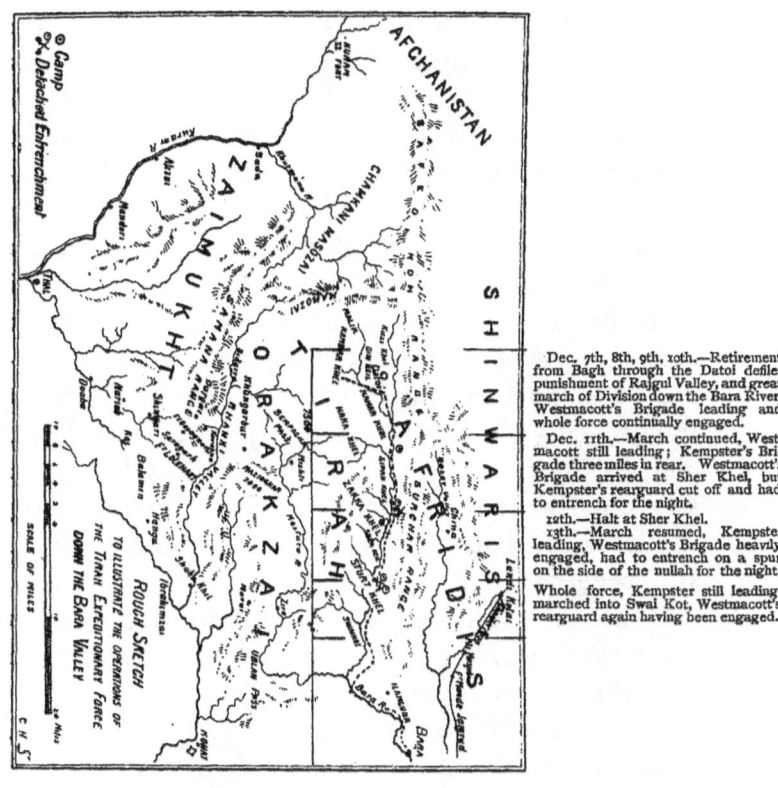

Dec. 7th, 8th, 9th, 10th.—Retirement from Bagh through the Datoi defile, punishment of Rajgul Valley, and great march of Division down the Bara River, Westmacott's Brigade leading and whole force continually engaged.

Dec. 11th.—March continued, Westmacott still leading; Kempster's Brigade three miles in rear. Westmacott's Brigade arrived at Sher Khel, but Kempster's rearguard cut off and had to entrench for the night.

12th.—Halt at Sher Khel.
13th.—March resumed, Kempster leading, Westmacott's Brigade heavily engaged, had to entrench on a spur on the side of the nullah for the night.

Whole force, Kempster still leading, marched into Swal Kot, Westmacott's rearguard again having been engaged.

cipated that General Lockhart would turn off into the Bazar Valley from below the Sipah country, and it may be—and the subsequent history of the day supports this theory—that they thought it better to let the leading force pass through, and to reserve themselves and their ammunition for the rear brigade, trusting to delay it so long that co-operation between the two brigades would be impossible.

Whatever the reason, General Westmacott's advance-guard barely fired a shot until the valley broadened out into the Aka Khel country. Here there was a change. The sheer, precipitous hills were found on the left, and the right rolled away in plateaux for quite a mile, this being the broadest portion of the valley in the hill country. On reaching Sher Khel village, which was the camp for the night, there was some small opposition from villages on either bank; but the advance-guard brushed such of the enemy as there were away, and it looked as if we were within sight of our goal without having severe fighting. The advance-guard of the 3rd Brigade almost caught up our rear-guard, and by four in the afternoon it seemed that the baggage of the rear brigade was coming along nicely, and that all would be in before nightfall. But they had had to come twelve or thirteen miles, and though the leading portion of the baggage was equal to the task, events proved that it was more than the rear could do.

As a matter of fact, the 3rd Brigade rear-guard, consisting of the Gordons, 1-2nd Gurkhas, and 2nd Punjab Infantry, were harassed by the enemy early in the day; and as the afternoon wore on they increased in numbers as only these frontier tribesmen can. As the flanking parties fell back to join the rear-guard, the enemy sprang up like the mountaineers of Roderick Dhu, and it was all the guns and troops could do to keep them at bay.

THE TIRAH EXPEDITION

Then, about three miles from camp, the baggage took a wrong road: leaving the river, they tried a plateau and became hopelessly mixed in the swampy rice fields. This caused a grave delay, for the enemy, seeing the opportunity they had waited for, outflanked the rear-guard, and began pouring a heavy fire into the baggage. The strain upon the force to supply flanking parties had been so severe that many men from the hospital escorts and baggage-guards had been withdrawn and used to dislodge the enemy from the commanding spurs. Thus, when the Pathans were almost among the baggage animals, panic seized the followers, and they deserted their animals and in some cases their doolies. As night began to fall Major Downman, of the Gordons, found himself with two weak companies of his regiment, two companies of the 1-2nd Gurkhas, a company of the 2nd Punjab Infantry, and details of the Dorsets, in a most serious situation: the guns not daring to be benighted had limbered up and pushed on, and the rear-guard remained with the enemy practically on all four sides of it, hampered with its own wounded—for men were falling fast—and stranded with doolies the native carriers of which had fled. In fact, men and officers were carrying the doolies themselves.

The enemy, growing more daring, were now among the bushes, a few yards alone separating the combatants, and there were no men left to guard the flanks. Captain Uniacke, retiring with a few of the Gordons, saw that there was only one course left: they must entrench for the night. He was in advance of the actual rear-guard, attempting to hold a flank, opposed to the fire of quite a hundred tribesmen in a village. That village was the only place which they could hope to defend with success, and Uniacke conceived the bold idea of rushing it. Collecting four men of his regiment, and shouting all he knew, they rushed at the doorway. In the dusk the enemy were uncertain of the numbers of their assailants, and, with their horror of the bayonet, fired one wild volley and fled. Captain Uniacke, to continue the ruse, climbed to the roof, shouted words of command as if he had a regiment behind him, and then blew his whistle continually to attract the rear-guard as they passed in the dark. The whistle was heard, and by driblets they fell back with the wounded upon the house. It was a poor place, but it was capable of defence. The wounded and dead, twenty-one in all, were brought in and placed under the only roof, and the force distributed for defence. But once they were behind walls the firing slackened, for the Pathans knew that there was loot lying in the palms of their hands all along the river bed.

As night wore on in Sher Khel camp, the greatest anxiety prevailed, especially when odd transport officers and units dribbled in and reported that the tribesmen were looting and cutting up followers within a mile of camp, and had no news to give of the four hundred men that composed the missing rear-guard. So anxious were the Headquarter Staff that Colonel Dixon was asked to send out a company of the Borderers to do what they could—this being the first time during the campaign that men other than the Gurkha scouts had been sent out at night. Lieutenant MacAlister took them out, and he went about a mile up the nullah, and was able to collect many followers and baggage animals, but he found

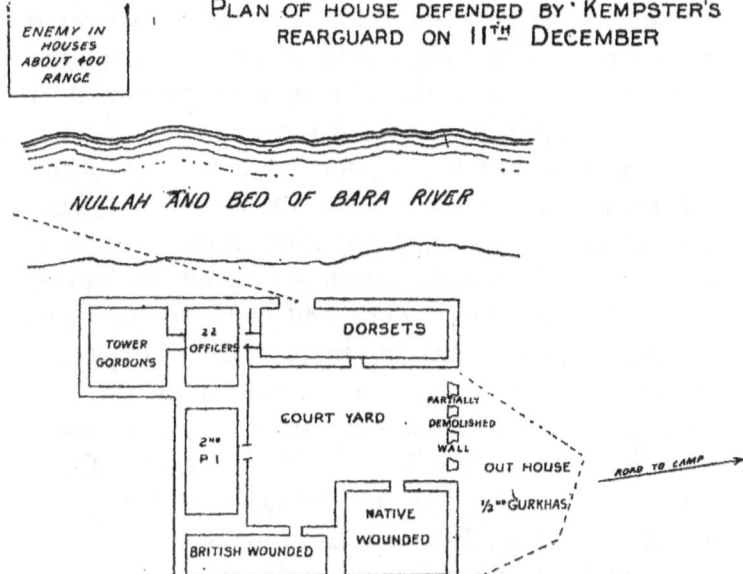

no sign of the enemy or the lost rear-guard, neither could he hear any firing.

Early in the morning of the 12th a company of the 2nd Punjab Infantry went out as a search party and got into communication with the rear-guard. They were safe in the house, but unable to move, being hampered with the wounded without means of moving them, and had the enemy all round them. The Borderers, Dorsets, and a Mountain Battery went out with General Kempster to bring them in. The defenders of the little blockhouse had had a terrible night, as, except where the wounded were laid, they had been unable to light a fire, and the exposure, wet to the waist as they were, had been terrible. Moreover, in the morning they became aware that the enemy commanded them through a gap in the wall, for the hillmen suddenly, as soon as it was light, poured in a volley which killed one and wounded four of the Gordons. They were brought into camp, together with as much of the baggage as could be found, but the enemy had secured a considerable amount, and had stripped many wretched followers, leaving them to die of exposure, and had shot others. The casualties of the day were: 3rd Brigade: one hundred and fifty animals, about one hundred followers. Combatants: forty-one, including Lieutenant Williams and Captain Norrie wounded; fourteen Gordons wounded, four killed; making the most serious day that the force had had since Saran Sur. The enemy were supposed to be chiefly Zakka Khels, Aka Khels, and Sepah Khels. As a matter of fact, it was not until the 11th that the enemy had actually realised that the force was retiring by the Bara Nullah, and they had now gathered to reap what benefit they could from the military disadvantages they knew the force to be labouring under. General Westmacott's great rear-guard action of the 13th showed in what force and spirit they could gather.

THE TIRAH EXPEDITION

Owing to the necessity of sending out part of the 4th Brigade to support the cut-off rear-guard of the 3rd Brigade, it was impossible to proceed on the 12th with the march to Barkai, so the whole force halted at Sher Khel, and the Sappers and Pioneers did their best to make ramps and roads out of camp into the riverway. Much of the missing baggage was recovered, but the Pathans had made a haul, and the last two miles of camp bore evidence of what had been the end of many of the missing followers. Some had been shot, others hacked to death, but the majority had died from exposure after having been robbed of all their clothes. The experience in the block-house had been terrible, for though there were two medical officers there, they could do little, as they were practically without appliances. Captain Norrie suffered terribly. He had been wounded early in the day, the upper part of his arm being shattered by a Dum-Dum bullet, but he bore up wonderfully in spite of the trying situation.

But back to the 12th. Throughout the day there were evidences that the enemy were still hanging about, for the outlying pickets were constantly fired into, but at no time did they show in force, though, as night fell, they crept up and fired into camp with great persistency, wounding several animals and followers. It was hoped that Barkai would be reached on the 13th and the dispositions were made accordingly. The order of the brigades was changed: the 3rd was to lead, having made over the second battery of artillery to the 4th for service in the rear-guard; it was also ordered that the flanking parties posted from the advance-guard were to remain in position until the baggage of the whole division was past. This was a change on the previous order of advance, when each brigade had been responsible for its own flanking parties. It was understood from the Political Officers that the force had only three miles of hostile country before it, that at the village of Guli Khel the end of the Aka Khel Afridis was reached, and the force, here turning off from the river bed into a camel path, would be in Stouri Orakzai country, which with the rest of the Orakzai was friendly.

The advance-guard of General Kempster's Brigade, consisting of the 2nd Punjab Infantry, and 1st and 2nd Gurkhas, marched out of camp at 7.30, and the scouts of the 5th Gurkhas were told off to burn and destroy all villages on either side of the nullah. The baggage of the division followed after General Kempster's mainguard. Directly the camp was left the Bara Nullah converged, and for half a mile the road lay through a narrow cutting. The drop being rapid, the Bara stream, already swollen by the melting snow, was literally a torrent, and the scene with the baggage in this cutting was one of extreme confusion. For, troubled by the memory of the past few days, a frenzied impetus had been engrafted in the generally apathetic followers, and men who had been used to dawdle and delay now showed an anxiety to press forward which it was almost impossible to control. And so, as the mass of baggage became heaped in the cutting, the scene became one

SAVING THE BAGGAGE IN THE REAR-GUARD ACTION

December 13

of terrible confusion. Once this defile was passed and the valley opened out again to a river reach, the baggage moved forward on a broad front with fevered despatch, but under perfect control. The last march on the Bara River found the country on the left more open, but steep and severe again on the right. The left inclined in easy slopes towards the enclosing range, and it was over one of these slopes that the Guli Khel camel road lay. The leading brigade had but little opposition. The flanking parties in places found stray groups of the enemy, who waited to be dislodged; and Lee-Metford sharpshooters again were present, killing two men of the 2nd Punjab Infantry early in the day. But the village of Guli Khel was reached, and the 3rd Brigade went over it without serious opposition. As the branching-off of this Guli Khel route has significance in relation to the tactics displayed by the enemy during the later part of this eventful day, the country will bear some minute description.

Guli Khel stands on the left bank of the Bara River, and immediately below it the nullah becomes a narrow gorge as the mountains close in, and, as in the gorge passed earlier in the day, the drop in the bed is considerable, and the many channels of water converging, the flow is very deep and rapid. The gorge, too, extends and winds for several miles, so by taking a road over a neighbouring saddle a very uninviting spot is avoided. The path up from the river bed is narrow, but sufficient to allow of two laden mules using it abreast: it traverses a wild

R

country covered thickly with close bush jungle growing to six or seven feet. This path winds for a matter of six or seven miles over a low kotal until the Bara River bed is again reached, and the first ford is Barkai.

As was said above, General Kempster's advance-guard was well into the camel road and the necessary hills were flanked by midday; in fact, his advance-guard was so far forward that by 3 P.M. it met the Oxfordshire Regiment, which was furnishing General Hammond's advance-guard, and which had come out seven miles from Swaikot to meet the force. But the baggage of a division moving on a big front is one thing, and the same transport filing out of a river cutting in pairs is another, and there was necessarily a lengthy block below Guli Khel. In the meantime matters had assumed a serious aspect in the rear.

General Westmacott's orders were to leave Camp Sher Khel, as soon after the baggage was out as possible. But long before the 3rd Brigade animals were through the first defile General Westmacott's outlying pickets were hotly engaged, and the breaking-up camp was surrounded by a general action. Whether goaded by hatred of the invader, or influenced by the success which attended their struggle with General Kempster's rear-guard, one can only surmise, but it was upon this day that the Afridi had gathered in strength, and showed that enterprise and recklessness which he was far famed for upon the frontier, and which hitherto in the campaign has been conspicuous by its absence. The

THE TIRAH EXPEDITION

enemy crept up to within a few yards of the pickets, and as the latter fell back upon the camp, the tribesmen fell into the positions they had left almost as soon as they were evacuated. Followers and baggage animals were constantly hit as they were loading up, and at about half-past ten the rear-guard regiments marched out of camp under cover of artillery fire. Amid the smoke of burning Sher Khel it was impossible to distinguish friend from foe; the rear company of the Borderers thought that they were clear, when a man appeared running towards them from out the smoke. He was one of their own men, and within twenty yards of his own company had been hit in three places. As another company of the Borderers was forming up six men appeared in the smoke of a house that had just been fired. Being unarmed they were taken for drabies and ordered to leave camp and join their sections; in answer they produced rifles from their skirts, dropped to their knees, and opened fire.

These few incidents, among many, show with what spirit the tribesmen commenced the day. General Westmacott's rear-guard was constituted as follows:—3rd Gurkhas under Lieutenant-Colonel Pulley; rear-guard, supported by the Borderers under Colonel Dixon, and 36th Sikhs under Major Des Vœux, Colonel Haughten being sick; No. 8 (British) and No. 5 (Bombay) Mountain Batteries, a wing of the Scots Fusiliers and the Northamptons forming the main body of the brigade. It was severe work holding the heights while the baggage was struggling through the first defile—how severe can be realised when within an hour the 3rd Gurkhas had expended their pouch ammunition, while by two o'clock each of the three regiments of the rear-guard had been forced to call up their first reserve mules. But the tribesmen, who were over-running the last camping ground like ants, were kept at bay until the last of the baggage was through the defile, and there the animals pushed on in a broad front as the valley widened out. But the extent of river bed to be traversed was only about three miles, and the baggage pressing forward at a fevered pace, the proximity and numbers of the enemy acting as an active stimulant to the followers and muleteers, it was not long before they reached the block caused by the narrowness of the path, and the whole river reach became blocked with animals and doolies. Wounded were coming in fast from the front, and this, with the knowledge that men with Lee-Metfords were skulking among the bushes on the mountainside, did not add to the composed feelings of the followers.

As a matter of fact, the enemy had realised that this block would take place, and it was evident as soon as the first defile was in their possession that they had conceived the bold idea of so enveloping the right of General Westmacott's Column right on retirement—as to force him to continue to follow the river bed, which would have plunged him into the lengthy gorge already described, and once benighted in such a place, the Pathans would have gone very near bringing total disaster upon the force. Thus General Westmacott had to direct all his

THE TIRAH EXPEDITION

energy in defending his right, as the enemy could move with the greatest rapidity along the plateau at the foot of the farther hill. Here the Gurkhas were constantly heavily engaged, and at one time Lieutenant West's company was so closely invested on a ridge that his ammunition ran out, and the Gurkhas had to retire with fixed bayonets, with the tribesmen at their very heels, upon a company of Borderers commanded by Major Mayne. By four in the afternoon the whole of the rear-guard regiments were in the fighting line supporting each other, and both batteries and the Borderers' Maxim were in continual action along the river bed. The Afridis for the first time were clearly taking the initiative, and during the long anxious wait in the river bed, while the baggage was filing up the path which was to take them to the kotal, groups of tribesmen even in the river bed were often within two hundred yards of the guns—men were falling fast, and each casualty reduced the fighting strength, as three or four men were required to carry the wounded to the rear.

But Borderers, 36th Sikhs, and Gurkhas stood manfully to the task, and at last the animals were up out of the river bed and the main object of the tribesmen frustrated. As the last of the rear-guard reached the plateau, the enemy pressed under the cover of the cliff, cutting off the nullah below them. But the worst was not yet passed, for the river reach had been more or less open; the country to be traversed now became a rolling plateau inclining upwards, intersected with ravines and thickly covered with low jungle; so dense was the jungle that it gave cover up to within four or five yards of the fighting line. Of necessity the flankers of the retiring force had to close in, for the tribesmen, nimble as cats, were up on the plateau almost as soon as the rear-guard. General Westmacott directed the line of retirement to hug the foot of the hills as much as possible, but in such a country the retirement had to be very slow, and it was getting dark before the camp of General Kempster's Brigade could be reached.

To be benighted in such a country with the column on the move meant disaster, so General Westmacott selected a ridge which he determined to hold for the night. The wearied men were just forming up. There were but four hundred and fifty rifles left of the tired rear-guard regiments, to which were added two weak companies of the Fusiliers and four of the Northamptons. There was a lull in the firing, and all were trusting that the Orakzai country having been reached the Afridi enemy would desist. But it was a vain hope, for suddenly there was a cry, and the officers had only just time to throw out their men and extend them along the range before the enemy were upon them. The Afridis had evidently collected for this *coup*, and they made a terrific rush, so that even among the brushwood more Afridis were seen than had ever been seen collected at close quarters before. It was a trying time, for they came under the cover of a sweeping fire. For a moment it seemed that the men who had been fighting all day would be enveloped, over-run, and swept away. It was but momentary. The officers threw themselves into the line, magazines worked freely, and the very bushes seemed to fade away before the hail of lead from the defending spur; from the very bayonet-point the tribesmen were swept back—back into the closing darkness, and they never tried a second rush. But their fire had been heavy, and Lieutenant West was among the many victims.

After this attack had been repelled the firing slackened and gave time for a makeshift camp to be arranged and for the wounded to be tended. When it is remembered that the rear-guard lost that day one officer killed and three wounded, eighteen men killed, eighty-three wounded, and six missing, it can be realised how severe was the engagement, and how ably conducted by the General, officers, and troops taking part, when one knows that not a single mule or pack of baggage was left behind.

After the rush on General Westmacott's hurriedly-formed camp was repulsed, the enemy sheered off and contented themselves with firing a few shots into camp, especially when the moon rose. But it was a terrible time in camp. There was neither water, food, nor blankets for the troops, but scant succour could be afforded to the wounded who had not been sent on to camp, and the men, worn out by the longest day that even the oldest campaigner remembered, had ever the tension of a possible second attack hanging over them. The camp, too, was full of stories of what had happened. Captain Short was carried in badly wounded, and it seemed evident that among the bushes some small parties had been cut off and annihilated; but at night it was impossible to make certain. A section of the Scots Fusiliers were reported missing, also some Sikhs of the Jhind Imperial Service; altogether it was a trying night, so great being the suspense that General Westmacott would not leave the sentry line, and took what rest he could at the heels of his in-lying pickets. Early in the morning the action recommenced, and the enemy tried hard to work in between the pickets on the hillsides and the moving force. But stubbornly disputing each successive ridge the rear-guard fell back, at times almost at hand-to-hand conflict with the tribesmen in the bushes. The kotal was reached, and even then the enemy did not stop, but continued to harass the retirement down to the river again. But here the picket posts of the 9th Gurkhas of the Peshawar Column were reached, and the action which had commenced on the 7th at Datoi was over at midday on the 14th at Barkai, the retirement from Tirah having been accomplished with the loss of one hundred and sixty-four killed and wounded, one hundred and eleven of whom were from General Westmacott's Brigade, known in the forces as the "Fighting Brigade."

As a military achievement this march of Lockhart's 2nd Division will live in the military history of the century. There may be those who believe that it is a small thing for a large force to march through the country of an enemy numerically their inferiors; but all who took part in that terrible day, December 13th, know too well what advantages lie even with an

THE TIRAH EXPEDITION 265

inferior force. Each single rifleman of the enemy, complete master of his weapon of precision, posted in a perfect situation, cragsman and mountaineer from his earliest youth, is equivalent in a defile valley such as the course of the Bara River to ten or more men hampered with baggage, supported by artillery, and retiring down a river bed. Nobody who was not there can conceive what was asked of the troops, British and Native, in that terrible march. Those who saw the men march into Swaikot can perhaps appreciate something, and those who saw the stream of wounded preceding them perhaps more.

There was no doubt about the force of the enemy; it was not half a dozen well posted marksmen, but wild tribesmen in thousands, men intoxicated with the fire of fanaticism, thirsting with a lust for the spoils of war, and maddened with the memory of what the invader had done for them. Of how steady our men stood, how Gurkha aided Borderer and Sikh supported Gurkha into that line of death, it is impossible to say enough; but the situation was such that if it had not been for the staunch coolness of the officers and magnificent example and clear direction of General Westmacott, the enemy were in sufficient force to have annihilated the rear-guard. I would not for a moment say that such an issue was ever imminent; it would be unfair upon the magnificent regiments responsible for the passage of the army. But this I will say, that General Westmacott's action was fought against superior numbers, and that the advantages which we held in magazine fire and artillery support were outbalanced by the disadvantages of the country traversed, and the fact that this country was being retired through. Moreover, the hillmen were practically fresh; the retiring force had been constantly engaged for six days in succession. With such conditions one mistake might easily have grown to a serious disaster. No mistake was made in the rear brigade : with perfect confidence in themselves and their General, each regiment supported the other, and then with one united effort, magnificent after so terrible a day, swept away the final blow which the enemy had calculated would completely break them. Never recently have the traditions of our service, British and Native, been better upheld than they were on December 13, 1897.

On arrival at Swaikot, General Lockhart issued the following order to G.O.C. the 4th Brigade : "To G.O.C. 2nd Division. General Lockhart will be obliged if you will convey to the Officer Commanding 4th Brigade his appreciation of the excellent work done by himself, his Staff, and the troops under his command, on December 13 and 14, when a very difficult operation was most successfully carried out. Sir William Lockhart regrets the many hardships to which the troops covering the withdrawal from Tirah were exposed, but they were unavoidable." The casualty list for the eight days is as follows: 3rd Brigade (General Kempster) December 10, 7; 11th, 41; 13th, 5—total 53. Fourth Brigade (General Westmacott) December 7, 4; 8th, 6; 9th, 3; 10th, 12; 11th, 4; 12th, 4; 13th, 70; 14th, 8—total 111.

THE TIRAH EXPEDITION 267

It has been impossible to estimate up to date the loss of followers and baggage animals in the action of the 11th, but in round numbers the 3rd Brigade lost one hundred and fifty animals and about one hundred followers on that date. But the loss of followers may, it is hoped, be less, as many units are known never to have rejoined their centres, but to have hung about and seized the first opportunity of pushing through to India. Over thirty of such deserters were apprehended at Swaikot.

To return to the 3rd Brigade: it had a quiet night on the 13th, and the force marched into Swaikot (Barkai) on the morning of the 14th. General Sir William Lockhart and Staff arrived first about 10 A.M., and the guards turned out to give full military honour. Then the advance-guard arrived. Colonel Mathias was marching at the head of the Gordon Highlanders. The troops in camp massed on each side of the roadway and cheered their campaign-stained comrades, and it was almost a pathetic sight to see men of the Inniskillings and Oxfords passing cakes and pieces of bread and cheese and hot cocoa to their battle-begrimed comrades. It was more a depressing sight than a military spectacle—rather it was the dark side of war—for the men were all drawn, pinched, dishevelled, and thoroughly worn. They were fit and hard, but they bore on their faces the undoubted marks of the awful time which they had just passed through. And then after the advance-guard came the dead and wounded, mostly carried on stretchers; the long line filed in, many carried on beds seized from the villages passed, others, with their pale drawn faces wincing in agony, riding rough hospital mules. In they came—officers, men, Highlanders, Lowlanders, Sikhs, Bombay Pioneers, and little Gurkhas, a quiet line which was allowed to pass in reverent silence. Thus they filed on until the head of the 4th Brigade appeared : the men who had covered themselves with glory in the last twenty-four hours, men even more marked by hardship, privation, and the anxiety of human strife than the Fighting Brigade that had proceeded them, because they were latest from the field; in fact, they were carrying their wounded of the morning with them. Thus the rear-guard marched in and encamped at Manmani, and the first phase of the Tirah Expedition was over—it had cost us thirteen hundred fighting men.

XXV

Khyber Pass reported deserted—Ali Musjid occupied without a shot being fired—Colour-sergeant Walker captured and retained as a hostage.

CAMP SHAHID MILLS, KHYBER,
December 24th.

IT was thought that possibly after the trying time in the Bara Valley the operations of opening out the Khyber and visiting the Bazar Valley would be left to General Symonds, as Sir William Lockhart was more than indisposed. But with his characteristic determination, the future Commander-in-Chief elected to bring the active operations of the winter campaign to a close in person. The following disposition of the forces was made. The 2nd Division was to hold the Bara Valley from Bara to Barkai, while the 1st Division and the Peshawar Column concentrated at Jamrud. It took a little over a week for the necessary commissariat arrangements to be completed, and on the 22nd the whole force was fully equipped. The Peshawar Column was to march up the Khyber and open the communications as far as Lundi Kotal, at once setting to work to reconstruct the dismantled posts. The 1st Division's destination was the Bazar

Valley, and General Lockhart was to accompany it there.

All reports from the pass and the opinions of the various officers who had conducted reconnaissances up as far as Fort Maude were that the Khyber was absolutely deserted, and that the re-occupation would be effected without the firing of a shot. On the morning of the 23rd General Hammond marched from Jamrud Fort to the head of the pass, Bagiari Dhara. As had been anticipated, there was no sign of an enemy, and the advance-guard wound its way unmolested up to Ali Musjid. Military precautions had been taken, and the Bagiari heights were occupied by a mountain battery and a strong picket of the 1st Gurkha Rifles. From this hill, which commands the whole pass to the full limit of nine-pounder range, a magnificent view presents itself. Behind you lies the Peshawar Vale, and in front of you the Khyber winds its tortuous way amid a labyrinth of low hills, and the great pass, with all its traditions and its points of recent pathetic interest, lies clearly mapped at your very feet.

Far away on either hand stretch the low hills—scenes of many an ancient fight, to say nothing of recent events—the Kohat Pass, the Jowaki country, the mouth of the awful Bara Valley that is still so marked in our memory. To the right lies the entrance to the Mohmund country, and the historical Shabkadr Plateau, where on four separate occasions the hill-men and the Indian army have come to close hostility; and then still farther right rises the black peak of the Malakhand, destined of recent years to

THE TIRAH EXPEDITION 271

mark the military history of the country; while behind one at the foot of Bagiari is Jamrud, tomb of some past Sikh General and now surrounded by a sea of dust-driven canvas. Away over the green pastures of fertile Peshawar tehsil winds the pillar of dust which marks the train of burden animals, feeding the long snake-like line now winding into the Khyber, past Hari Singh Ke Burj until it is lost in the plantations which surround Peshawar city. The view is one of pathetic interest, for of a truth from the days of Alexander may the Bagiari Dhara be called the Gate of War!

Thus has Ali Musjid been occupied again without a shot being fired, a move which has been expected for months, but which for some reason the authorities have refused to take. Whether the good gained by the gentle hint which the relinquishing was evidently meant to convey to the Amir has outbalanced the loss of prestige which certainly took place, I must leave for others to argue and decide, but there is no doubt that the effect was great, for even in Jedda and Yembo it was publicly declared that the British arms had been reversed, and the garbled reports did not arrive without embellishments, reporting disaster and ruin to the Kafir and success to Islam. Be that as it may, General Hammond occupied Ali Musjid on the 23rd, and to-day General Lockhart has marched with the 1st Division and encamped beyond the Shagai heights, the brigades halting at the spots from which to commence their separate marches into the Bazar Valley to-morrow.

General Lockhart, who is still far from well,

accompanies General Hart's Brigade taking the Chura Khandas route, General Symonds goes with General Gaselee viâ the Alarchi. The expedition is rationed for a week, and two days' rations are to be pushed up by General Hammond to meet it at Lundi Kotal. At this period prophecy is unprofitable, but there seems a general impression that the tribesmen, upon the evacuation of Tirah, have been able to come together, and having discussed the situation are inclined to patch up the quarrel. There is no doubt, gainsay it who may, that they have all been reduced to the greatest straits by the occupation; moreover, the continued closure of the Khyber has brought gentle reminders from across the northern border, that it is not a war favoured of the Faithful. Thus probably, though we can hardly anticipate a pacific exit from Bazar, it is possible that the presence of a force in the Bara Valley, prepared to take the aggressive in the spring, will be sufficient to bring the campaign to a close.

The fact that Colour-sergeant Walker was captured and kept alive by the Zakka Khels has been pathetically proved, as a letter has come in from him. It is a manly sort of letter for a man in his terrible position, and to add to his trouble he has been hit by a bullet about an inch above the elbow. Apparently the tribesmen are treating him well. But it is a ticklish position for the Political Officers, as the Zakkas are bent upon playing their prisoner off as a hostage. Colonel Aslam Khan, of the Khyber Rifles, has received several letters from the Zakka Khel Jirgah, and it may be that they are only temporising to save the destruction of their village; but, as I said before, all prophecy is unfruitful. The weather has changed for the better. It threatened to rain two days ago, but it is bright again now, though we may possibly spend a "seasonable" Christmas on the pass to-morrow.

XXVI

Christmas Day and letters in camp—Account of Chena village—Enemy engage the Yorks in a smart flanking skirmish—Sir William Lockhart's plan of campaign changed—End of winter campaign and its result.

FORT JAMRUD,
December 28th.

THE force is practically back from the Bazar Valley, that is, headquarters are in Jamrud, the 2nd Brigade at Lala Chena in the Khyber, and the 1st Brigade at Chura in the Malikdin end of the Bazar Valley. As shown in a previous letter, the division had concentrated at Lala Chena the day following that on which General Hammond's Column had marched up the Khyber, namely, Christmas Eve, and the whole force had been distributed into three columns, General Hammond to open out the Khyber up to Lundi Kotal, and, if necessary, to co-operate with the column returning over the passes from Bazar; General Symons with General Hart's Brigade to take the Alarchi route into the valley by Karamna, Burg, and Walai; General Gaselee, with his brigade, accompanied by army headquarters, entering by the Chura Pass, and timed to arrive at Walai simultaneously with General Symons' Column.

The general move was made on Christmas morning, and as the 2nd Brigade wound into the big nullah at the foot of Ali Musjid Fort, a dull and dreary Christmas dawned. There was a great block of transport in the nullah, as the different columns, on leaving Lala Chena camp, branched off from this point. Thus there was ample time to direct one's attention to the historical memories of the place.

There stood Ali Musjid, the conical hill which for thousands of years has been the turning key of probably the most bloodstained mountain highway in the world. There it stood, just as the plundering hands of the tribesmen had left it four months ago. The defences, as far as solid masonry and stonework are concerned, were intact, except in the places where the tearing away of woodwork had moved the mortar with it. Wherever roofs and penthouses had stood, the red stone of the uprights was blackened and smoke-begrimed; and thus stood Ali Musjid, a well-preserved skeleton of what it had been and what it will shortly be again. The Chura road branched out from the Khyber to the south, and an excellent baggage track wound over the low Khyber country. It was a bleak country to be crossed, bleak as are all the collection of small hills which lie between the Bara River and the Kuki Khel country; and the path wound upwards for seven miles before anything but scrub jungle and bare rock was visible.

But the road was good, as the rock is soft and shaley, and as before the Khyber days this was one of the principal routes to Afghanistan, years of traffic have worn a decent path. After the seventh mile a low kotal was crossed, and the path dropped down to the Bazar River. All this was Malikdin territory, and opposition was not anticipated, especially as we were due to camp in the vicinity of the village of one. Yar Mahamad, a Malik who had surrendered certain of the captured mule drivers. As the river was neared, the country lost its arid appearance, and adjacent to the stream were strips of green field hedged with trees. Chura boasted half a dozen walled dwellings and as many towers, and there were a certain number of the cave dwellings of which we have heard so much. For the most part they are but holes caused by the action of water in the peculiar shaley soil. The marks of smoke at their entrances and the litter of straw show that they are used as habitations; but they can be but squalid, uncomfortable dwellings at the best. Some few of the larger ones were walled at the entrances, and had wooden doors.

The camp formed in the terraces close to the river bed, the army headquarters occupying the house of an unkindly Malikdin Khel. Owing to the narrow front with which the baggage had to advance, the rear-guard was not into camp until late; but a post came on, and this is an incident well worthy of notice. Nearly every one at headquarters either received a Christmas card or home letter that Christmas Day, which is a golden advertisement for Mr. Van Someren and the Field Postal Service. Somehow, even though the force was on light service scale, bottles of good wine circulated that night,

THE TIRAH EXPEDITION

plum puddings for the first time graced Bazar Valley tables, and the combustible nature of the houses of the invaded made excellent bonfires. Thus in spite of the grotesque surroundings, the traditions of the season were maintained. The original plans had been for General Gaselee's Brigade to march to Walai on the 26th, but the knowledge of the route and country to be traversed was so meagre that in the next twenty-four hours after leaving Chura the whole complexion of the expedition was changed. General Gaselee, with the Yorks and Gurkha scouts as advance-guard, started down the bed of the Bazar River, which was a cutting perhaps a hundred yards across, narrowing eventually about three miles from camp into a steep cliffed gorge known as the Thanda Thangi.

Up to the Thangi in the immediate vicinity of the river the country was wooded, fertile, and picturesque; but once the gorge was through, the real barren nature of the Bazar country began to declare itself. The force pushed on rapidly, as there had been no opposition, and the baggage was able to move in a broad front without a check. After the gorge there was no water, the road becoming simply the dry bed of a nullah. But, throughout, the slopes and spurs which lead to the nullah readily lent themselves to the covering of the passage of the force. About midday, when it was more or less expected that General Hart's advance-guard would be made and Walai reached, the nullah suddenly turned to the left past a precipitous bank for several hundred yards, and then skirted the highest and steepest continuation of the Bara watershed that we had yet struck. On the right a distinct roadway led up to a couple of hundred feet to a length of sky line which looked like a plateau.

Once on this sky line and you are in the Bazar Valley proper—a huge rolling plain lies before you. As far as eye can reach it stretches away to the Afghan border, while to right and left its boundaries must lie ten miles apart. This was the home of the Zakka Khels. Once in the Bazar Valley it is easy to appreciate the causes which have outlawed the Zakka Khels, even among their own tribes; for their valley is a fit type of the "desolation of desolation:" it is one arid, bare, rocky wilderness, and as you stood at the entrance, not a vestige of human habitation or existence could be seen, save for the weary track which faltered its way among the rocks and boulders. But for occasional nullahs it is an absolute rolling plain, much more so than Maidan or any of the Tirah valleys; in fact, the Bazar Plain is the first ground that cavalry could usefully operate over that we have seen since the Mohmund plateaux. Down the middle of the valley runs a solitary spur, perhaps a thousand feet high, and the guides pointed out this as the covering hill to Chena, the principal Zakka Khel centre. It was then evident that the movement of the force had been more rapid than had been anticipated, for we were not timed to reach Chena until the 27th. But, as it was early yet and the baggage well up, Sir William Lockhart resolved to push on the three miles across the open plain to Chena. Of General

THE TIRAH EXPEDITION

Symons with the 1st Brigade there was no news, and it being cloudy, helio communication was not practicable.

Chena village, which we had been led to believe was a huge settlement and emporium of all the wealth of the princes of Himalayan robbers, proved itself to be in keeping with the desolate plain in which it stood. A collection of walled houses nestle on the banks of a nullah at the foot of the solitary spur, overlooking, perhaps, half a dozen acres of arable land, the only sign of cultivation that was visible in the whole valley. The majority of houses are in themselves poor ones, many being semi-caves and natural shelters. There were some walled and towered defences of great strength for their class, which showed that the place, if not overflowing with bandits' gains, was at least looked upon as a robbers' stronghold. But it could in no wise be called an important spot, and bore no resemblance to the emporium and settlement which had been promised. The 3rd Sikhs and Yorks occupied it without a shot being fired, and it was found that everything that was movable had been taken away, the fodder stacks even having been burned.

But there were tribesmen about, for, as a York picket fell in from the crest of the high hill, before mentioned as being the first direct spur of the Bara watershed, they were immediately followed up by a party of riflemen who had been waiting this opportunity, and a smart flanking skirmish ensued, in which the Yorks lost one killed and two wounded. The same party of tribesmen also fired into the

4th Gurkha rear-guard as they closed up from the sheer cliff in the nullah to the plateau crest line, killing one Gurkha rifleman and wounding another. The spot chosen for the camp was the same spot where General Maud's force encamped during the Afghan War, and in which, the *Gazetteer* says, they spent such an unpleasant night. At first it seemed that we were also to spend an unpleasant night, for as the pickets were taking up their positions for the night along the solitary spur, the extreme left picket of the Yorks was fired into at about a thousand yards, and two men were hit, one poor fellow dying during the night. Major Logan-Home, who had climbed the spur to try and find communication with General Hart's Column, also reported that with a telescope he could see armed bodies of men moving on both sides of the plain. Helio or flag communication was impossible, but a runner came through from the missing brigade, and reported them to be at Karamna and Burg, having found great difficulty in crossing the dividing range by the Alarchi route.

Having seen this much of the Bazar Valley, Sir William Lockhart changed his plan of campaign, and, instead of halting for a day at Chena, it was in orders that night that on the morrow the 2nd Brigade would, after having destroyed and razed Chena, return to the Khyber by the same route along which it had advanced, the 1st Brigade marching in its rear from Walai. There were several reasons for this move. In the first place there was nothing beyond Chena to destroy; secondly, seeing how easy the Chura route was, it was not considered advisable to make the connecting passes between the Bazar Plain and the Khyber of easier passage than they are at present. Also by the Alarchi route there is not sufficient water for the following of a brigade, let alone a division.

A bitterly cold night was spent at Chena, for though it did not actually rain until the next day, yet a piercing wind swept across the plain and chilled every one to the bone. The camp had been laid with all due precautions, the rear protected by the outlying pickets on the spur, the front by a nullah. But though trouble was expected, except for the first York picket engagement there was no molestation, and the return march was commenced at daybreak. The Sappers had been at work late into the night preparing for the demolition of the strongholds, and as the baggage streamed across the plain explosion after explosion told how well they were doing their work. Large charges were used, and as the rear-guard of the 3rd Sikhs led out Chena was a mass of blazing ruins. With their heads turned homewards and in a broad front the baggage simply slanted along, and about ten, just before the Tangi, the 4th Gurkha advance-guard met General Symons and the advance outposts of General Hart's Brigade. This column had found the Alarchi route much more difficult than had been expected, and part of the road, which had been very precipitous, had been carried away. This so delayed the progress of part of the force that the rear-guard did not reach Karamna until midday 26th, though the advance-guard had arrived there on Christmas Day. This part of the force spent a very unpleasant Yuletide on the pass top. There was certain desultory fighting, especially on arrival at Karamna, and a few casualties in the 30th Punjab Infantry, though no determined resistance was anywhere met with. Karamna was found to be a fortified village much like Chena, and not knowing the movements of the main column, General Symons did not destroy it, but proceeded to Burg, a similar village. From Burg the pickets pushed out, and made connection with the main body as described. Orders were then given for the 1st Brigade to encamp the night at Karamna, and, destroying it and Burg on the following day, to follow the 2nd Brigade viâ Chura to Lala Chena and the Khyber.

It appears that a party of about a hundred tribesmen, probably the men of Burg and Karamna, were hanging upon General Hart's right flank, for, as General Gaselee's rear-guard of the Queen's and 3rd Sikhs were retiring down the Bazar Nullah they suddenly heard yells and shouting on their right in retirement, and saw that a party of tribesmen had rushed a knoll which had recently been evacuated by one of General Hart's pickets. The unexpected falling in of this picket left General Gaselee's right exposed, and the rear-guard had a smart engagement for an hour before the flanking parties could make the passage secure. The Derajat Battery came into action, but the Queen's had six casualties and the 3rd Sikhs two before the Thangi was passed, after which there was no opposition. The rear-

THE TIRAH EXPEDITION

guard earlier in the day had evacuated Chena without opposition, though the tribesmen swarmed into the plain within range; yet they seemed more desirous of saving what wood they could from the flames than of engaging the invader. As far as the 2nd Brigade was concerned, hostilities ceased when the Thanda Thangi was passed and the force quietly encamped at Chura, in its original camping ground of Christmas Day. The night was an uncomfortable one, for the long-threatening rain came, and every one more or less got wet through. Army headquarters marched in the morning for Jamrud Fort, the brigade only making Lala Chena, and Sir William Lockhart left Ali Musjid by tonga for Peshawar. With the return of General Symons' and General Hart's Brigade (details not yet to hand) the active operations may be said to cease for the winter, Sir William Lockhart having gone direct to Pindi.

Thus ended the first phase of the campaign, which at one time was to have lasted a month, and which now promises to open again in the spring. The object of the invasion was to exact reparation from the tribesmen for their unprovoked attacks upon posts within the Peshawar and Kohat Borders. So far the military portion of the operations have been a success: Tirah has been invaded, every valley of the country has been traversed, and in those where the fines have not been paid the country has been swept with fire and sword. For four months the inhabitants have been fugitives from their homes, and the whole of an important frontier has been fully mapped and surveyed. There has been no means of dealing the enemy a crushing defeat; but the castigation has been so severe that all but a very few clans, the most recalcitrant of the nation, have sued for peace. Those that have opposed us to the end are clans which have little to lose, except their lives, by their dealings with us, and everything to lose by disarmament. But the Government of India have determined to make no discrimination, and unless there is an unconditional surrender on the part of all sections which aided or abetted the attacks upon our border, operations will recommence when the snow in Tirah has melted. To this end a force remains in occupation of the Bara Valley, and a division of three brigades holds the Khyber from Lundi Kotal to Jamrud.

XXVII

The Tirah Field Force.

THE MAIN COLUMN.

FIRST DIVISION.

First Brigade.

2nd Battalion The Derbyshire Regiment.
1st Battalion The Devonshire Regiment.
2nd Battalion 1st Gurkha (Rifle) Regiment.
30th (Punjab) Regiment of Bengal Infantry.
No. 6 British Field Hospital.
No. 34 Native Field Hospital.

Second Brigade.

2nd Battalion The Yorkshire Regiment.
1st Battalion Royal West Surrey Regiment.
2nd Battalion 4th Gurkha (Rifle) Regiment.
3rd Regiment of Sikh Infantry, Punjab Frontier Force.
Sections A and B of No. 8 British Field Hospital.
Sections A and C of No. 14 British Field Hospital.
No. 51 Native Hospital.

Divisional Troops.

No. 1 Mountain Battery, Royal Artillery.
No. 2 (Derajat) Mountain Battery.
No. 1 (Kohat) Mountain Battery.

Two Squadrons 18th Regiment of Bengal Lancers.
28th Regiment of Bombay Infantry (Pioneers).
No. 3 Company Bombay Sappers and Miners.
No. 4 Company Bombay Sappers and Miners.
One Printing Section from the Bombay Sappers and Miners.
The Kapurthala Regiment of Imperial Service Infantry.
The Maler Kotla Imperial Service Sappers.
Section A of No. 13 British Field Hospital.
No. 63 Native Field Hospital.

Second Division.

First Brigade.

1st Battalion The Gordon Highlanders.
1st Battalion The Dorsetshire Regiment.
1st Battalion 2nd Gurkha (Rifle) Regiment.
15th (The Ludhiana Sikh) Regiment of Bengal Infantry.
No. 24 British Field Hospital.
No. 44 Native Field Hospital.

Second Brigade.

2nd Battalion The King's Own Scottish Borderers.
1st Battalion The Northamptonshire Regiment.
1st Battalion 3rd Gurkha (Rifle) Regiment.
36th (Sikh) Regiment of Bengal Infantry.
Sections C and D of No. 9 British Field Hospital.
Sections A and B of No. 23 British Field Hospital.
No. 48 Native Field Hospital.

Divisional Troops.

No. 8 Mountain Battery, Royal Artillery.
No. 9 Mountain Battery, Royal Artillery.
No. 5 (Bombay) Mountain Battery.
Machine Gun Detachment, 16th Lancers.
Two Squadrons 18th Regiment of Bengal Lancers.
21st Regiment of Madras Infantry (Pioneers).

THE TIRAH EXPEDITION 287

No. 4 Company Madras Sappers and Miners.
One Printing Section from the Madras Sappers and Miners.
The Jhind Regiment of Imperial Service Infantry.
The Sirmur Imperial Service Sappers.
Section B of No. 13 British Field Hospital.
No. 43 Native Field Hospital.

LINE OF COMMUNICATION.

22nd (Punjab) Regiment of Bengal Infantry.
2nd Battalion 2nd Gurkha (Rifle) Regiment.
39th (Garhwal Rifle) Regiment of Bengal Infantry.
2nd Regiment of Punjab Infantry, Punjab Frontier Force.
3rd Regiment of Bengal Cavalry.
No. 42 Native Field Hospital.
No. 52 Native Field Hospital.
The Jeypore Imperial Service Transport Corps.
The Gwalior Imperial Service Transport Corps.
Ordnance Field Park.
Engineer Field Park.
British General Hospital, of five hundred beds, at Rawalpindi.
Native General Hospital, of five hundred beds, at Rawalpindi.
    No. 1 Field Medical Store Depôt. (For First Division.)
    No. 2 Field Medical Store Depôt. (For Second Division.)
    No. 5 Veterinary Field Hospital.
    No. 11 British Field Hospital, No. 25 British Field Hospital, No. 47 Native Field Hospital, No. 64 Native Field Hospital, for sick and wounded returning from the field.

THE PESHAWAR COLUMN.

2nd Battalion The Royal Inniskilling Fusiliers.
2nd Battalion The Oxfordshire Light Infantry.
9th Gurkha (Rifle) Regiment of Bengal Infantry.

45th (Rattray's Sikh) Regiment of Bengal Infantry.
57th Field Battery, Royal Artillery.
No. 3 Mountain Battery, Royal Artillery.
9th Regiment of Bengal Lancers.
No. 5 Company Bengal Sappers and Miners.
No. 5 British Field Hospital.
No. 45 Native Field Hospital.
British General Hospital, of two hundred and fifty beds, at Nowshera.
Native General Hospital, of five hundred beds, at Nowshera.

THE KURRAM MOVABLE COLUMN.

12th Regiment of Bengal Infantry.
The Nabha Regiment of Imperial Service Infantry.
3rd Field Battery, Royal Artillery, four guns.
6th Regiment of Bengal Cavalry.
One Regiment of Central India Horse.
Section D of No. 3 British Field Hospital.
No. 62 Native Field Hospital.
Section B of No. 46 Native Field Hospital.
Native General Hospital, of two hundred beds, at Kohat.

THE RAWALPINDI RESERVE BRIGADE.

2nd Battalion The King's Own Yorkshire Light Infantry. (At Rawalpindi.)
1st Battalion The Duke of Cornwall's Light Infantry. (At Rawalpindi.)
27th Regiment (1st Baluch Battalion) of Bombay (Light) Infantry, 2nd Regiment of Infantry, Hyderabad Contingent, Jodhpur Imperial Service Lancers, No. 12 British Field Hospital. (Already ordered to Rawalpindi.).
No. 53 Native Field Hospital. (At Rawalpindi.)
The above-mentioned troops will move on the field service strengths, establishments, &c., as laid down in the Field

THE TIRAH EXPEDITION

Service Equipment Tables for the different branches, except that the number of British Officers with Regiments of Native Cavalry and Native Infantry will not be increased above the authorised peace establishment.

COMMANDS AND STAFF.

Army Staff.

Lieutenant-General Commanding the Force, General Sir W. S. A. Lockhart, K.C.B., K.C.S.I.

Aide-de-Camp, Lieutenant F. A. Maxwell, 18th Bengal Lancers.

Aide-de-Camp, Second-Lieutenant J. H. A. Annesley, 18th Hussars.

Orderly Officer, Second-Lieutenant G. R. de H. Smith, Central India Horse.

Orderly Officer, Second-Lieutenant E. H. E. Collen, Royal Artillery.

Deputy-Adjutant-General, Chief of the Staff, Brigadier-General W. G. Nicholson, C.B.

Assistant-Adjutant-General, Brevet-Lieutenant-Colonel E. G. Barrow, 7th Bengal Infantry.

Assistant-Quartermaster-General, Major G. H. W. O'Sullivan, R.E.

Deputy-Assistant-Adjutant-General, Captain J. A. L. Haldane, Gordon Highlanders.

Assistant-Quartermaster-General for Intelligence, Colonel G. H. More-Molyneux, Assistant-Quartermaster-General.

Deputy-Assistant-Quartermaster General for Intelligence, Captain E. W. S. K. Maconchy, D.S.O., 4th Sikhs.

Field Intelligence Officer, Captain F. F. Badcock, D.S.O., 1st Battalion 5th Gurkhas.

Principal Medical Officer (with the temporary rank of Surgeon-Major-General), Surgeon-Colonel G. Tomson, C.B., Indian Medical Service.

T

Secretary to Principal Medical Officer, Surgeon-Major W. A. Morris, Army Medical Staff.

Brigadier-General Commanding Royal Artillery, Brigadier-General C. H. Spragge, Royal Artillery.

Brigade-Major Royal Artillery, Captain C. de C. Hamilton, Royal Artillery.

Orderly Officer, Royal Artillery, Major H. F. Mercer, Royal Artillery.

Ordnance Officer.

Brigadier-General Commanding Royal Engineers, Brevet Colonel J. E. Broadbent, R.E. (with temporary rank of Brigadier-General).

Brigade-Major Royal Engineers, Captain S. L. Craster, R.E.

Orderly Officer Royal Engineers, to be nominated by the Brigadier-General Commanding Royal Engineers.

Superintendent Army Signalling, Major G. J. N. Logan-Home, 1st Bedfordshire Regiment.

Headquarter Commandant, Captain R. E. Grimston, 6th Bengal Cavalry.

Assistant-Judge-Advocate-General, Captain F. J. S. Lowry, 29th Bombay Infantry.

Principal Provost Marshal, Lieutenant-Colonel E. Balfe Deputy-Judge-Advocate-General.

Commissariat Transport Officer, Captain G. W. Palin, Assistant-Commissary-General.

Staff Surgeon (from the Force).

Inspecting Veterinary Officer, Veterinary Lieutenant-Colonel B. L. Glover.

Chief Survey Officer, Brevet-Colonel Sir T. H. Holdich, K.C.I.E., C.B., R.E.

Principal Chaplain, Reverend E. T. Beatty.

Chief Superintendent of Post Offices.

Inspector of Post Offices.

| Lieut. E. H. E. Collen, R.A. *(A.D.C.)* | Major-Gen. Lord Methuen, C.B. | Capt. J. A. L. Haldane | Lieut. J. H. Annesley *(A.D.C.)* |

| Mr. White-King *(Political Officer)* | Lieut. G. R. de H. Smith, C.I.H. *(A.D.C.)* | Brig.-Gen. Nicholson, C.B. *(Chief of the Staff)* | Lieut. Maxwell, *(A.D.C.)* | Sir William Lockhart, K.C.B., K.C.S.I. | Sir Richard Udney, K.C.S.I. *(Chief Political Officer)* |

GENERAL SIR WILLIAM LOCKHART'S PERSONAL STAFF

THE TIRAH EXPEDITION

Main Column.

First Division.

Commanding (with the local rank of Major-General), Brigadier-General W. P. Symons, C.B.

Aide-de-Camp, Captain A. G. Dallas, 16th Lancers.

Assistant-Adjutant-General, Lieutenant-Colonel C. W. Muir, C.I.E., 17th Bengal Cavalry.

Assistant-Quartermaster-General, Major E. A. G. Gosset, 2nd Derbyshire Regiment.

Deputy-Assistant-Quartermaster-General for Intelligence, Captain A. Nicholls, 2nd Punjab Infantry.

Field Intelligence Officer, Lieutenant C. E. E. F. K. Macquoid, 1st Lancers, Hyderabad Contingent.

Principal Medical Officer, Surgeon-Colonel E. Townsend, Army Medical Staff.

Lieutenant-Colonel Commanding Royal Artillery, Lieutenant-Colonel A. E. Duthy, Royal Artillery.

Adjutant Royal Artillery, Captain W. K. McLeod, Royal Artillery.

Divisional Ordnance Officer, Captain A. R. Braid, Royal Artillery.

Commanding Royal Engineers, Lieutenant-Colonel H. H. Hart, Royal Engineers.

Adjutant Royal Engineers, Captain O. M. R. Thackwell, Royal Engineers.

Field Engineer, Major J. A. Ferrier, D.S.O., Royal Engineers.

Assistant Field Engineer, Lieutenant J. F. N. Carmichael, Royal Engineers.

Assistant Field Engineer, Lieutenant W. H. Bunbury, Royal Engineers.

Assistant-Superintendent Army Signalling, Captain H. T. Kenny, 2nd Bombay Lancers.

Provost Marshal, Captain H. W. G. Graham, D.S.O., 5th Lancers.

Field-Treasure-Chest Officer (from the Division).
Staff Surgeon (from the Division).
Roman Catholic Chaplain, Reverend Father N. J. Winkley.
Divisional Commissariat Officer, Major W. R. Yielding, C.I.E., D.S.O., Assistant-Commissary-General.
Assistant to Divisional Commissariat Officer, Lieutenant C. H. Corbett, 18th Hussars.
Divisional Transport Officer, Captain F. C. W. Rideout, Assistant-Commissary-General.
Assistant to Divisional Transport Officer, Captain A. W. V. Plunkett, 2nd Battalion The Manchester Regiment.

First Brigade of First Division.

Commanding, Colonel I. S. M. Hamilton, C.B., D.S.O. (with the temporary rank of Brigadier-General). Later: Brigadier-General R. Hart, V.C., C.B.
Orderly Officer, Captain C. O. Swanston, 18th Bengal Lancers.
Deputy-Assistant-Adjutant-General, Captain A. G. H. Kemball, 1st Battalion 5th Gurkhas.
Deputy-Assistant-Quartermaster General, Captain H. R. B. Donne, 1st Norfolk Regiment.
Brigade Commissariat Officer, Captain A. Mallaly, Deputy-Assistant-Commissary-General.
Assistant to Brigade Commissariat Officer, Lieutenant H. I. Nicholl, 1st Bedfordshire Regiment.
Brigade Transport Officer, Captain E. de V. Wintle, 15th Bengal Lancers.
Provost Marshal (from the Brigade).
Brigade Signalling Officer (from the Brigade).
Veterinary Officer, Veterinary Lieutenant H. T. W. J. Tatam.

Second Brigade of First Division.

Commanding, Brigadier-General A. Gaselee, C.B., A.D.C.

THE TIRAH EXPEDITION 293

Orderly Officer, Lieutenant A. N. D. Fagan, 1st Lancers, Hyderabad Contingent.

Deputy-Assistant-Adjutant-General, Major W. Aldworth, D.S.O., 1st Bedfordshire Regiment.

Deputy-Assistant-Quartermaster-General, Major A. A. Barrett, 2nd Battalion 5th Gurkhas.

Brigade Commissariat Officer, Lieutenant C. S. D. Leslie, Deputy-Assistant-Commissary-General.

Assistant to Brigade Commissariat Officer, Captain H. de la P. Gough, 16th Lancers.

Provost Marshal (from the Brigade).

Brigade Signalling Officer (from the Brigade).

Veterinary Officer, Veterinary Lieutenant W. F. Shore.

Second Division.

Commanding, Major-General A. G. Yeatman-Biggs, C.B.

Aide-de-Camp, Captain E. St. A. Wake, 10th Bengal Lancers.

Orderly Officer, Captain R. G. Brooke, 7th Hussars.

Assistant-Adjutant-General, Lieutenant-Colonel R. K. Ridgeway, V.C.

Assistant-Quartermaster-General, Major C. P. Taiscopp, D.S.O., Royal Artillery.

Deputy-Assistant-Quartermaster-General for Intelligence, Major R. C. A. B. Bewicke-Copley, King's Royal Rifle Corps.

Field Intelligence Officer, Captain H. F. Walters, 24th (Baluchistan) Regiment of Bombay Infantry.

Principal Medical Officer, Surgeon-Colonel G. McB. Davis, D.S.O., Indian Medical Service.

Lieutenant-Colonel Commanding Royal Artillery, Lieutenant-Colonel R. Purdy, Royal Artillery.

Adjutant Royal Artillery, Captain H. D. Grier, Royal Artillery.

Divisional Ordnance Officer, Captain H. F. Head, Royal Artillery.

Commanding Royal Engineers, Lieutenant-Colonel C. B. Wilkieson, R.E.

Adjutant Royal Engineers, Captain T. Fraser, R.E.

Field Engineer, Captain F. H. Kelly, R.E.

Assistant Field Engineer, Lieutenant W. A. Stokes, R.E.

Assistant Field Engineer, Lieutenant C. B. L. Greenstreet, R.E.

Assistant-Superintendent Army Signalling, Captain G. C. Rigby, 1st Wiltshire Regiment.

Provost Marshal, Captain W. C. Knight, 4th Bengal Cavalry.

Field Treasure-Chest Officer, Lieutenant W. M. Grimley, 20th Punjab Infantry.

Staff Surgeon (from the Division).

Roman Catholic Chaplain, Reverend Father A. Vanden Deyssel.

Divisional Commissariat Officer, Lieutenant-Colonel B. L. P. Reilly, Assistant-Commissary-General.

Assistant to Divisional Commissariat Officer, Lieutenant H. Macandrew, 5th B. C.

Divisional Transport Officer, Major H. L. Hutchins, Assistant-Commissary-General.

Assistant to Divisional Transport Officer, Major H. R. W. Lumsden, 3rd Bengal Infantry.

First Brigade of Second Division.

Commanding (with the temporary rank of Brigadier-General), Colonel F. J. Kempster, D.S.O., A.D.C.

Orderly Officer, Lieutenant G. D. Crocker, 2nd Royal Munster Fusiliers.

Deputy-Assistant-Adjutant-General, Major H. St. Leger Wood, 1st Dorsetshire Regiment.

Deputy-Assistant-Quartermaster-General, Major H. S. Massy, 19th Bengal Lancers.

Brigade Commissariat Officer, Lieutenant D. H. Drake-Brockman, D.A.C.G.

THE TIRAH EXPEDITION 295

Assistant to Brigade Commissariat Officer, Lieutenant F. W. Birch, 29th Punjab Infantry.

Brigade Transport Officer, Lieutenant R. A. N. Tytler, 1st Gordon Highlanders.

Provost Marshal (from the Brigade).

Brigade Signalling Officer (from the Brigade).

Veterinary Officer, Veterinary Lieutenant C. Rose.

Second Brigade of Second Division.

Commanding, Brigadier-General R. Westmacott, C.B., D.S.O.

Orderly Officer, Lieutenant R. C. Wellesley, Royal Horse Artillery.

Deputy-Assistant-Adjutant-General, Captain W. P. Blood, 1st Royal Irish Fusiliers.

Deputy-Assistant-Quartermaster-General, Captain F. J. M. Edwards, 3rd Bombay Light Cavalry.

Brigade Commissariat Officer, Captain E. Y. Watson, Deputy-Assistant-Commissary-General.

Assistant to Brigade Commissariat Officer, Lieutenant N. G. Fraser, 4th Bombay Cavalry.

Brigade Transport Officer, Captain W. H. Armstrong, 1st East Yorkshire Regiment.

Provost Marshal (from the Brigade).

Brigade Signalling Officer (from the Brigade).

Veterinary Officer, Veterinary Lieutenant F. W. Wilson.

LINE OF COMMUNICATION.

General Officer Commanding, Lieutenant-General Sir A. P. Palmer, K.C.B.

Aide-de-Camp, Lieutenant F. L. Galloway, R.A.

Orderly Officer, Lieutenant Deane, 12th Bengal Cavalry.

Orderly Officer, Lieutenant H. O. Parr, 7th Bengal Infantry.

Assistant-Adjutant and Quartermaster-General, Captain

(temporary Major) J. W. G. Tulloch, 24th Bombay Infantry.

Deputy-Assistant-Adjutant and Quartermaster-General, Captain I. Phillips, 1st Battalion 5th Gurkhas.

Principal Medical Officer (with the temporary rank of Surgeon-Colonel) Brigade-Surgeon-Lieutenant-Colonel W. E. Saunders, Army Medical Staff.

Senior Ordnance Officer, Colonel C. H. Scott, Royal Artillery.

Section Commandant, Captain O. B. S. F. Shore, 18th Bengal Lancers.

Section Commandant, Captain St. G. L. Steel, 2nd Bengal Lancers.

Section Commandant, Captain F. de B. Young, 6th Bengal Cavalry.

Lieutenant-Colonel Commanding Royal Engineers, Lieutenant-Colonel J. W. Thurburn, Royal Engineers.

Adjutant Royal Engineers, Captain H. V. Biggs, Royal Engineers.

Field Engineer, Captain C. H. Cowie, Royal Engineers.

Assistant Field Engineer, Lieutenant H. S. Rogers, Royal Engineers.

Assistant Field Engineer, Lieutenant R. P. T. Hawksley, Royal Engineers.

Assistant Field Engineer, Lieutenant A. E. Turner, Royal Engineers.

Provost Marshal, Major L. S. Peyton, 14th Bengal Lancers.

Staff Surgeon (from the Force).

Commissary-General, Colonel L. W. Christopher, Commissary-General.

Assistant to Commissary-General, Captain H. S. G. Hall, Assistant-Commissary-General.

Chief Transport Officer, Major H. Mansfield, Assistant, Commissary-General.

THE TIRAH EXPEDITION 297

Assistant to Chief Transport Officer, Captain T. H. Smith. 12th Bengal Cavalry.

Veterinary Inspector, Veterinary Captain F. W. Forsdyke.

STAFF AT THE BASE.

Base Commandant, Colonel W. J. Vousden, V.C., Indian Staff Gorps.

Deputy-Assistant-Adjutant and Quartermaster-General, Major A. W. J. Allen, 1st East Kent Regiment.

Commandant British Troops Depôt, Major A. de B. V. Paget, 2nd Durham L.I.

Adjutant and Quartermaster British Troops Depôt, Captain A. F. Bundock, 2nd Battalion South Lancashire Regiment.

Commandant Native Troops Depôt, Captain S. M. Edwardes, D.S.O., 2nd Bombay Infantry (Grenadiers).

Adjutant and Quartermaster Native Troops Depôt, not known yet.

Base Ordnance Officer, Captain M. W. S. Pasley, Royal Artillery.

Officer in Charge of Engineer Field Park, Captain U. W. Evans, R.E.

Base Medical Officer (Officer in Charge of Kohat Native General Hospital).

Base Commissariat Officer, Major H. R. Marrett, Assistant-Commissary-General.

Department Assistants to Base Commissariat Officer— Captain W. H. D. Rich, Assistant-Commissary-General; Lieutenant F. W. H. Forteith, Deputy-Assistant-Commissary-General; Lieutenant L. H. Marriet, Deputy-Assistant-Commissary-General; Lieutenant H. G. P. Beville, Deputy-Assistant Commissary-General.

Department Assistant (for Transport) to the Base Commissariat Officer, Captain H. N. Hilliard, Deputy-Assistant-Commissary-General.

Regimental Assistants to Base Commissariat Officer—Captain W. P. M. Pollok, 18th Hussars; Captain H. Smyth, 1st Battalion Cheshire Regiment; Lieutenant T. E. Bayley, 20th Hussars; Lieutenant C. G. E. Ewart, 5th Bengal Cavalry; Lieutenant E. N. Davis, 3rd Infantry, Hyderabad Contingent.

The Peshawar Column.

Commanding, Brigadier-General A. G. Hammond, C.B., D.S.O., V.C., A.D.C.

Orderly Officer, Lieutenant H. D. Hammond, Royal Artillery.

Assistant-Adjutant and Quartermaster-General, Brevet-Lieutenant-Colonel F. S. Gwatkin, 13th Bengal Lancers.

Deputy-Assistant-Adjutant and Quartermaster-General, Major C. T. Becker, 2nd King's Own Scottish Borderers.

Field Intelligence Officer, Captain F. H. Hoghton, 1st Bombay Infantry (Grenadiers).

Principal Medical Officer, Brigade-Surgeon-Lieutenant-Colonel R. G. Thomsett, Army Medical Staff.

Lieutenant-Colonel Commanding Royal Artillery, Lieutenant-Colonel W. M. M. Smith, Royal Artillery.

Adjutant Royal Artillery, Captain F. R. Drake, Royal Artillery.

Brigade Ordnance Officer, Major T. E. Rowan, Royal Artillery.

Field Engineer, Major E. C. Spilsbury, R.E.

Assistant Field Engineer, Lieutenant C. B. Farwell, R.E.

Assistant-Superintendent Army Signalling, Lieutenant C. E. Cobb, 1st E. York Regiment.

Provost Marshal (from the Column).

Field Treasure-Chest Officer (from the Column).

Staff Surgeon (from the Column).

Brigade Commissariat Officer, Lieutenant H. H. Jones, Deputy-Assistant-Commissary-General.

Assistant to Brigade Commissariat Officer, Lieutenant V. R. Pigott, 1st Battalion Cheshire Regiment.

Brigade Transport Officer, Lieutenant C. Charlton, Royal Horse Artillery.

Veterinary Officer, Veterinary Lieutenant F. U. Carr.

The Kurram Movable Column.

Commanding (with rank and pay of Colonel on the Staff), Colonel W. Hill, Indian Staff Corps.

Orderly Officer, Captain R. O. C. Hume, 1st Border Regiment.

Deputy-Assistant-Adjutant-General, Major E. F. H. McSwiney, D.S.O., 1st Lancers, Hyderabad Contingent.

Deputy-Assistant-Quartermaster-General, Captain C. P. Scudamore, D.S.O., 1st Royal Scots Fusiliers.

Principal Medical Officer, Brigade-Surgeon-Lieutenant-Colonel W. R. Murphy, D.S.O., Indian Medical Service.

Brigade Ordnance Officer, Lieutenant D. R. Poulter, Royal Artillery.

Field Engineer, Captain J. A Gibbon, Royal Engineers.

Assistant Field Engineer, Lieutenant E. A. Tandy, Royal Engineers.

Assistant-Superintendent Army Signalling, Lieutenant C. R. Scott-Elliot, 4th Madras Pioneers.

Staff Surgeon (from the Column).

Brigade Commissariat Officer, Captain C. F. T. Murray, Assistant-Commissary-General.

Assistant to Brigade Commissariat Officer, Captain P. H. Rogers, 2nd Yorkshire Light Infantry.

Brigade Transport Officer, Captain H. W. C. Colquhoun, 24th Madras Infantry.

Provost Marshal (from the Column).

Veterinary Officer, Veterinary Lieutenant W. N. Wright.

THE RAWALPINDI RESERVE BRIGADE.

Commanding, Brigadier-General C. R. Macgregor, D.S.O.

Orderly Officer, Second Lieutenant E. W. C. Ridgeway, 29th Punjab Infantry.

Deputy-Assistant-Adjutant-General, Major Sir R. A. W. Colleton, Bart., 1st Royal Welsh Fusiliers.

Deputy-Assistant-Quartermaster-General, Captain H. Hudson, 19th Bengal Lancers.

Field Intelligence Officer.

Senior Medical Officer (from the Brigade).

Staff Surgeon (from the Brigade).

Brigade Commissariat Officer, Lieutenant E. G. Vaughan, Deputy-Assistant-Commissary-General.

Brigade Transport Officer, Lieutenant K. E. Nangle, 3rd Infantry, Hyderabad Contingent.

Provost Marshal (from the Brigade).

Brigade Signalling Officer (from the Brigade).

Veterinary Officer, Veterinary Lieutenant W. S. Anthony.

The Staffs and Departments will be directed to assemble at the following stations on receipt of orders:

Army Staff, Divisional Staff of Second Division, Staff of Kurram Movable Column, Staff of Line of Communication, at Kohat.

All the Staffs of First Division, except those of Second Brigade.

First and Second Brigade Staffs of Second Division, Staff of Peshawar Column, at Peshawar.

Staff of Reserve Brigade, at Rawalpindi.

www.ingramcontent.com/pod-product-compliance
Lightning Source LLC
Chambersburg PA
CBHW031249230426
43670CB00005B/100